SOCIAL POLICY REVIEW 15
UK and international perspectives

Edited by Catherine Bochel, Nick Ellison and
Martin Powell

First published in Great Britain in July 2003 by

The Policy Press
Fourth Floor, Beacon House
Queen's Road
Bristol BS8 1QU
UK

Tel +44 (0)117 331 4054
Fax +44 (0)117 331 4093
e-mail tpp-info@bristol.ac.uk
www.policypress.org.uk

British Library Cataloguing in Publication Data
A catalogue record for this book is available from the British Library

ISBN 1 86134 470 8 hardback
A paperback version of this book is also available

Catherine Bochel is a Senior Lecturer in Social Policy, Department of Policy
Studies, University of Lincoln, **Nick Ellison** is a Senior Lecturer in the Department
of Sociology and Social Policy, University of Durham, and **Martin Powell** is a Senior
Lecturer in Social Policy, Department of Social and Policy Sciences, University of
Bath.

Cover design by Qube Design Associates, Bristol.
Front cover: photograph of GLA building, London, supplied by Toby Melville, *The
Guardian*, PA Photos.

The right of Catherine Bochel, Nick Ellison and Martin Powell to be identified as
editors of this work has been asserted by them in accordance with the 1988 Copyright,
Designs and Patents Act.

Printed and bound in Great Britain by Hobbs the Printers Ltd, Southampton.

Contents

List of tables and figures

Tables

Figures

Notes on contributors

Giuliano Bonoli is Associate Professor in the Department of Social Work and Social Policy, University of Fribourg, Switzerland.

Denis Bouget is Professor in Economics at the University of Nantes and Director of the Maison des Sciences de l'Homme in Nantes, France. He is Chair of COST A15: Reforming Social Protection Systems in Europe.

Mick Carpenter is Reader in Social Policy at the Department of Sociology, University of Warwick, UK.

Benoît Gay-des-Combes is a Research Assistant in the Department of Social Work and Social Policy, University of Fribourg, Switzerland.

Jane Falkingham is Professor of Demography and International Social Policy at the University of Southampton, UK.

David Gladstone is Senior Lecturer and Director of Undergraduate Programmes at the School for Policy Studies, University of Bristol, UK.

Ian Greener is a Lecturer in Management Studies at the University of York, UK.

Pamela A. Holcomb is a Senior Researcher at the Urban Institute, Washington DC, USA, and has spent many years engaged in policy-related research pertaining to welfare reform, employment, training and other social welfare programmes.

Ian Holliday is Professor and Head, Department of Public and Social Administration at the City University of Hong Kong.

Kirk Mann is Senior Lecturer in Social Policy and Sociology at the University of Leeds, UK.

Karin Martinson is a consultant to the Urban Institute, Washington DC, USA, and has spent many years engaged in policy-related research pertaining to welfare reform, employment, training and other social welfare programmes.

Richard Parry is Senior Lecturer in Social Policy at the University of Edinburgh, UK.

Debora Price is studying for a PhD at the Centre for Research on Ageing and Gender at the University of Surrey, UK, and a barrister specialising in the resolution of financial issues following separation and divorce.

Katherine Rake is Director of the Fawcett Society, UK.

Herman M. Schwartz is Professor and Director of Graduate Studies in the Department of Politics, University of Virginia, USA.

Paul Wilding is Emeritus Professor of Social Policy at the University of Manchester, UK.

Introduction: the year in social policy

Catherine Bochel, Nick Ellison and Martin Powell

UK developments

One of the characteristics of the past 12 months that might strike the casual observer of social policy is the sheer number and range of issues that have been covered in the media, among the most prominent of which have been immigration and asylum seekers, and the government's handling of these; the public services, including both funding and pay; the outcome of the Laming enquiry into the death of Victoria Climbié, with its wide-ranging recommendations for improved partnership and coordination between a range of public services; education, with higher education joining school education in a more prominent position on the government's agenda than in recent years; and sustained attention to pensions, with companies continuing to move from final salary schemes to money purchase schemes, while falls in the stock market further eroded the pension plans of many people.

Outside the social policy agenda, but nevertheless with significant implications for social policy, the dominant issues remained those associated with the aftermath of 11 September, with debates over the likelihood and the rights and wrongs of war with Iraq overshadowing other news stories, while the fear of terrorism continued to make itself felt through events abroad, such as the Bali bombing and, at home, the heightened security measures in place in and around airports as well as discussions in the media about the extent to which the public should be informed about possible terrorist threats. The strength of feeling against a war was demonstrated in February 2003 when the largest demonstration ever seen in Britain took place in London, dwarfing that of the Countryside Alliance the previous autumn.

The state of the economy was also an issue of some concern, in part due to doubts about the extent to which the UK could insulate itself from the downturn in the world economy, and given the slowdown, the ability of the government to meet its planned levels of expenditure on public services, as well as the concerns over pensions noted above and explored later in this chapter. In addition, rises in house prices meant that questions of affordability for key workers, particularly in the south east of England, remained, while the extent to which regional inequalities in house prices would widen or narrow regularly featured in the media. The related topic of the levels of personal borrowing and debt of the British public also emerged, often being linked to the rising value of houses encouraging borrowing.

For social policy, however, the state of the public services over the year was arguably the dominant issue, although approached from a number of different perspectives. Resourcing was one of these, with Gordon Brown in July 2002 announcing a £61 billion boost over three years for public spending. Education was the main beneficiary of this, although housing, policing, overseas aid and defence also showed significant gains. But the Chancellor continued the New Labour mantra linking spending with 'performance' (but see Parry, this volume). However, only four months later he admitted that the government would have to borrow an extra £30 billion over the next five years to fulfil its plans, a discrepancy he attributed to the global economic slowdown. On a less positive note, the pressure on resources was highlighted by strikes among local government workers, rail workers and fire fighters, with the government emphasising the need for restraint, and in the case of the last group, remaining adamant that any pay deal over 4 per cent must be financed through 'modernisation' of the service. However, in early 2003 general practitioners were offered the possibility of pay increases of up to 50 per cent for adopting the new contracts offered by the government, although here too change was demanded, in particular a move to rewarding practices for the quality of care they deliver to patients rather than simply the number of patients that they treat.

The resourcing of education was also a prominent issue, with attention particularly focusing on higher education. By mid-2002 it appeared that the government was taking seriously the cries of the higher education sector that it was under-resourced, although ministers appeared unsure how to respond and the media was full of conflicting and changing stories of government proposals. In early 2003 the publication of the White Paper, *The future of higher education* (DfES, 2003), set out the government's thinking, with proposals for a graduate contribution scheme together with the introduction of grants for the worst-off to replace the existing fees and loans. From 2006 universities were to be able to charge top-up fees of up to £3,000 a year for each course, upfront tuition fees would be abolished, and repayment would be deferred until after graduation, paid through the tax system and linked to the ability to pay. At the same time, a greater concentration of research funding within a few universities seemed likely, and universities were being further encouraged to follow one or two of the three strands of excellence in research, teaching or widening participation, the last to be encouraged by a requirement for individual universities to draw up access agreements and the appointment of an independent access regulator to oversee these.

While higher education moved closer to the centre of the government's agenda, the state of school-age education also remained under scrutiny, particularly in the autumn of 2002 when around 100,000 students had their A level grades reviewed following differences of interpretation by the exam boards and the regulatory body, the Qualifications and Curriculum Authority, although eventually only 1,945 students' grades were actually altered. Shortly afterwards the Secretary of State for Education, Estelle Morris, resigned, saying that she felt she was not up to the job, following previous crises including the vetting of new teachers by the Criminal Records Bureau and a perhaps ill-timed intervention over the exclusion of a student from a school in Epsom, as well as an admission that government targets for literacy and numeracy for 11 year olds had not been met. In contrast with many recent political resignations, she was generally seen as going with grace and some sense of dignity.

A child was at the centre of perhaps the most significant government public enquiry of the past year. Lord Laming's 2003 report into the death of eight-year-old Victoria Climbié called for a major reform of children's services in England and for a national agency to be established for children and families to coordinate policy and monitor local children's services. Perhaps the most damning indictment of the report was over the failure of agencies either to cooperate or to take responsibility for the case, despite previous enquiries also having highlighted failings of collaboration and coordination. The government responded, promising a new range of policies for children at risk including children's trusts to take responsibility for coordinating health and social care at local level and new national guidelines for the care of children.

The debates noted in *Social Policy Review* in recent years about immigration, and particularly asylum seekers, continued in 2002/03, with added impetus arising from the concerns of some following the 11 September attacks on the US. Although the Sangatte refugee camp near Calais, the focus of much previous attention, finally closed in December 2002 following an agreement between the British and French governments, there remained a significant level of public debate on the issue, with some politicians and sections of the media making more or less explicit links to the threat of terrorism. The government appeared uncertain how to respond, with some vacillation over the requirements for entry, treatment of asylum seekers and how to accommodate them until their cases had been considered, but with a general trend towards harsher treatment such as removing entitlements to benefits if people did not apply for asylum immediately on entry to the UK. Debate in the media to a large extent promoted an anti-immigration stance and contributed to public campaigns against government plans to house asylum seekers in or near local communities. In a development seen by some as related, the Home Secretary, David Blunkett, published a Green Paper (Home Office, 2002) designed to stimulate debate on 'entitlement' cards, seen by some as a form of identity card, which would be used to access services such as healthcare or benefits.

However, despite the challenges facing the government in social policy and elsewhere, the lack of a coherent and credible opposition meant that New Labour has so far been under less pressure than might otherwise have been the case. Under Ian Duncan Smith the Conservatives remained divided on the extent to which they should 'modernise' or shift to the right and, despite the apparent growing public anxiety over many of the government's policies, seemed unable to close the gap in the opinion polls. Similarly, the Liberal Democrats, for whom Charles Kennedy appeared to be establishing himself as a credible leader and who have claimed in recent years to be the 'effective' opposition, seemed unable to catch up with the Conservatives. However, the local government elections and those for the Scottish Parliament and National Assembly for Wales due in May 2003 appeared to give all parties much to play for.

International developments

Outside the realms of terrorism and war the main international concerns of previous *Reviews* such as the debate on globalisation continue to run (see, for example, the chapters by Bouget and Schwartz in this volume). Similarly, institutions such as the World Bank and the International Monetary Fund continue to express concerns about the 'p-words' of poverty and participation. In the US the implications of the welfare changes of the Clinton presidency continue to work through, such as the time limits on welfare (see Holcomb and Martin, this volume), while relatively little has yet appeared on the domestic agenda of the Bush presidency, although in early 2003 proposals to abolish taxes on the estates of the very wealthy after death were opposed by some of the country's richest citizens, including Bill Gates senior.

Even when moving to the European scale it is impossible to summarise, or even list, all of the major developments in European social policy (for example, see the *Journal of European Social Policy* digests and the vast but chaotic Europa website [http://europa.eu.int]); the focus here, therefore, is upon a few main themes.

If a week is a long time in politics, then five years represents an epoch for social democracy. In the late 1990s, when most of the EU states were governed by centre-left coalitions, it was possible to write of the "magical return of social democracy" (see Bonoli and Powell, 2003: forthcoming). Since then the magic appears to have worn off, with the right making progress in a series of elections in countries such as Austria, Denmark, France, Italy and the Netherlands. The nadir for the left was perhaps April and May 2002 when nearly 6 million French electors voted for Jean-Marie Le Pen in the first round of the Presidential elections, eliminating the socialist candidate, Lionel Jospin; and the LPF, the party of the assassinated Pim Fortuyn, won 1.6 million votes and 26 of the 150 seats in the Lower House in the Netherlands, subsequently forming part of a centre-right coalition. Only New Labour in Britain, with its second landslide victory in 2001, resisted this shift. Some New Labour supporters were quick to advise continental Social Democrats that they had to 'modernise', with Peter Mandelson insisting that the common factor behind the left's retreat in Europe was immigration and crime. Tony Giddens in *The Guardian* in April and May 2002 considered that the third way could help the left beat the far right with policies on reform of labour markets and welfare systems and the need to address issues traditionally dominated by the right, such as crime and immigration: policies have to be "tough on immigration, but tough on the causes of hostility to immigrants". Since then the Social Democrats in Germany and Sweden have clung to power by their fingertips, although since regional elections in January 2003 the Christian Democrats in Germany have the power to block many social policy reforms in the Bundesrat. The Social Democrats in the Netherlands made significant gains in the election of January 2003, which was caused by the failure of the previous coalition, and may (at the time of writing) enter a grand coalition with the Christian Democrats. However, the electoral success of the right appears to have left its mark on the Social Democrats, who feel that they have to respond to populist agendas on immigration and crime.

Turning from issues in individual countries towards the wider EU, the moves towards European citizenship continue. It has generally been claimed that the social elements of citizenship have been most problematic, with limited additional (EU) rights that supplement those of member states (for example, Kleinman, 2002; see also Threlfall in *SPR 14*). However, there are a number of moves that could make European social citizenship more visible. First, many commentators argue that the Lisbon Summit of March 2000 "marked a watershed in the Europeanization of employment and social policy" (for example, Hemerijck, in Esping-Andersen et al, 2002, p 209). The Portuguese presidency of the EU championed the 'Open Method of Co-ordination' (OMC) to regulate social policy (de la Porte and Pochet 2002; Esping-Andersen et al, 2002). In contrast to 'hard' laws such as the Maastrict convergence criteria, this 'soft' approach consists of common guidelines, national action plans (NAPs), peer reviews, joint evaluation reports and recommendations. It was first used in the sphere of employment, but is now spreading to social inclusion, healthcare and pensions, with seasoned Euro-observers expressing some surprise that pensions, generally considered the ideal example of subsidiarity, are at the centre of discussions of European social debate (see for example, *Journal of European Social Policy* Digest, vol 11, no 4, 2001). However, the National Action Plans on social inclusion – NAPinclus (not of course to be confused with the NAPemps!) – submitted to the Commission in June 2001 varied significantly in length, detail and targets. For example, some countries used the 50 per cent of median income poverty level, while others used the 60 per cent level (see Atkinson et al, 2002; European Commission, 2002). This process will, no doubt, become more consistent in the future. A report prepared at the request of the Belgian presidency of the Council of the European Union (Atkinson et al, 2002) produced 33 recommendations, including 7 level 1 indicators, 14 level 2 and a number of level 3 indicators to be determined by individual member states. However, it is less than clear whether OMC represents old wine in new bottles. At root, it combines two old but far from vintage concepts. First, benchmarking shares the problems of performance indicators (see Parry, this volume). Second, policy learning goes back at least as far in social policy as David Lloyd George's visit to Bismarck's social insurance scheme at the turn of the 20th century. Moreover, governments have previously signed up to targets of symbolic politics. For example, the British Conservative government supported the WHO target of reducing health inequalities by 25 per cent. A further result of the Belgian presidency was the commissioning of a report on the evolving architecture of European welfare states (Esping-Andersen et al, 2002).

Second, the Franco-German initiative for dual citizenship announced in January 2003 was presented as a model and as an initial step towards the goal of future European citizenship. However, on closer inspection, most of the citizenship rights seemed to be more civil and political (such as allowing citizens to vote in each other's national elections) rather than the more elusive social rights.

Third, the enlargement process clearly has major implications for European citizenship, and is one of the issues that prompted the formation of the Convention on the Future of Europe headed by Valéry Giscard d'Estaing (http://european-convention.eu.int). In a speech in Barcelona in February 2003, Romano Prodi, the President of the European Commission, claimed that the document could become Europe's first fully-fledged constitution. It sets out in almost 50 articles the EU's values, objectives and powers. Much of the wording is inevitably vague. For example, 'values' include 'human dignity', 'fundamental rights' and 'tolerance' (an intolerance of intolerance?), while 'objectives' include the 'promotion of economic and social cohesion'. Again, civil and political rights are clearer than social rights, while there is an intriguing mention of the 'duties' of citizenship. However, the f-word (Federal) is sufficient to ensure that battle lines between Europhiles and Eurosceptics are being drawn.

Despite all this talk of citizenship, it is far from clear, given the close link between labour markets and welfare policies (Andersen and Jensen, 2002; Sarfati and Bonoli, 2002), whether 'social citizenship' constitutes a separate, 'decommodified' sphere or whether it derives largely from employment. *SPR 13* noted the key phrase of 'social policy as a productive factor' and the Joint Report on Social Inclusion (European Commission, 2002, p 11) points to the "dual role of social policy" both as a productive factor and a key instrument to reduce inequalities and promote social cohesion. But it stresses *the key role of participation in employment* especially by groups that are under-represented or disadvantaged in it, in line with the objectives of the European employment strategy. The document's discussion of key risk factors and core challenges goes beyond the labour market, and it claims that:

> The overarching challenge for public policy is to ensure that the main mechanisms which distribute opportunities and resources – the labour market, the tax system, the systems providing social protection, education, housing, health, and other services – become sufficiently universal in the context of structural changes to address the needs of those individuals, who are most at risk of poverty and social exclusion and to enable them to access their fundamental rights. (p 25)

However, the document appears to shift uneasily between a productivist (or universal breadwinner) and universal citizenship discourse (or SID versus RED to use the terms of Ruth Levitas), and is opaque on the issue of unpaid care as opposed to paid work. As in all Eurospeak, the devil is in the detail.

Pensions, ageing and social policy

An innovation in this edition of *Social Policy Review* is the inclusion of a special section dedicated to the consideration of a particular dimension of social policy in which there is much current interest. Pensions have been chosen for *SPR 15* not only because the Labour government has just published a Green Paper (DWP, 2002), focusing on future pension arrangements in the United Kingdom, but also because the 'pensions problem' has become a national and international issue. Irrespective of regime-type, governments in the advanced industrial world are engaged in similar processes of rethinking their pensions policies. In particular, these attempts to recast current policies involve not only the adjustment of existing levels and sources of provision, but the reconceptualisation of prevailing understandings of 'ageing' and 'retirement'. This is not the place to discuss the complexities of policy changes that herald greater privatisation in pensions provision, changes in funding arrangements from 'defined benefit' to 'defined contribution' systems and/or attempts to adjust official retirement ages. However, changes of this kind strike at a vital part of the logic that underpins – or *underpinned* – the post-war Keynesian welfare state: protection against the 'risk' of old age. In this way, the 'pensions issue' becomes a significant symbolic focus of contemporary welfare state change.

There are at least four dimensions of social policy study involved here:

• how alterations to pensions arrangements affect poverty and inequality in old age;
• the way in which such changes point up issues of welfare governance;
• how the changing shape of pension arrangements illuminates debates about the classification of welfare systems;
• how particular policy changes – specifically the drift towards private solutions – exposes vulnerable populations to the fortunes of the global capital market.

These dimensions will be briefly explored in turn.

With respect to the dramatic alterations currently being made to pensions arrangements, these clearly impact upon all sections of society – the economically active population, those nearing retirement and those who are already retired. From a social policy standpoint, a major focus of impact has to be the new inequalities that such changes create or compound. Obviously pensions policies have always affected the structure of poverty and inequality in old age, as Titmuss (1963) famously recognised. But recent policy changes in countries as ostensibly different as Denmark, Germany and the UK to raise insurance contributions, reduce benefit levels and/or to rely more heavily on occupational and private alternatives have changed the traditional parameters of disadvantage both within retired populations as well as between these populations and the economically active (see Jackson, 1998; Barr, 2001; Myles, 2002). For example, individual decisions about retirement have been affected by the tightening of early retirement policies, decisions to reduce retirement benefits, and so on. Equally, rising payroll taxes imposed to bolster existing pension schemes threaten to raise labour costs and so induce employers to lay off workers or forego expansion, contributing to unemployment – and creating a vicious circle of ever-rising contributions and falling employment levels. Increased contribution rates can alter the balance among generations either because those in work have to pay more to finance *their own* provision in old age (in defined contribution systems) or to support the pensions of the already retired (in pay-as-you-go, defined benefit systems). There are intragenerational difficulties as well: for instance, women tend to work less but live longer, suggesting that "they ... tend to be disproportionately affected by reforms that reduce or restructure public sector benefits" (Myles, 2002, p 147).

The implications for contemporary understandings of social citizenship are wide-ranging because the extent to which citizens in mature welfare states can expect to be protected from poverty in old age is no longer clear. To be sure, much depends on the nature of the welfare regime: the Green Paper on pensions (DWP, 2002) recently published in the UK suggests that, outside minimal state support, responsibility for retirement provision is to be left to individuals and their families – surely a marked retreat from the logic of the Beveridgean welfare state. Elsewhere, there has been noticeable public hostility to proposed reforms in the Christian Democratic countries of continental Europe – and particularly to the threat of creeping privatisation (Anderson and Meyer, 2003: forthcoming). The general point, however, is that changes to accepted pensions arrangements can damage the social fabric as trust in hitherto accepted welfare systems begins to erode in the face of new inequities and changing forms of exclusion.

If changing pensions policies are likely to affect understandings of citizenship and trust in welfare states, they also point up issues of welfare 'governance' – *how* decisions to alter existing arrangements are made (Pierson, 1996, 2001; Bonoli, 2000; Bonoli and Palier, 2001). The core of Pierson's argument, in particular, is that welfare state programmes tend to be 'path dependent' – welfare arrangements become institutionalised and self-reinforcing over time – which means that the potential scope of reform is likely to be constrained by the embedded preferences of key actors (see Green-Pedersen and Haverland, 2002). Partly for this reason, public provision is popular with trade unions and others keen to protect the 'social wage', including certain segments of electorates with a particular investment in public services. But there is a tension here because paying for welfare programmes by increased taxation (or higher insurance contributions) does not go down well in an era of high unemployment and population ageing. As mentioned above, changes to pension arrangements, perhaps more than to other areas of welfare systems, run directly into deep-rooted assumptions about the kind of support those who have 'contributed' (in financial *and* social terms) can expect in old age. It is consequently not surprising that efforts by political parties to alter pensions policies disrupt accepted understandings of the methods, scope and generosity of provision that in some cases have been assumed for at least two generations.

Of course, it is possible that Pierson and others overestimate the influence of path dependent processes. After all, it is being suggested here that social policies *have* indeed changed – even in the supposedly sclerotic Christian Democratic regimes of continental Europe. But this is precisely the point: shifting pensions arrangements, perhaps more than other areas of social policy, throw these complex debates into relief, forcing researchers to rethink the complexities of welfare governance.

So far as the exercise of welfare state classification is concerned, recent attempts (Goodin and Rein, 2001; Hinrichs, 2001) to take account of changes to post-war systems of protection in old age suggest a move away from Esping-Andersen's (1990) accepted tripartite typology of welfare regimes. Now, to be sure, it is important not to confuse a welfare regime with a particular sub-system of welfare, as Esping-Andersen (1999) reminds us. However, pensions arrangements, together with employment policies, constituted a core component of his original typology and, to this extent, recent policy changes are likely to loosen prevailing perceptions of regime classification. Certainly, Karl Hinrichs' (2001) work on Bismarckian and Beveridgean pensions systems, for example, introduces a new, 'dynamic' approach to changing arrangements for provision in old age, which permits new forms of comparison which cut across 'accepted' categories. In addition, recent work by Goodin and Rein (2001; see also Ploug, 2002) suggests a 'blurring' of distinctions among pension systems and the mix of 'pillars' that comprise them as the scope for 'novel combinations and recombinations' increases.

Last but not least, it is worth briefly considering the relationship between changes to pension systems and 'globalisation'. On one view, of course, no discernible relationship exists. Those (for example, Hirst and Thompson, 1999; Hay, 2001) who dismiss globalisation as exaggerated or, at best, a necessary 'myth' masking welfare state retrenchment, generally argue that welfare state change – and particularly pension change – is a function of internal economic reorganisation associated with the shift towards a post-industrial economy. On this reading, pensions are primarily a 'domestic' issue, the argument being that governments remain in a position to decide on methods of provision and also remain accountable to their electorates for any changes they decide to make. There is certainly more than an element of truth in this view – after all *national* governments have indeed embarked on far-reaching *national* reforms in recent years. But this argument needs to be treated with a degree of caution. To counter it by suggesting that the demographic shift towards ageing populations in the advanced democracies is itself a 'global' phenomenon may be a rather cheap shot, although it is important to be aware of the ubiquity of concern and the desire for change that population ageing has produced (see OECD, 1996, 1998, 2000). Of more significance are two factors that impinge directly on pensions. First, as Bonoli and Gay-des-Combes make clear in this volume, global economic pressures have an impact on the shape of labour markets, which necessitate new pensions policies. For example, 'atypical' workers – particularly female part-timers – now comprise a much larger segment of the workforce and at least some of the responsibility for the decline of the 'white, male, blue-collar breadwinner' can be traced to the effects of 'globalisation'. Equally, the demand for greater workforce 'flexibility' may be at least partly a function of increasing global competition.

Second, and more significantly, the turn to private sector solutions in countries as supposedly different as the UK, Sweden and Germany, clearly opens pension systems, and pensioners themselves, to the risks associated with the global financial marketplace. These risks partly relate to the complex world of capital flows and the intricacies of a system well beyond the capacity of ordinary individuals to understand, let alone to control (see Held et al, 1999). One point in particular is worth noting, however: pension fund mismanagement is extensive and appears to be increasing. In the US, large-scale investment by certain American pension funds in Enron's off-balance-sheet partnerships and 'special purpose entities' raises the question as to why "pension-fund managers [were] prepared to risk their members' savings in such patently unsafe measures" (Blackburn, 2002, p 32). The British case is no less alarming. In an environment where New Labour appears reluctant to recreate a system of state provision in old age, companies' funds are being closed or altered in ways that, as Timmins (quoted in Blackburn, 2002, p 43) has commented, will appear "to many members – those in their forties and fifties ... like theft". The closure of defined benefit schemes has clearly hit private sector employees hardest – but, as Blackburn (2002, p 44) argues, "public sector pensions are increasingly vulnerable as the public–private boundary is broken down by outsourcing and privatisation".

References

Andersen, J.G. and Jensen, P.H. (eds) (2002) *Changing labour markets, welfare policies and citizenship*, Bristol: The Policy Press.

Anderson, K. and Meyer, T. (2003: forthcoming) 'The third way in welfare state reform? Social democratic pension politics in Germany and Sweden', in G. Bonoli and M. Powell (eds) *Social democratic party politics in contemporary Europe*, London: Routledge.

Atkinson, A., Cantillon, B., Marlier, E. and Nolan, B. (2002) *Social indicators: The EU and social inclusion*, Oxford: Oxford University Press.

Barr, N. (2001) *The welfare state as piggy bank*, Oxford: Oxford University Press.

Blackburn, R. (2002) 'The Enron debacle and the pension crisis', *New Left Review*, vol 14, March April, pp 26-51.

Bonoli, G. (2000) *The politics of pension reform*, Cambridge: Cambridge University Press.

Bonoli, G. and Palier, B. (2001) 'How do welfare states change? Institutions, and their impact on the politics of welfare state reform in Western Europe', in S. Liebfried (ed) *Welfare state futures*, Cambridge: Cambridge University Press, pp 57-76.

Bonoli, G. and Powell, M. (2003: forthcoming) *Social Democratic Party policies in contemporary Europe*, London: Routledge.

de la Porte, C. and Pochet, P. (eds) (2002) *Building social Europe through the open method of co-ordination*, Brussels: Peter Lang.

DfES (Department for Education and Skills) (2003) *The future of higher education*, London: The Stationery Office.

DWP (Department for Work and Pensions) (2002) *Simplicity, security and choice: Working and saving for retirement*, Cm 5677, London: The Stationery Office.

Esping-Andersen, G. (1990) *The three worlds of welfare capitalism*, Cambridge: Polity Press.

Esping-Andersen, G. (1999) *The social foundations of postindustrial economies*, Oxford; Oxford University Press.

Esping-Andersen, G. with Gallie, D., Hermerijck, A. and Myles, J. (2002) *Why we need a new welfare state?*, Oxford: Oxford University Press.

European Commission (2002) *Joint report on social inclusion*, Brussels: EC.

Goodin, R. and Rein, M. (2001) 'Regimes on pillars: alternative welfare state logics and dynamics', *Public Administration*, vol 74, no 4, pp 769-801.

Green-Pedersen, C. and Haverland, M. (2002) 'The new politics of scholarship of the welfare state', *Journal of European Social Policy*, vol 12, no 1, pp 43-53.

Hay, C. (2001) 'Globalization, social democracy and the persistence of partisan politics: a commentary on Garrett', *Review of International Political Economy*, vol 7, no 1, pp 138-52.

Held, D., McGrew, A., Goldblatt, D. and Perraton, J. (1999) *Global transformations*, Cambridge: Polity Press.

Hinrichs, K. (2001) 'Elephants on the move: patterns of public pension reform in OECD countries', in S. Liebfried (ed) *Welfare state futures*, Cambridge: Cambridge University Press, pp 77-103.

Hirst, P. and Thompson, G. (1999) *Globalization in question*, Cambridge: Polity Press.

Home Office (2002) *Entitlement cards and identity fraud*, London: The Stationery Office.

Jackson, W. (1998) *The political economy of ageing*, Aldershot: Edward Elgar.

Kleinman, M. (2002) *A European welfare state?*, Basingstoke: Palgrave.

Laming, Lord. (2003) *The Victoria Climbié inquiry: Report of an inquiry*, London: The Stationery Office.

Myles, J. (2002) 'A new contract for the elderly?', in G. Esping-Andersen with D. Gallie, A. Hemerick and J. Myles (eds) *Why we need a new welfare state*, Oxford: Oxford University Press, pp 130-73.

OECD (Organisation for Economic Co-operation and Development) (1996) *Ageing in OECD countries: A critical policy challenge*, Paris: OECD.

OECD (1998) *Maintaining prosperity in an ageing society*, Paris: OECD.

OECD (2000) *Reforms for an ageing society*, Paris: OECD.

Pierson, P. (1996) 'The new politics of the welfare state', *World Politics*, vol 48, no 1, pp 141-79.

Pierson, P. (ed) (2001) *The new politics of the welfare state*, Oxford: Oxford University Press.

Ploug, N. (2002) *The re-calibration of the Danish old-age pension system*, Working Paper, Copenhagen: Danish National Institute of Social Research.

Sarfati, H. and Bonoli, G. (eds) (2002) *Labour market and social protection reforms in international perspective*, Aldershot: Ashgate.

Titmuss, R. (1963) 'The social division of welfare', in R. Titmuss (ed) *Essays on the welfare state*, London: George Allen and Unwin, pp 34-55.

Part One:
UK social policy

This section examines some of the major concerns of the current New Labour government's social policy from a number of different perspectives. David Gladstone begins by examining community care and integration over a long time scale, and shows that 'community care' (unlike sexual intercourse) did not begin in 1963 between the end of the *Chatterley* ban and the Beatles' first LP. While the 19th century saw a significant degree of institutional expansion, recent historical research has begun to question the pervasiveness of institutional segregation in earlier periods. Family and community care remained important, with great permeability of the boundaries between institution, family and community, and with movement in and out of specialist institutions. Moreover, the inter-war period saw the development of a type of institution along the lines of the colony model, much different from the barrack-like institutions that had developed in the 19th century. However, Gladstone shows that mechanisms of control could exist 'outside the walls' of institutions. He concludes that integration, far from being a creation of policies from the 1960s, can be seen as one of the most important continuities that link contemporary issues and debates about the locus of care to much earlier periods of British social policy.

In the following chapter Richard Parry analyses the 'invest and reform' strategy, focusing on the 'big idea' of Public Service Agreements (PSAs). He argues that the strategy misappropriates both words: 'investment' is seen as any current expenditure the government chooses to favour, while 'reform' disguises moves towards a more rigorous and market-oriented public sector labour market. If one of the favoured services is 'education, education, education', then the larger increase for the other priority might justify 'NHS, NHS, NHS'. However, with only small increases in other areas such as social security and with increases in the size of the economy, public spending as a percentage of GDP was lower in 2001/02 than it was in 1997/98. Parry views PSAs as a blunt instrument. For example, it is difficult to detect failure to achieve the PSA targets as they change in number and composition over time. Moreover, success appears to be defined by the spending departments rather than the Treasury, and the result of failure is that 'support and advice' are offered, rather than the 'name and shame' approach taken to some aspects of public services.

In the final chapter in Part One, Ian Greener explores the evolution of 'choice' in the NHS. Choice was not an issue considered in the traditional producer-dominated NHS, but, from its first uses in documents by Sir Keith Joseph in the 1970s, it increased in importance so that it appeared some 40 times in *Working for patients* – the 1989 White Paper that introduced the internal market in the NHS. Having set out to 'abolish' the internal market, New

Labour appears to have rediscovered 'choice' in their NHS Plan. However, following Titmuss' concerns about markets in healthcare, and by differentiating consumer and customer markets, Greener demonstrates the contradictions and confusions in New Labour's policies. He suggests that like the Conservatives' experiments with markets in the 1990s, New Labour's attempt to use patient choice as the driver of health reform is a mistake and that there remains a need to develop a more meaningful approach to the operationalisation of patients' views in the NHS.

ONE

Thinking historically about integration

David Gladstone

Introduction

Exactly 40 years ago, in 1963, the Ministry of Health of Macmillan's Conservative government produced its *Health and Welfare* White Paper (Ministry of Health, 1963). Its significance lay in its subtitle: the development of community care. Together with the Hospital Plan of the preceding year, it refocused the objectives and activities both of hospital care within the NHS and services for adults provided by the local authority health and welfare departments, the precursors of the modern social services departments. The Hospital Plan proposed a reduction in the number of beds in hospitals for the mentally ill and mentally handicapped, and ultimately their long-term closure. The White Paper represented the obverse of that commitment. Services for adults who had hitherto been institutionalised were instead to be provided by an expanded local authority service staffed by professional workers. Like the Ten Year Plans proposed for hospitals, local authority health and welfare departments were also required to submit ten-year plans for their subsequent growth and development. The 1963 White Paper thus represented not only the transition from institutional provision to day care and domiciliary services, but also an expansion of increased government welfare activity, which had begun some years earlier in school-age education, into the sectors of health and social care.

Such policies seemed indicative of a revolutionary break with the past, and a significant change in where care was to be delivered. The isolated segregation of the institution would be replaced by a new policy of integration that would enable those adults with special needs arising from their disabilities to maintain a contact and connection with the ordinary life settings and experiences of the majority of the population (King's Fund Centre, 1980). Integration was thus a means of achieving the principle of normalisation (Wolfensberger, 1972).

Subsequent research has significantly challenged that optimistic vision of the early 1960s. Well-attested evidence has highlighted that the rundown and closure of long-stay hospitals far outstripped the development of alternative community services. Over the past 40 years successive governments, in various ways and with varying success, have struggled to make a reality of the ambiguous concept of community care. As a policy objective it has been underpinned by the idea that "it is better, wherever possible, to provide help and support for people living in their own homes, with their own families, in their own neighbourhoods, rather than in institutions" (Bell, 1965, p 419). If there has been some consistency in its principles, however, there have been significant changes of emphasis in its practice. To the initial descriptor of change *care in the community* symbolised by the planned expansion of statutory personal welfare services in the 1960s was added in the 1980s the New Right's gloss of *care by the community*, an attempt to stimulate a more active role for the other suppliers in the mixed economy of welfare: the informal networks of family and friends, and the independent sector of voluntary and commercial organisations. A further change best described as *care by contract* was heralded by the introduction of the quasi-market into personal care in the early 1990s, and with it a significant increase in the purchasing and regulatory role of local authorities in place of direct service provision.

Though the means of *Making a reality of community care* (Audit Commission, 1986) may have changed over the past 40 years, there has been a considerable consistency in the value of integration underlying the policy. That consistency is customarily explained by reference to its opposite: the warehousing of segregation and the scandals associated with isolation and separation. "How is it that institutions established to care for the sick and helpless can have allowed them to be neglected, treated with callousness and even deliberate cruelty?" (Martin, 1984, p xi). Some of the answers to those questions lie in the reports of the official inquiries into conditions in long-stay hospitals for people with learning disabilities of the 1960s and 1970s, and the more recent reports of children's residential homes. Their story too has been remarkably consistent. Separation and segregation have created a regime of opportunity in which physical, mental and sexual abuse has occurred: a stultifying and repressive environment that has impacted on the personal and social development of its inmates and hampered them profoundly, not least in terms of educational performance and achievement, and of adjustment to an ordinary life. Significantly, it was Enoch Powell, the Minister of Health responsible for the 1963 White Paper, who provided a characteristically vivid image of the impact of the institutions: "There they stand: isolated, majestic, imperious, brooded over by the gigantic water tower and chimney combined, rising, unmistakable and daunting out of the countryside: the asylums which our forefathers built with such immense solidity" (cited in *The Independent Magazine*, 1988). Forty years later many of those immensely solid asylum institutions have been demolished altogether, or else converted into upmarket apartment-style homes complete with security gates and on-site leisure and recreational facilities. In short, a type of 21st-century segregation: an asylum or place of refuge for those who can afford to pay for it.

But, in addition to the evidence about the impact of more recent policy initiatives, recent historical research has begun to question the pervasiveness of institutional segregation in earlier periods. Specifically it has:

- adduced evidence highlighting the role of families and communities in the care of 'the different' in the early modern period and beyond;
- highlighted the historical specificity of the institutional solution in the 19th and first half of the 20th centuries;
- produced data indicating the movement into and out of specialist institutions: "the casting out and bringing back" (Walton, 1985) that characterised the Victorian asylums and which challenges the concept of the total institution (Goffman, 1961);
- highlighted the greater permeability of the boundaries between institution, family and community in the past.

Thus, rather than the 1960s signifying a defining moment – at least in theory – between institutional and domiciliary care, the historical evidence now highlights the coexistence of the two, both in Victorian England and in the England of the first half of the 20th century.

Community care is thus not only an ambiguous concept, as many writers have suggested (for example, Means and Smith, 1998), it also has a longer antecedent history than many have allowed. Community care, however it may have been redefined in the 1960s, was not the creation of that decade. On the basis of the historical evidence, it now seems more appropriate to think of it as a shift in the balance of an already existing continuum of institutional and domiciliary care. In short, the new historiography posits that while there is incontrovertible evidence for the growing importance of the institutional solution in Victorian England, the emphasis it has received has served only to distort and distract from the continuities of integration and the practice of care provided by families and communities within a broader mixed economy of welfare supply.

Thinking historically about integration, therefore, suggests the need to:

- abandon any lingering notion of a radical discontinuity between the different loci of care;
- map, more comprehensively than hitherto, the institutional *and* family-based alternative strategies of care, control and confinement that existed in the past for those at risk;
- recognise that "the boundary between the asylum and the larger society was always somewhat more porous than an earlier generation of studies had allowed or implied" (Scull, 1999, p 302).

There is, of course, incontrovertible evidence for the growing importance of the institutional solution in Victorian England, a solution that left the architectural legacy that Enoch Powell described. Poor Law workhouses, 'model' prisons, residential homes for children as well as the asylums for idiots and imbeciles (to use the contemporary terminology) were all a feature of that period. As a result, "the history of institutions in this country has been dominated by destitution, madness and criminality" (Parker, 1988, p 8). It is also a history of institutions increasing in scale and size, as new buildings were added and the number of inmates and staff increased. That is in sharp contrast to both the tradition of small-scale residential institutions of earlier centuries, and to the experience of other European countries, such as France, which had developed larger institutions earlier (Crowther, 1981, p 65). Furthermore, it underscores Roy Porter's (1992, p 279) observation that:

> In English rural communities as late as the seventeenth and eighteenth centuries
> ... families aided by parish relief were still typically expected to assume
> responsibility for their non-compos mentis relatives who might be kept at
> home, in a cellar or hidden away in a barn, or sometimes under the care of a
> servant.

Historians have explained the shift towards the institutional solution in different ways. Scull's (1979) explanation centred on the capture of psychiatric practice by the medical profession. Their professional self-interest and ambition were the drivers towards institutional development and expansion which, linked to a perceived unwillingness or inability of traditional carers to cope with disturbed relatives in the conditions of capitalist industrial society, led to the institution rather than the family as the epicentre of care.

An alternative view sees the segregation which the institution offered as creating a safe environment – especially but not only for children – in which new traits of character could be established, freed from the corrupting influences of parents and surroundings. Institutions thus served a dual purpose: on the one hand protecting the community from those who were different and by whom they felt threatened; on the other, providing a period of corrective character training for their inmates. The institutional panacea, that is to say, cannot be separated from the Victorian notion of character. It was a period when "the social discourse of the state and of voluntary societies and of philanthropic individuals came to centre around ways to develop character ... in which the passions were habitually mastered by reflection, the pressures of the present controlled by the perspective of the future" (Weiner, 1990, p 38).

However such growth is explained, the Census of 1911 recorded a higher proportion of the British population as living in various forms of state institution than at any time before or since (Harris, 1993, p 218). It is against that background that this chapter seeks to explore both the institutional solution for those with a learning disability *and* the alternative strategies of care, control and confinement that have been obscured by an earlier obsessive concern with institutional provision.

Explaining institutional expansion

Institutional provision in the 19th century was a feature both of voluntary activity and state supply. The creation of the five voluntary institutions for idiots in England occurred between the end of the 1840s and the late 1860s, each of them based on the initial model created by the Charity for the Asylum for Idiots established in Highgate in London in 1847 by the Rev Dr Andrew Reed, a non-conformist minister and established charity organiser. Those charitable asylums owed their origin, at least in part, to the pioneering work of Itard and Seguin in Paris where their experiments appeared to have confirmed the notion of the educable idiot. Such an initial mood of optimism, however, had given way by the end of the century to a more pessimistic scenario in which the asylums were less a flowing stream of trainable cases and more a stagnant pool of longer-stay residents, who embodied "the faces of degeneration" (Pick, 1989). By 1900 there was far less confidence in educating them to earn a living outside the institution, and more factors than there had been encouraging them to stay. Those in specialist institutions, however, were a minority. Far more of those defined as idiots were "intermingled with criminals, lunatics, indigents and others in workhouses, lunatic asylums and prisons" (Gelband, 1979, p 359). The only other specialist provision was that provided after 1867 by the Metropolitan Asylums Board in specialist asylums at Darenth, Leavesden and Caterham. By the beginning of the 20th century the numbers in those three asylums were almost double those in the five voluntary asylums combined.

By that time mental deficiency had become a major social problem and an integral element of the social question of late 19th- and early 20th-century Britain that centred on fear of the poor and a concern about national efficiency. Against that background it is not surprising that historical explanations for the growth of institutional segregation have focused on the eugenics movement. More recent historical analysis, however, has also directed attention to other factors.

Even though the Eugenics Education Society was itself not founded until 1907, the significance of eugenic ideas in shaping the debate about the 'faces of degeneration' cannot be ignored. The basic tenets of the Eugenics movement are well enough known: a concern with the declining birth rate among the middle classes and respectable working classes compared to the continuing higher rates among the poorest. As a result, "the poor were not only deteriorating themselves but disproportionately lowering the average physical, moral and mental capacity of the nation" (Perkin, 1989, p 54). The links between such concerns and mental deficiency were all too obvious:

> Because of their mental defect they sank within society to join the residuum: lacking moral restraint they bred unchecked with similarly weak-minded individuals; and their offspring were brought up in such a socially and morally impoverished environment and inherited such weak mental powers, that they perpetuated the vicious circle of decline. (Thomson, 1998, p 22)

Mental deficiency, that is to say, became a symbolic representation and focus for the wider ideological and political debates and concerns of the time that commanded wide-ranging support among the political and intellectual elites. As such it significantly shaped the features of the 1913 Mental Deficiency Act.

But more recent historians have also identified other factors that were important in the shaping of that legislation which for the first time introduced powers of compulsory detention over those who were judged to be unable to support and look after themselves in the wider community.

Of these, the first was the changing discourse around prisons and punishment. The Victorian prison system had been established on the premise that crime was a wilful act that could be deterred by a system of just and penal servitude. It was "essentially seen as the expression of a fundamental character defect stemming from a refusal or an inability to deny wayward impulses or to make proper calculations of long run self-interest" (Weiner, 1990, p 11). Though crime rates declined in the second half of the 19th century, there was at that time a growing interest and concern with recidivists and regular offenders. The increasing number of prison doctors perceived these habitual criminals either as professional criminals or else as weak-minded, with seemingly no wilful control over their actions and characters that appeared unreformable. By the end of the 19th century, the link between mental deficiency and criminal tendencies seemed incontrovertible. The Chairman of the Prison Commission was convinced that men turned to crime because of physical and mental as well as moral defectiveness (Gattrell, 1990). "Whereas early Victorian policy makers had seen in crime a threat to civilisation by a flood of wilfulness, their Edwardian successors found in criminality a message of the weakness of the individual and the ineffectuality of his unaided will" (Weiner, 1990, p 365). That reinterpretation was to have a significant effect on diversifying the penal regime, and not inconsiderable implications for mental deficiency institutions under the legislation of 1913.

Whereas the debate about prisons was about men, the contemporaneous concern with purity was about women in workhouses and Rescue Homes. Tredgold (cited in Walmsley et al, 1999) cites research from this time showing that mentally defective women were abnormally fertile, that their offspring were likely to be below average in physical and mental fitness, and that at least 40 per cent of those admitted to Rescue Homes between 1909 and 1913 were mentally deficient. Not only was the mentally deficient woman seen as the biological source of mental deficiency, she was also seen as a deep threat to existing middle-class and respectable working-class notions of sexuality and familial morality. It is this, Simmons (1978, p 394) suggests, which accounts for "the near hysteria which characterises discussions about the social problem of the mentally deficient woman". But it is interesting that:

> Feminists who had been outraged by the affront to personal liberty posed by the Contagious Diseases Acts in the 1860s and 1870s, were curiously silent about the Mental Deficiency Act of 1913 which permitted the permanent

exclusion of feeble-minded unmarried mothers dependent on poor relief; indeed women child care workers and asylum attendants played a prominent role in the campaign that gave rise to this measure. (Harris, 1993, pp 29-30)

The public concern of the late 19th and early 20th centuries thus has to be explained not only by reference to the Eugenics movement but also in relation to other contemporary debates surrounding the gendered nature of character development and change. "The reasons for the passage of the 1913 Act and for the form that it took must, therefore, be found in the way the participants interpreted the social problem of the time" (Simmons, 1978, p 387).

The Act, as one recent assessment has concluded:

> automatically targeted individuals who were the subject of moral, social or eugenic concern. In practice, therefore, the Act provided far more than a system of specialised care for the mentally disabled and retarded: it also provided an administrative machinery whose influence had the potential to regulate the moral, social and eugenic boundaries of good citizenship. (Thomson, 1998, p 247)

Constructing the population

Such specialised and segregated care was predicated on an incipient but developing classification, which, in the process, constructed a definition of difference, a legitimising of 'the other'.

Such a classification operated in two milieux in the case of those with a learning disability. There was, first of all, a developing differentiation that occurred in the environment outside the institution. But there was also a classification that operated within the asylum itself. This suggests, as recent research has indicated, that classification and therefore segregation involved a number of agents. These might be concerned with education and schooling or the medical practitioners who operated as asylum superintendents. But parents and families were also among those who recognised difference and sought the refuge of an institution. Classification, that is to say, was a multifaceted process, involving a number of professional and other agents.

It is appropriate to begin with the wider milieu of school and asylum. Schooling for children between the age of five and ten became compulsory in 1880. As a result, the school became something of a social laboratory concerning child development, aided by the system of payment by results that had been introduced by the Revised Code in 1862. Payments to schools were made on the basis of those pupils who passed an annual examination and proceeded from one defined standard to the next. But not all children made such a progression. Some remained in 'Standard 0'. The impact was clear, as Rose (1985, p 102) observes: "Normal children were those capable of benefiting from normal schools, feeble-minded children were those capable of benefiting from special schools, idiots and imbeciles were incapable of benefiting from schools at all".

Compulsory schooling and the operation of payment by results had thus facilitated an emergent and hierarchical classification. In the 1890s such a classification became the basis for the development of special, and therefore, different types of school, outside the conventional elementary school sector, for those defined as feeble-minded.

Its principle was well expressed in the 1898 Report of the Defective and Epileptic Children Committee of the Education Department:

> From the normal child down to the lowest idiot there are degrees of deficiency
> of mental power and it is only a difference of degree which distinguishes the
> feeble-minded children from the backward children who are found in every
> school...and from the children who are too deficient to receive proper benefit
> from any teaching which the school can give. (cited in Rose, 1985, p 99)

Not surprisingly, legislation the following year opened up "a continuum of deficiency that had no sharp dividing line and required specialised expert diagnosis and treatment" (Weiner, 1990, p 200). It was nonetheless a continuum that separated out those who were capable of progressing at a 'normal' rate through the elementary school system from others who were not. For them, the development of special schools for a variety of specific categories such as the blind or the feeble-minded became part of the response to difference. It made more likely that those "who are too different to receive proper benefit of any teaching" (Weiner, 1990, p 200) would be treated differently. Increasingly, that meant in a segregated environment.

Almost from their inception in the mid-19th century the voluntary asylums contained a larger number of boys than girls, though, after the 1913 Act introduced the category of moral deficiency, that was to change. In the earlier period, however, one asylum superintendent offered a cogent explanation for the preponderance of boys in his institution:

> Weak minded girls with a certain amount of intelligence are more amenable
> to treatment at home, and in some instances may even be helpful to their
> mothers in small things, while boys soon get beyond maternal control and,
> being allowed more freedom out of doors, too often become troublesome to
> their neighbours and the public, and their seclusion is then called for. (WCA,
> 1894, p 4)

Between their admission from the age of six until the customary time of discharge at 15, however, both boys and girls were to be trained in productive occupations and skills: productive in the sense of both being of value to the financial viability of the institution, and of producing some improvement in their residents' employment opportunities on their return to the community. In the changed employment and ideological context of the late 19th century that pattern changed. A larger number were retained in the institutions after the age of 15. They thus had less opportunity to show whether their training had enabled them to compete effectively in the 'open' labour market. At the same time, however, they served as a valuable resource in contributing to the economic survival of the growing institutions.

The classification system that established difference was not only external to the institution. Medically qualified personnel, often in their role as medical superintendents, carried out an assessment that for the potential inmate served as a bridgehead between family and institution.

Before the introduction of any specialist and apparently objective scientific intelligence testing, the broad parameters of such assessment related to age, likelihood of improvement and financial guarantees. Application forms asked about the child's mental condition, sensory abilities and general health as well as the circumstances of the family, the health and intelligence of other children and whether there was any history of insanity, idiocy or epilepsy in the family. Testimonials were requested from family and friends and established figures in the local community. Meanwhile, the medical examination consisted of a number of indicators. These included "whether he can speak, count, read, write, walk, dress himself, feed himself, whether he has the use of his hands, is mischievous, what his temper is, what the cause of his idiocy is and so forth" (Pycroft, 1882, pp 10-11). This was an examination designed to detect those likely to be capable of the training and improvement that the asylums offered. Those who were not, failed the test, were excluded and returned whence they came. This was part of the "casting out" (Walton, 1985, p 132) that characterised the 19th-century asylum. And, as the financial viability of the voluntary institutions came to rely more on economic self-sufficiency and producing goods for sale, so there was what one superintendent described as a "judicious weeding out" (WCA, 1898, p 14) of those unlikely to benefit either themselves or the institution from the training that was offered.

The significance of this selection process was cogently expressed by the Chairman of the Western Counties Idiot Asylum at its Annual General Meeting in 1914:

> The Committee are most determined to keep this House full of the same class of patients we have always had.... We spent a tremendous lot of money on rooms and appliances for teaching and are not going to have them wasted by a lot of blithering idiots who cannot learn. We are going to take the very highest class of mental defectives and teach them to the best of our ability. (cited in Radford and Tipper, 1988, p 52)

In the light of the developments in special education mentioned earlier, and one year after the 1913 Mental Deficiency Act, that looked increasingly a forlorn aspiration.

Decisions about admission and discharge involved families as well as the agents of the emergent professions. Threats to the family and the ways in which behaviour patterns threatened family stability and respectability and increased the attention of neighbours and the wider community, have all been identified as factors of difference which might precipitate the request for institutional admission (Mitchell and Hirst, 1999; Suzuki, 1999). Meanwhile, recent research also highlights the role of the family in sometimes requesting discharge or, more usually, their unwillingness to accept the return of a family member who was professionally deemed suitable to return to the family and community (Walsh, 1999; Wright, 1999). As a result, trans-institutionalisation became more prevalent, especially between the specialist asylums and the workhouses.

Outside the walls

The 1913 Act widened the category of mental deficiency with its distinction between idiots, imbeciles, the feeble-minded and moral imbeciles. It also placed an obligation on local authorities to provide specialist institutions, and formalised the arrangements governing admission and the possibility of discharge. But there was a significant gap between the rhetoric of a more total institutionalisation and the reality of continuing permeability between the institution and the community. Part of that was due to the First World War, which "seriously impeded the efforts of the Board of Control to get the Local Authorities to set aside funds for the construction of specialised institutions" (Simmons, 1978, p 400). The continuing financial austerity that followed the short-lived post-war boom continued the process. At that same time "changes in some of the major elements of the initial conceptualisation of feeble-mindedness led to a further reconceptualisation of the problem" (Simmons, 1978, p 400).

Together, these factors created a milieu that was considerably different to that growing institutionalisation prefigured in the 1913 Act. As recent research has highlighted, greater use was made of the provisions, such as those in legislation passed in 1927, enabling the authorities – the Board of Control, the local Mental Deficiency Committees and the voluntary societies acting as their agents – to regulate and control people outside of the institution. These measures included:

- licensing – the grant of leave of absence to an inmate provided the home to which they were going was approved;
- guardianship – the placing of a defective in the control of a suitable person, for example, a relative or employer;
- supervision – which entailed the visiting and overseeing of defectives in their own homes, a duty entrusted to either professional staff such as health visitors, school nurses or mental welfare workers, or voluntary workers working for local mental welfare associations, and required the submission of regular reports to the local authority Mental Deficiency Committee.

The interwar statistical data show a significant increase in the numbers in institutions. This was a period of institutional growth, often on the colony model: a collection of smaller living units with shared central administrative facilities, in contrast to the barrack-like large-scale institutions that had developed in the 19th century. It thus represented a development of – or even a return to – the therapeutic raison d'etre of the voluntary asylums at their inception. But it also continued a controlling tradition:

> Segregation from the outside community could be justified for eugenic reasons and because the moral instability and social inefficiency of these individuals was a threat to the community. At the same time, the colony promised a sheltered environment in which defectives could be protected from the community and would be better able to contribute to their own support. (Thomson, 1998, pp 117-18)

In addition to the growing numbers in institutions and their changing role, however, the data also show an even greater increase in those under supervision, from approximately 16,000 in 1926 to nearly 44,000 in 1939. The increasing numbers of those outside the formal walls of the asylum certainly gave an added significance to the interwar discussion of voluntary sterilisation, which, by that time, "had become the ideological leading edge of the eugenics movement" (Macnicol, 1989, p 154).

The 1929 Wood Report on Mental Deficiency revealed a substantial increase in the estimated scale of the problem, highlighted the variable rates of certification between different parts of the country, and revived "the idea that mental deficiency was a national threat" (Thomson, 1998, p 210). It was against such a diagnosis that the 1934 Brock Committee recommended an ultimately unattainable policy of sterilisation "as a modern and scientific way of dealing with social problems":

> Facts must be faced. It is idle to expect that the section of the community least capable of self-control will succeed in restraining one of the strongest impulses of mankind. The mere suggestion is so fantastic that it carries its own refutation. Without some measure of sterilisation these unhappy people will continue to bring into the world unwanted children, many of whom will be doomed from birth to misery and defection. (cited in King, 1999, pp 66-7)

But the issue was not confined to a national level. As Dorothy Atkinson's research in Somerset has shown, it was a pertinent issue for its county council committee members (Walmsley et al, 1999). The context was the escalating cost of providing segregation in suitable institutions and the county's declared objective to develop alternative community-based provisions. That, however, merely focused attention on the hereditarian argument and the anticipated increased demand from defective children in the next generation. It was this scenario, polarised around socialisation or segregation, that led the committee to advocate sterilisation as a means of avoiding compulsory segregation for life in an institution, and as a condition of discharge from the institution for both women and men. The debate surrounding sterilisation has thus to be located in the context of the developing community – rather than institutional – character of the interwar years.

That community ethos, however, is capable of varied interpretation. On the one hand, it offered an alternative to the institution through the development of day schools and occupation centres, as well as the various alternatives to complete confinement in an institution that were mentioned earlier. But the velvet glove of apparent progressiveness masked the iron fist of continuing surveillance, the sanction of admission or return to the institution, and the preferences about sterilisation expressed by local authorities that would have curtailed personal and individual freedom. As Desmond King (1999) has argued, it neatly points the tension between liberalism and illiberal social policy.

Conclusion

Recent historical research has begun to redefine our understanding of the institutional solution and community care, as well as the relationship between them. Much recent research evidence, has suggested that, although institutional provision expanded in the Victorian period, the family constituted the primary locus of care for the learning disabled, both prior to and in lieu of institutional confinement. Wright's (1998) research into the pre-institutional experience of 475 children admitted to the first of the voluntary asylums at Earlswood showed the primacy of the co-residing family: the significant burden of care that fell disproportionately on mothers and elder daughters and the controlling role that was the especial province of fathers and sons. Such a finding neatly encapsulates the pivotal role of family members as well as illustrating the gendered character of community care in the past, as much as in the present. Meanwhile, in the interwar years, requests for institutional admission tended to be linked to particular identifiable circumstances in the life course: "the ageing, retirement or death of parents, the arrival of new siblings and the ageing of defectives" (Thomson, 1998, p 261). Moreover, despite the increase of institutional provision that characterised that time, there is also evidence of the persistence of family care, despite the fact that "the authorities were reluctant to allow the parents or families of defectives to serve as guardians in the community" (Thomson, 1998, p 169). Some families, however, could and did resist officialdom, most usually those perceived by the authorities to be 'good' or 'respectable'. (Walmsley and Rolph, 2001). For the remainder, the situation was a paradox. On the one hand was their central role in care giving and supervision. On the other was their vilification as social problem families in some of the literature of the interwar years. As in the Victorian period, "families were the very bedrock of the system. They were often poor families and were vilified in the public writing of the eugenicists, yet they were needed and relied on to be the primary providers of care in the community" (Walmsley et al, 1999, p 202). In the mixed economy of personal welfare it seems, *plus ça change, plus ça même chose*.

Both these examples illustrate the coexistence of institutional and domiciliary-based care and control even at the time of the 19th- and early 20th-century great confinement. This is not to underestimate the significance of the institutional solution on the life experience of many of those with learning disabilities who were incarcerated within the walls of the asylum. But it is to recognise also that "the rise of the Victorian asylum and moves towards institutional care may be something of an anomaly when seen in a longer time span" (Welshman, 1999, p 206). Once the significance of that interpretation is acknowledged, integration, far from being a creation of policies in the 1960s and subsequent decades, can be seen to be one of the important continuities that link contemporary issues and debates about the locus of care to much earlier periods of British social policy. At the heart of that continuity is the ambiguity that Thomson (1998, p 169) identifies as central to the 1913 Mental Deficiency Act; "that care was intended to protect the defective from the community, yet also to protect the community from the defective". Dated terminology apart, that remains one of the dilemmas and uncertainties in the contemporary practice of integration.

References

Audit Commission (1986) *Making a reality of community care*, London: HMSO.

Bartlett, P. and Wright, D. (1999) *Outside the walls of the asylum*, London: The Athlone Press.

Bell, K.M. (1965) 'The development of community care', *Public Administration*, vol 43, no 4, pp 419-35.

Crowther, M.A. (1981) *The workhouse system 1834-1929*, London: Batsford.

Gatrell, V. (1990) 'Crime, authority and the policeman-state', in F.M.L. Thompson (ed) *The Cambridge social history of Britain 1750-1950*, vol 3, Cambridge: Cambridge University Press, pp 243-310.

Gelband, H.S. (1979) 'Mental retardation and institutional treatment in 19th-century England', University of Maryland PhD thesis (unpublished).

Gladstone, D. (1996) 'The changing dynamic of institutional care: the Western Counties idiot asylum 1864-1914', in D. Wright and A. Digby (eds) *From idiocy to mental deficiency*, London: Routledge, pp 134-60.

Goffman, E. (1961) *Asylums*, Harmondsworth: Penguin.

Harris, J. (1993) *Private lives, public spirit*, Oxford: Oxford University Press.

Hirst, D. and Michael, P. (1999) 'Family, community and the lunatic in mid-19th-century North Wales', in P. Bartlett and D. Wright (eds) *Outside the walls of the asylum*, London: The Athlone Press, pp 66-87.

Horden, P. and Smith, R. (1998) *The locus of care*, London: Routledge.

King, D. (1999) *In the name of liberalism*, Oxford: Oxford University Press.

King's Fund Centre (1980) *An ordinary life: Comprehensive locally-based residential services for mentally handicapped people*, London: King's Fund Centre.

Macnicol, J. (1989) 'Eugenics and the campaign for voluntary sterilisation in Britain between the wars', *Social History of Medicine*, vol 2, no 2, pp 147-69.

Martin, J. (1984) *Hospitals in trouble*, Oxford: Basil Blackwell.

Means, R. and Smith, R. (1998) *Community care: Policy and practice*, Basingstoke: Macmillan.

Melling, J. and Forsythe, B. (1999) *Insanity, institutions and society 1800-1914*, London: Routledge.

Miller, E.J. and Gwynne, G.V. (1972) *A life apart*, London: Tavistock.

Ministry of Health (1963) *Health and welfare: The development of community care*, London: HMSO.

Parker, R. (1988) 'An historical background to residential care', in I. Sinclair (ed) *Residential care: the research reviewed*, London: HMSO, pp 1-38.

Perkin, H. (1989) *The rise of professional society*, London: Routledge.

Pick, D. (1989) *Faces of degeneration: A European disorder c1848-c1918*, Cambridge: Cambridge University Press.

Porter, R. (1992) 'Madness and its institutions', in A. Wear (ed) *Medicine in society*, Cambridge: Cambridge University Press, pp 277-304.

Pycroft, G. (1982) *An address on idiocy*, Starcross: Western Counties Asylum.

Radford, J. and Tipper, A. (1988) *Starcross: Out of the mainstream*, Toronto: NIMR.

Rose, N. (1985) *The psychological complex: Psychology, politics and society in England 1869-1939*, London: Routledge and Kegan Paul.

Scull, A. (1979) *Museums of madness*, London: Allen Lane.

Scull, A. (1999) 'Rethinking the history of asylumdom', in J. Melling and B. Forsythe (eds) *Insanity, institutions and society 1800-1914*, London: Routledge, pp 295-315.

Simmons, H. (1978) 'Explaining social policy: the English Mental Deficiency Act of 1913', *Journal of Social History*, vol 11, no 3, pp 387-403.

Suzuki, A. (1999) 'Enclosing and disclosing lunatics within the family walls', in P. Bartlett and D. Wright (eds) *Outside the walls of the asylum*, London: The Athlone Press, pp 115-31.

The Independent (1988) Magazine Issue of 29 October, p 47.

Thomson, M. (1998) *The problem of mental deficiency*, Oxford: Clarendon Press.

Tizard, J., Sinclair, I. and Clarke, R. (1975) *Varieties of residential experience*, London: Routledge and Kegan Paul.

Walmsley, J., Atkinson, D. and Rolph, S. (1999) 'Community care and mental deficiency 1913 to 1945', in P. Bartlett and D. Wright (eds) *Outside the walls of the asylum*, London: The Athlone Press, pp 181-203.

Walmsley, J. and Rolph, S. (2001) 'The development of community care for people with learning difficulties 1913 to 1946', *Critical Social Policy*, vol 21, no 1, pp 59-80.

Walsh, O. (1999) 'Lunatic and criminal alliances in 19th-century Ireland', in P. Bartlett and D. Wright (eds) *Outside the walls of the asylum*, London: The Athlone Press, pp 132-52.

Walton, J. (1985) 'Casting out and bringing back in Victorian England: pauper lunatics 1840-70', in W.F. Bynum, R. Porter and M. Shepherd (eds) *The anatomy of madness*, vol 2, London: Tavistock, pp 132-46.

WCA (Western Counties Asylum) (1898) *Annual report*, Starcross: Western Counties Asylum.

Weiner, M. (1990) *Reconstructing the criminal*, Cambridge: Cambridge University Press.

Welshman, J. (1999) 'Rhetoric and reality: community care in England and Wales 1948-74', in P. Bartlett and D. Wright (eds) *Outside the walls of the asylum*, London: The Athlone Press, pp 204-226.

Wolfensberger, W. (1972) *The principle of normalisation in human services*, Toronto: NIMR.

Wright, D. (1998) 'Familial care of "idiot" children in Victorian England', in P. Horden and R. Smith (eds) *The locus of care*, London: Routledge, pp 176-97.

Wright, D. (1999) 'The discharge of pauper lunatics from county asylums in mid-Victorian England', in J. Melling and B. Forsythe (eds) *Insanity, institutions and society 1800-1914*, London: Routledge, pp 93-112.

TWO

Invest and reform: spending review 2002 and its control regime

Richard Parry

Introduction

The Treasury's spending review of 2002 was Labour's third spending announcement, following those of 1998 and 2000, to confirm real-terms increases in non-cash social policy going way beyond those thought sustainable in the previous 25 years. Despite uncertainties about the ability of the British economy to sustain these rates of growth, Gordon Brown delivered the high-spending approach and redefined 'investment' away from capital spending to whatever current spending he chose to define as socially valuable. As well as spending plans, the review consolidated a new control regime – instead of the old annual cycle, a biennial cycle setting plans for three years and so superseding the final year of the old plans. The way that the plans were determined confirmed the dominance of the Treasury in the UK core executive. Two continuing Treasury-run initiatives, the welfare-to-work 'New Deals' and tax credits for work, pensions and childcare, extend means-tested benefits to most of the population and implicate the Treasury in the details of social policy.

Alongside investment is 'reform', New Labour's big idea of public service agreements (PSAs) as initially set out in two White Papers both entitled *Public services for the future: Modernisation, reform, accountability* (Cm 4181, 1998, and Cm 4315, 1999) and revised alongside the spending reviews of 2000 and 2002. The PSAs express the new contractual relationship with spending departments in which reform, modernisation and service delivery are expressed in negotiated objectives and targets.

This chapter attempts to locate the process and outcome of spending review 2002 in the history of Treasury control in Britain and our understanding of the balance between spending commitment and policy success. It reviews the place of Gordon Brown in the history of the development of Treasury power and asks whether the spending increases can deliver their objectives – the 'invest' side – and evaluates the PSAs and the lower-level service delivery agreements and the widespread scepticism they have encountered – the 'reform' side.

Gordon Brown in the Treasury

Much academic and especially journalistic commentary on the Treasury is critical of its controlling tendencies, but an alternative view (developed in Deakin and Parry, 2000) suggests that its informed involvement in social policy issues should be developed in order to balance its preoccupation with spending control. Gordon Brown, Chancellor of the Exchequer since 1997, has promoted this perspective. He has established an utter domination because of his length of time in the office, the Prime Minister's lack of interest and expertise in economics, and above all because of the consonance between Brown's rigorous, intellectual and moralistic personality and the Treasury's own mentality. A self-estimated superior politician has encountered a similar department. The Treasury building now bears Brown's imprint with its refurbished open-plan section opened in 2002 by Alan Greenspan, Chairman of the US Federal Reserve and the Western world's guardian of sound money. Brown suffered a personal tragedy in January 2002 when his infant daughter Jennifer died after two weeks of life. Brown took a month off (delaying the Budget until April) and, after his evident joy at her birth, his stony countenance was resumed. The 'iron chancellor' image is apt, but the impression of boredom with lesser mortals characteristic of both Brown and the Treasury may yet stand in the way of his assumption of the Labour leadership.

In the event, 2002 emerged as the year when Brown's legendary economic touch started to elude him. After years of favourable outcomes on economic growth and tax revenues, including the avoidance of potential trouble in 2000 and 2001, Brown included optimistic growth forecasts in his April 2002 Budget. This was of particular significance because it set the macroeconomic framework for the 2002 spending review to be announced in July. In order to gain a political advantage, the highest-ever real-terms health increases were committed in April following the Wanless report (HM Treasury, 2002a). Education followed in July, and the total sums committed required the use of Brown's golden rule that the surpluses accumulated early in the current economic cycle could be offset against later deficits.

By the autumn the economic projections were unsustainable. In his pre-Budget report in November, Brown nearly halved his growth estimate and doubled his deficit projection for 2002. He presented this as a cyclical blip that would be corrected by better figures in future years, and in a speech in February 2003 was defiantly expressing confidence that "tested in adversity our system will demonstrate its credibility and resilience" (Brown, 2003, p 4). But the numbers looked more reminiscent of the structural fiscal picture of the mid-1970s or early 1990s: advance commitments to spending increases that could not be altered in response to falling revenues, and likely to result in a mixture of higher taxes and expensive borrowing in years to come.

The rhetoric of 'reform'

'Reform' is a New Labour word that covers ambivalent political intentions. Janet Newman has set out a model of governance that operates on two dimensions of difference – differentiation/decentralisation versus centralisation/ vertical integration, and continuity/order versus innovation/change (2001, Figure 2.1). The combination of the less progressive variables (centralisation and continuity) provides her 'hierarchical' model, based on formal authority and tending to control, standardisation and accountability. This fits the traditional role of the Treasury well, and suggests an explanation for the way that progressive Labour rhetoric can be turned into a top-down model of governance. Despite its unprecedented spending increases, Labour has often been condemned for the constraining effect of its spending regime. The Treasury, as the archetypal totally centralised department, is skilled at devising planning mechanisms, but less good at understanding policy outcomes in the real world.

A further Treasury theme is that of economic rationality. In the past decade, it has embraced a coherent set of objectives on stability and efficiency that have persisted across the change of government; in the words of an unpublished 1996 working paper *Strategic considerations for the Treasury 2000-05*, "Treasury officials have a high level of commitment to the efficiency of the market mechanism; to neo-classical welfare economics and to the utilitarian ethics on which they are based" (Deakin and Parry, 2000, p 84). Stated Treasury objectives have been modified under Labour to embrace employment and social justice issues, but they remain a comfortable part of what Sanderson (2002, p 2), following Bronk, calls the 'modernist-rationalist project', "a strong framework of morality, social cohesion and evidence-based government intervention". It contrasts with constructivist or postmodernist explanations in which everything is subjectively contingent, and there is no uncontested objective 'knowledge' from which policy conclusions can be drawn. But Labour's rationality is ultimately constrained by the demands of political presentation and election winning.

'Invest and reform' is a slogan that misappropriates two words. Investment is applied not just to capital expenditure with a long-term return, but to any current expenditure the government chooses to favour. Reform is not so much structural reform of government or public services as a more rigorous and market-orientated public sector labour market. Sometimes when the trade-off is offered investment is rejected – notably in the way that hospital consultants in England and Wales rejected more money in 2002 in order to resist tighter control of their working schedules by health service managers. The PSAs are an ambitious attempt to commit government departments to measurable targets of policy success and failure, but they are easier to set in place as a conceptual structure than to carry through to achievement.

The evolution of the spending review structure

Labour's new structure of spending control evolved in an unsystematic way. The underlying strategy, commonly adopted by incoming administrations, is that of zero-based budgeting: setting spending limits in the light of the government's own priorities rather than inherited patterns, and redirecting presumed savings. This approach buys time, but eventually it has to be replaced by something more resilient. In Labour's case, this was a three-stage process:

Stage 1 (1997/98): Conservative plans owned by the Labour Treasury

Gordon Brown broke with Labour tradition by playing the Chancellor even before he assumed office, announcing in January 1997 that he would observe Conservative spending plans for both 1997/98 and 1998/99. Brown was not so much laying down a principle as preventing his colleagues from conducting a debate about spending with the Treasury. In his first Budget he was quite prepared to raise some spending limits, embark upon a 'welfare to work' programme of his own financed from a tax on 'windfall' profits of public utilities, and without warning remove tax relief on the dividend income of pension funds. With Tony Blair prepared to devolve the spending area to Brown, the Treasury was left free to set up a contractual relationship with departments – agreement over policy in return for freedom from detailed control. The approach coupled a strategic grip on policy, tilted in a market-orientated direction, with a disposition to withdraw from time-consuming appraisal of detailed spending items.

Stage 2 (1998/99): a three-year real-terms regime introduced

Labour's comprehensive spending review of 1997/98 embodied the new Treasury approach and also allowed them to become involved with detailed policy through 'cross-departmental reviews'. During the review, the Treasury moved to a multi-year approach. Forward estimates for three–four future years had always been set, but subject to annual revision. The difference here was that public expenditure was divided into annually managed expenditure (AME, the biggest components being social security benefits and debt interest) and departmental expenditure limits (DEL); the latter were set for three years (1999-2002) with year-end flexibility, so that 'underspends' could be carried over. No spending review was planned for 1999 but a rolling forward of the three-year plans was set for 2000 when a new system of resource accounting and budgeting took effect. Public sector agreements seemed an afterthought. Discussed only briefly in the comprehensive spending review White Paper and not all issued until 1999, they were accompanied by a rather indiscriminate set of output and performance analyses by department.

Stage 3 (2000-02): the institution of a two-year spending cycle

The decision to hold a spending review in 2000, though presented as a consequence of the move to resource accounting and budgeting, also aligned the spending control cycle with the electoral cycle. By getting spending decisions out of the way it cleared the decks for the 2001 General Election that was nearly a replay of the 1997 result. A much-refined set of public service agreements was published at the same time as the review. By this time, the excessively 'lean' approach of stage 1 was still leaving an unhelpful legacy: total public spending as a share of GDP fell in Labour's first three years and remained below 40 per cent of GDP until 2002/03. The next review in 2002 saw the abandonment of caution: higher increases in spending were rolled forward to cover a period when the economic cycle was likely to have turned down. An ambitious and possibly imprudent spending track, presented positively by the Chancellor, was in place and does mark a break with Treasury traditions.

The development of the Treasury's own social policy

Until the mid-1990s the Treasury had an unimaginative view of social policy. It was seen as a source of insatiable demand that had to be restrained as much as possible but with limited hope of containment. Being economists, the Treasury had a horror of producer interest dominance in an imperfect market, of providing apparently 'free' goods without understanding their opportunity costs, and of a deadweight burden of paying people to do what they were doing anyway. Hence the Treasury liked pay control, charging, and means testing. They especially liked the private finance initiative of 1992 (now public–private partnerships) not just because it saved short-term money, but because it required an accurate specification of requirements and risks and the chance of exporting risks to the private sector. Much of the sense of disappointment by 'old Labour' forces in the Blair government stems from the continuing influence of this orthodoxy.

One change of perspective came from the Treasury's fundamental review of running costs in 1994. Written by Jeremy Heywood, now Tony Blair's principal private secretary, it set out a picture of a Treasury unloved by its spending department partners and unimaginative in its handling of public resources (Deakin and Parry, 2000, Chapter 4). For the first time, the review set out a positive vision of Treasury engagement with the supply-side levers of the welfare state, especially in education. The initial impact of the review was in a cull of senior management posts and empowerment of 'Young Turk' team leaders. But it set the scene for a new push into social policy once Gordon Brown became Chancellor. With the power to set interest rates transferred to the Bank of England almost immediately, the capacity was there to move into a concern with individual microeconomic behaviour.

Gordon Brown's approach is work-centred. It asserts the value of labour market participation as both an economic and social good. This is applied particularly to the route from education into employment. One part of New Labour's policy – welfare-to-work, or the New Deal – was a self-contained exercise because of the windfall tax. It allowed a more ambitious package of job subsidy and training support to under-25s, and later other policies on the same 'brand' such as those for lone parents. Income from the windfall tax ceased in 1999; spending from it was meant to end in 2000/01 but was stretched out over two more years before the programmes were absorbed into mainstream expenditure. In the event, only £1.48 billion of the £5.2 billion windfall fund was spent on the New Deal for Young People against the initial estimate of £3.15 billion (HM Treasury, 2002d, Table 4.1); but this is still more than New Deal expenditure on the older unemployed and lone parents. New Deal money and its 'brand' was extended to a wide range of policies, including educational capital expenditure, emphasising how the money served as a funding source for Brown's preferred projects rather than a challenge to general trends in the labour market. These policies have been run by other departments – until 2001 Social Security and Education and Employment, but then joined in the Department of Work and Pensions, whose Secretaries of State (Alistair Darling and then Andrew Smith) came directly from being Chief Secretary to the Treasury. The National Insurance Contributions Agency was also merged into the Inland Revenue, whose ministerial head is the Chancellor. In terms of both political ownership of the policies, and domination of the relevant institutional landscape in Whitehall, the Treasury is dominant.

More significant was the unheralded work on the relationship between taxes and benefits that took the Treasury firmly into social security territory, where because of the spending magnitudes involved they had already engaged with the details of benefit rules. The new thinking was set out in a series of papers, 'The modernisation of Britain's tax and benefit system' (an initial one on work incentives chaired by former Barclays Bank chief Martin Taylor). This was supported by a new Treasury team on Work Incentives, Poverty and Income Distribution. With this work the Treasury fully engaged with issues about social security that had been a source of frustration for so long. The use of tax credits allowed the income tax system to be used to pay and withdraw benefit. The rate at which the new tax credits were withdrawn as income rises (initially 55 per cent) was less than the poverty trap levels of previous rules but greater than the marginal rate of income tax. By 2003 the tax credit regime – now called Working Tax Credit and Child Tax Credit – was extended to 25 per cent and 85 per cent of households respectively (HM Treasury, 2002b). Although Labour made notable increases in universal child benefit, the primary approach was an old Treasury one of quite precise calibration of means testing to induce maximum impact on behaviour (and political credit) at minimum cost. The problems this approach will always cause of low take-up and low benefit to many recipients have been evident in Brown's programmes. For many, they offer only a marginal advantage over the existing benefit structure (including means-tested housing benefit and council tax benefit) or the normal workings of the labour market (which may seem preferable to the semi-compulsion of the welfare-to-work schemes).

A final aspect of the Treasury's own social policy under Labour is the definition of cross-cutting issues for study in the spending reviews and sometimes specific budgets associated with them. The Treasury's role in these is well hidden, as other departments who provide the ministerial lead administer the budgets. In fact, the choice of subjects and chairing of the review was firmly in Treasury hands. In the first review, the Treasury focused on preschool children in a Jesuitical-style 'grab them early' approach that led to the Sure Start programme. In the 2002 spending review there were seven cross-departmental reviews, and the social policy ones were on Children at Risk, Tackling Health Inequalities, and The Role of the Voluntary Sector in Public Services (HM Treasury, 2002c, Chapter 24). The weakness of cross-cutting reviews is in the gap between identifying an issue and launching policies large enough in scale to do anything about them. But implicitly they set up a client-centred approach to policy that can override departmental interests and can mobilise the concerns of Treasury ministers and officials.

The spending record: the shift from social security to service increases

It is ironic that the 'longest suicide note in history' – Labour's election manifesto of 1983 – included what was then seen as the profligate promise to increase spending on health and social services by 3 per cent a year in real terms. Under the Conservatives, any real-terms increases at all were presented as a generous concession, while social security spending consistently rose above targets.

Under Labour, the position has been reversed. This was less to do with Labour's own social policy as with the getting to grips with the main drivers of expenditure under the Conservatives – invalidity and disability benefits and income support for the unemployed. The core social security budget was contained by demarcating help for the young unemployed in the welfare-to-work budget, and channelling most of the enhanced family support through the income tax system. After arguments with statisticians, the costs of tax credits were made transparent rather than lost as a tax expenditure.

Enough time has passed to assess Gordon Brown's record on spending. This record has rested upon a consistent inaccuracy – year by year, government revenues have been underestimated and government expenditure overestimated. The first is caused by a technical failure to relate economic growth and changing employment patterns to the revenue from income tax, VAT and corporation tax, failures that are not systematic – in the 1980s there was a mysterious shortfall in VAT – but in the era of healthy growth under Gordon Brown tax revenues showed unexpected buoyancy. The second is the result of spending departments' caution over many years of tight spending control, and in particular their failure to carry through capital investment schemes. In 2002 the estimate for gross investment in 2001/02 was cut from £29.9 billion in the April Budget, already

Table 2.1: Labour's record: social spending in real terms (total managed expenditure by function) 1997/98 to 2001/02

£bn 2000/01 prices	Conservative inheritance		Labour's own plans			
	1997/98	1998/99	1999/00	2000/01	2000/02	change
Education	40.1	40.7	41.7	44.1	49.4	+23.2
Health	45.6	46.6	49.6	52.6	56.7	+24.3
Social security	104.4	103.6	105.1	105.4	109.1	+4.5
Total managed exp	346.8	347.5	350.7	367.2	382.5	+10.2
As % GDP	39.4	38.4	37.4	38.2	39.3	

Note: the pre-Budget report (November 2002) shows the latest provisional outturn for 2001/02 expenditure only £0.3 billion less than the estimate in the June 2002 source used for this table.

Source: Public expenditure statistical analyses 2002-03, Cm 5401, Table 3.4

after the end of the financial year, to £26.5 billion in the November pre-Budget statement (HM Treasury, 2002d, Table B5).

Table 2.1 shows the effect of this: it will not be until 2002/03 that spending goes above 40 per cent of GDP where it was in the last Conservative year (November 2002 estimates are 40.2 per cent in 2002/03 and 41.5 per cent in 2003/04 (HM Treasury, 2002d, Table B14)). The two years of spending plans inherited from the Conservatives were notably austere, and it was not until the pre-election year 2000/01 that Labour was able to feed through its spending priorities. Over the whole period, education and health expanded by nearly a quarter in real terms, over twice the rate of public expenditure as a whole, and in all but the final year social security spending was nearly static.

Future spending allocations as set out in spending review 2002 are given in Table 2.2 (covering four years against five in Table 2.1). These are not fully comparable with earlier plans: the price base is different, full resource budgeting has been introduced (which increases spending figures by charging for capital consumption), and plans incorporate an agreed treatment of the tax credits that will become an important part of social security transfers. The pattern remains the same, but health gains an edge over education, and income transfers start to build up again.

Comparing the three spending review plans in two categories with comparable data (Table 2.3), we can observe a ratcheting up of the growth rates from review to review coupled (in the handover years) with a sharper injection of funds that is compensating for a slow spending performance. Taken together, they amount to a major resource injection.

The evolution of public service agreements

There is a long history of semi-contractual relationships between the Treasury and spending departments. In the early 1990s the 'Portillo' fundamental

Table 2.2: Spending plans in the 2002 spending review

£bn 2002/03 prices	02/03	03/04	04/05	05/06	change
Health (UK)	68.1	73.0	78.2	84.0	+23.3
Education (UK)	53.7	57.1	59.8	63.5	+18.2
Work and pensions	7.0	7.3	7.4	7.3	+4.3
Social security benefits and credits	114.7	120.9	124.0	125.9	+9.7
Total DEL[a]	239.6	256.9	266.1	279.3	+16.6
Total AME[a]	178.7	186.4	191.8	195.0	+ 9.1
Total managed expenditure	418.4	443.3	457.9	474.3	+13.4
As % GDP	39.9	41.1	41.4	41.9	

[a] Only DELs (the departmental expenditure limits set for three years) are published in real terms; AME (annually managed expenditure, including social security) has been calculated using the same implied deflators. Social security benefits and credits include some non-social security tax credits.

Source: HM Treasury, (2002c, Tables A.4 and A.11)

expenditure reviews had put in place a policy framework to underwrite expenditure strategies. In the mid-1990s 'concordats' were negotiated as a basis for working relationships between the Treasury and the spending departments. But the PSAs themselves were not an original part of Labour's strategy; they were more a reaction to the dangers of letting go of expenditure in the new three-year regime. It is surprisingly difficult to chase down what part they have actually played in spending decisions. Neither meeting them nor failing

Table 2.3: The three spending review plans on health and education

% annual real terms increase	99/00	00/01	01/02	02/03	03/04	04/05	05/06
Health (England) 1998:	+5.5	+4.7	+4.0				
2000:	+8.3	+6.5	+7.4	+5.7			
2002:			+8.4	+7.4	+7.2	+7.3	
Education 1998:	+5.1	+5.9	+4.4				
(UK) 2000:	+10.3	+5.4	+5.3	+5.4			
2002:				+6.3	+4.7	+6.2	

Source: Parry and Deakin (2003, Table 3), and Table 2.2 above

to meet them has any automatic consequences on expenditure authorisations. They are meant to be monitored constantly by the Cabinet Committee on Public Expenditure and Public Services (PSX) but this is thought to meet infrequently. They are in theory a joint exercise between the Treasury and the Cabinet Office, but this gets caught up in the Blair versus Brown fissure in the government.

The control mechanism was described by former Treasury spending director Gill Noble in 2000 as follows:

> the main carrot and stick of the PSA framework is that performance against targets is monitored quarterly. That is reported back to the PSX committee. PSX has meetings with the ministers who are missing their targets … if the performance does not match the targets, one of the parliamentary committees will ask the ministers to account for that. That is quite a strong stick. (Scottish Parliament Finance Committee, 2000, p 136)

But the stick is a blunt one. The 1998 PSA White Paper conceded that:

> should a target not be met there is no question of money being deducted from the budget for that department. Nor will additional funding over and above that already allocated be made available simply because a department is failing to meet its targets, but support and advice will be given by the committee. (Cm 4181, 1998, p 2)

Targets are meant to help departments to achieve the government's objectives, and to highlight where they need special help to do so, but in the cynical world of expenditure politics no one is going to embrace them as a neutral mechanism.

Hence it is not surprising that the Treasury has been defensive about the centrepiece of their strategy. In evidence to the Treasury Select Committee in 1999 (HC 378) academic critics such as Colin Talbot scorned the way the concept has been used, and the reaction of MPs, Commons committees and journalists has been generally sceptical (see also Talbot, 2000). In autumn 2002 the Commons Public Administration Committee launched another investigation into public sector targets; in evidence to it on 16 January 2003 Suma Chakrabarti, Permanent Secretary at the Department for International Development, admitted that:

> undoubtedly in the first spending review of this government in 1998, when I was at the Treasury, we wrote down far too many targets … and what has happened with each spending review is there has been a learning process, so it has come down to 160 and now 130 over time and I think rightly so. (Q 619)

On 18 July 2002 Gordon Brown, in evidence to the Treasury Committee, had been unable to give a coherent defence of the way PSAs were used and had to admit that the government was channelling money into the areas it considered as priorities, not the ones where the PSA record showed that it had been most usefully spent. This was illustrated in an exchange about the Home Office:

> Q 320 (Andrew Tyrie, Con); Is there any level of failure to perform on the Home Office's target that might have led you to alter the 5.6 per cent real terms increase? Any level at all?

> Brown: Again, your point seems to be that the public should somehow suffer through having less police, that we are not meeting all our objectives. Surely the important thing is to bring in a process of reform which guarantees that the public will get the best service.

What do PSAs look like?

Public service agreements consist of objectives and targets that are meant to be SMART – specific, measurable, achievable, relevant and timed. They are not contracts in any legal sense, and are not fully auditable documents because much of the delivery detail has been kept out of departmental annual reports. The National Audit Office's major (and generally positive) review of the first two rounds of PSAs reported difficulties in translating PSA targets into operational targets and linking them with other planning systems and service providers' priorities (National Audit Office, 2001, p 34).

Below the PSA are a second level of targets – originally called output and performance analyses (OPA), and subsequently service delivery agreements (SDAs). The OPA document (HM Treasury, 1999) attempted to set out a structure of PSA targets, indicators for measuring progress against them, and performance against productivity targets, but departmental presentation was inconsistent. Some OPAs were in effect additional targets, some reworkings of them in different language. Not all departments provided a full methodology of the performance measures, and some entries were cursory. The service delivery agreements are better, but again not consistent in presentation and tending to confuse indicators of success with delivery mechanisms that in many cases involve other agencies. There are also technical documents for each department that define the targets and the way they are to be measured more precisely, and departmental investment strategies on plans for capital investment related to the achievement of stated departmental objectives.

At the highest level, we can get a sense of what the Treasury is prepared to commit itself to by looking at its own social policy targets (Table 2.4), matters where it is not just negotiating with departments but is prepared to take, or at least share, responsibility itself. The 1998 targets were quite soft, a matter of putting in place policies to which Labour was committed, but the later ones took on board a commitment about child poverty that might well be hard to achieve later on. Social policy targets are held jointly with the responsible department (now Work and Pensions): fine for Labour's vision of joined-up

Table 2.4: The Treasury's own social policy targets

1998
• put in place policies to reduce structural unemployment over the cycle;
• put in place policies to allocate all the proceeds of the windfall tax so that, by May 2002, 250,000 under-25 year olds move off benefit and into work;[a]
• maintain a minimum income guarantee for pensioners and severely disabled people;[a]
• provide an income guarantee of at least £190 a week for working families by October 1999

2000
• increase employment over the economic cycle;
• make substantial progress towards eradicating child poverty by reducing the number of children in poverty by at least a quarter by 2004.[a]

2002
• demonstrate progress by spring 2006 on increasing the employment rate and reducing the unemployment rate over the economic cycle;[a]
• reduce the number of children in low-income households by at least a quarter by 2004, as a contribution towards the broader target of halving child poverty by 2010 and eradicating it by 2020.[a]

[a] Targets held jointly with the spending department
Source: PSA White Papers, 1998, Cm 4181; 2000, Cm 4808; 2002, Cm 5571

government, but raising problems of accountability if things go wrong. It may also be a smart strategy for the spending department; in his evidence mentioned above Suma Chakrabarti explained how he had promoted a joint paper with the Treasury on the best evidence-based indicators of the value of foreign aid, so that the Treasury would own the DfID PSA targets (Q 653).

The NAO found a major shift towards outcome indicators in the first two PSAs – from 15 per cent of the 387 1999/2002 ones, to 68 per cent of the 160 2001/04 ones (2001). For a departmental example, we can look at Health (Table 2.5), which has tried systematically to set outcome indicators that are not just reports of health service activities or plans. Nearly half of the 2002 targets seek outcomes. After some rather exposed targets in 1998 (on size of waiting lists and in emergency admissions) the 2000 and 2002 PSAs are very consistent, and rather long term. They caused no complications at the 2001 election but might do so at the next.

The Health example makes it clear that the 2002 PSAs were updates of the 2000 ones, supplemented by some new policy initiatives. What is striking is the long timescale of some of the objectives. The department's technical note stretched out some of these even further: targets to be achieved 'by' or 'from' a calendar year typically refer to 31 December of the year, and the mortality improvements by 2010 are actually the average of 2009, 2010 and 2011, which will not be known until July 2012. How and when corrective action might be taken to avert missed targets is unclear.

Table 2.5: Health PSA social policy targets 2000 and 2002 compared

Maintained
- reduce mortality rates by 2010 from heart disease by at least 40% and from cancer by at least 20% (both for under-75s) and from suicide and undetermined injury by at least 10%;
- reduce the maximum wait for an outpatient appointment to three months and the maximum wait for inpatient treatment to six months by the end of 2005;
- guaranteed access to a primary care professional within 24 hours and to a primary care doctor within 48 hours from 2004;
- all hospital appointments pre-booked by 2005 [2002 PSA: the end of 2005];
- outcomes for care leavers at least 75% of those achieved by all young people in the same area, and at least 15% of children in care attain five good GCSEs, by 2004;
- increase participation of problem drug users in drug treatment programmes by 55% by 2004 and by 100% by 2008.

Dropped
- two thirds of all outpatient appointments and inpatient planned admissions will be pre-booked by 2003/04 [in addition to 2005 target as above].

Added
- achieve progressive further cuts with the aim of reducing the maximum inpatient and day case waiting times to three months by 2008;
- reduce the under-18 conception rate by 50% by 2010;
- increase by March 2006 the number of those supported intensively to live at home to 30% of the total being supported by social services at home or in residential care;
- by 2010 reduce inequalities in health outcomes by 10% as measured by infant mortality and life expectancy at birth.

Source: PSA White Papers, 1998, Cm 4181; 2000, Cm 4808; 2002, Cm 5571

PSAs and SDAs as political mechanisms

We can distinguish PSAs on two dimensions – *location of responsibility for delivery* (government at various levels and agencies, individual behaviour, national trends, international trends) and *timescale* (by the next spending review, by the next election, by the next election but one, or a longer period outside the time horizon of government). There are many considerations of rational policy-making and political tactics within these dimensions. As Powell (2002, p 238) points out in his analysis of Labour's first term promises, there is confusion in the analysis of targets, especially the relation between manifesto pledges and PSAs. Unlike the local government approach of best value, it is scarcely possible to see the PSAs as a coherent strategy for managing quality and service delivery (Boyne et al, 2002).

In 1999 Treasury official Adam Sharples set out the position as follows:

> The accounts of the department are clearly financial statements which have to be subject to an audit in the normal way. The Public Service Agreements and the measures that are attached to these agreements are closer to policy statements, they are statements of what it is that the Government and the departments are seeking to deliver in policy terms. The Government has

accepted – and I think it is sticking its neck out on this – a transparent process of accountability for those services in committing itself to publishing each year a report on progress against those targets. (House of Commons Treasury Committee, 1999, p 37)

Sharples was right about the government sticking its neck out, and in the event the progress reports are actually the departmental annual reports published as command papers every spring, supplemented from 2002 by autumn performance reports (also White Papers but of varying formats and publication dates) updating progress. Each department has presented its subsidiary documents in a different way. The only consistent documents produced by the Treasury have been the PSA White Papers of 1998/99, 2000 and 2002. Below that level, it requires detailed investigation for each department and an understanding of their own plans and strategies to discern what is going on. From April 2003 the Treasury promises comprehensive web-based reporting of the 2003–06 targets.

Notions of an overall success rate against PSAs are hard to pin down because of the varying timescales for achieving them and the decreasing use of intermediate targets towards the final goal. Rhetoric about being 'on course' puts off the evil day until after the next spending round or next General Election; departmental reports are becoming expert in euphemisms like 'nearly met' and 'some slippage'. In his uncomfortable evidence session to the Treasury Committee on 18 July 2002, Gordon Brown bandied about the figure of an 87 per cent success rate but basically handed over responsibility to departments:

Q 305 (David Laws, Lib Dem): Who has measured that 87 per cent of the targets have been met? Is that the Treasury's own estimate?

Brown: What is going to happen is that departmental reports will be published and then a final reckoning can be made.

This line undermines the contractual basis of the PSAs in which, in the principal-agent terminology used to describe contract or employment relationships, the Treasury is meant to be the 'principal' and the spending department its 'agent'. The PSAs aptly illustrate Lane's point that "the key problem in agency relationships is to define a contract that motivates the agent to work for the principal at the same time as the principal pays a compensation that corresponds to the effort of the agency" (2000, p 132). At the departmental level, it is clear that important targets are not being met: for instance, the Department for Education and Skills' November 2002 report revealed failure to meet the 2002 targets on literacy, numeracy and truancy (DfES, 2002, p 6). These were 1998 targets coming home to roost. But this brings us back to the original philosophy of the PSAs: it is not the achievement that matters but the effort in trying. Once it was confirmed that departments would not be punished or rewarded in future allocations for their record in previous ones, the government's approach could only be that of putting more money into its own priority areas. Paradoxically, a performance shortfall could be seen as evidence of the intractability of the problem and hence a demand for further resources: this is evident in both criminal justice and education, areas in which the cabinet ministers are political heavyweights identified with Blair rather than Brown.

Problems of delivering spending increases

There is a wider problem of delivering on spending plans in terms of both the effective commitments of the sums authorised and the achievement of objectives. Whereas in many systems, as in the USA, the government's plans are the beginning of the story as negotiations lead to amendments and additions, the Treasury plans are the effective decisions. But they are not assured of implementation. There are delicate problems of macroeconomic management in which actions have unsuspected consequences. For instance, pension policy has been affected by the taxation of pension funds' assets, the other fiscal stratagem of 1997 alongside the much more successful windfall tax, and by the running of fiscal surpluses that have obviated the issue of long-term government bonds that might have tempted pension funds out of equities before the stock market fell. The resultant weakening of the pension system prompted the government's pension review published in December 2002 (Cm 5677).

The very fast increases planned for labour-intensive social services are particularly prone to capacity constraints. This operates for straightforward microeconomic reasons. Professional skills require training and so cannot be increased rapidly. Even though government is a near-monopoly purchaser, it does not seek to operate a totally uniform national pay policy nor seek to control the recruitment policies of individual hospitals or schools. Just as the Conservatives did before them, Labour's policy seeks to identify the best-performing hospitals, schools and local authorities and give them the freedom and the means to increase their input of resources in a tight labour market. Resource expansion can mean that productivity and efficiency gains can slow or disappear, as seems to be happening in health (Le Grand, 2002).

Labour has tended to neglect these considerations. The health review the Treasury commissioned under Derek Wanless – coming to grips with the issue itself, and not leaving it to the Health Department – delivered a fairly unambiguous warning about what might happen under the spending increases the Chancellor implemented:

> Given the expected workforce supply over the next few years, the Review believes that its projections for UK real terms spending growth of 7.1 to 7.3 per cent a year over the next five years are at the upper end of what could sensibly be spent. Indeed, to be wisely spent, they would represent a very considerable management challenge. The risks of spending being ineffective rises with the spending growth rate. The figures already incorporate assumptions that the significant workforce expansion planned for the next

few years is fully delivered, that Information and Communication Technology spend can be doubled and spent productively, and that waiting times and National Service Frameworks commitments are met. (HM Treasury, 2002a, para 5.17)

In the event, the Chancellor implemented the 7 per cent-plus annual increases without addressing Wanless's concerns and in the face of evidence in 2002/03 of difficulty in gearing up NHS activity to meet the government's targets.

Conclusion

PSAs express the mechanistic trend of New Labour – setting a structure that appears to have non-partisan rationality. It fits in well with the self-confident style of the Treasury. Permanent Secretary (from 2002) Gus O'Donnell and spending chiefs Nick Macpherson and Adam Sharples are sharp and outgoing, and O'Donnell's predecessor Andrew Turnbull is now Head of the Home Civil Service at the Prime Minister's right hand. Traditional Treasury positions are still asserted: on the euro, and on the sanctity of aggregate Treasury control of expenditure. The argument in 2002 with the Health Department on foundation hospitals was on a classic issue of setting up public sector organisational forms that are independent players on the capital and labour markets and so evade Treasury constraint. The dispute was settled by a reaffirmation of overall Treasury control of the health budget.

For spending departments, life is always simpler when money is flowing around. Their position has also benefited from two phenomena: the Treasury's decision in the 1990s to behave more fraternally to spending agencies, with less rudeness and fewer brutal demands; and the Blair–Brown fissure in the government. Because of the latter, the concept of the PSX Committee system, serviced by the Treasury and the No 10's Performance and Innovation Unit, monitoring spending and compliance has never really worked as intended. The last thing Gordon Brown has wanted is frequent Cabinet-level debates about his economic policy intentions, and the big spenders go straight to Blair and his team. After the 2001 election the Performance and Innovation Unit became the Strategy Unit, responsible for longer-term strategy. Michael Barber's Delivery Unit then became the agent for focusing on the most urgent demands for securing PSA targets. In late 2002 the Unit decided to move its physical (but not organisational) location into the Treasury.

The invest and reform strategy, and the mechanisms of the spending reviews and the public service agreements, have provided a structure of rationality to a Labour decision to spend – and if necessary to tax – in an attempt to make the core elements of the British welfare state deliver on their potential. The PSAs do not function as performance-related public expenditure, and the spending reviews are political struggles rather than synoptic evaluations. They let the Treasury do what it is prepared to do, and their novelty and resilience should not be exaggerated.

References

Boyne, G., Gould-Williams, J.S., Law, J. and Walker, R.M. (2002) 'Best value – total quality management for local government?', *Public Money and Management*, vol 22, no 4, pp 9-16.

Brown, G. (2003) 'A modern agenda for prosperity and social reform', speech to the Social Market Foundation, 3 February, London: HM Treasury, press notice 12/03.

Deakin, N. and Parry, R. (2000) *The Treasury and social policy: The contest for control of welfare strategy*, London: Macmillan.

DfES (Department for Education and Skills) (2002) *Autumn performance report 2002*, Cm 5689, London: The Stationery Office.

House of Commons Treasury Committee (1999) *Public service agreements*, seventh report 1998-99, HC 378, London: The Stationery Office.

HM Treasury (1999) *The government's measures of success: Output and performance analyses*, London: HM Treasury.

HM Treasury (2002a) *Securing our future health – Taking a long-term view*, final report of Derek Wanless and the Health Trends Review Team, London: HM Treasury.

HM Treasury (2002b) *The child and working tax credits*, The modernisation of Britain's tax and benefit system No 10, London: HM Treasury.

HM Treasury (2002c) *Opportunity and security for all: Investing in an enterprising, fairer Britain – New public spending plans 2003-06*, Cm 5570, London: The Stationery Office.

HM Treasury (2002d) *Pre-budget report 2002*, Cm 5664, London: The Stationery Office.

Lane, J-E. (2000) *New public management*, London: Routledge.

Le Grand, J. (2002) 'Further tales from the British National Health Service', *Health Affairs*, vol 21, no 3, pp 116-27.

National Audit Office (2001) *Measuring the performance of government departments*, HC 301, 2000-1, London: The Stationery Office.

Parry, R. and Deakin, N. (2003) 'Cross-cutting coordination: concordat style – the changing role of the Treasury in controlling public expenditure in Britain', in J. Wanna (ed) *Controlling public expenditure: The changing roles of central budget agencies – better guardians?*, Cheltenham: Edward Elgar.

Powell, M. (ed) (2002) *Evaluating New Labour's welfare reforms*, Bristol: The Policy Press.

Sanderson, I. (2002) 'Evaluation, policy learning and evidence-based policy making', *Public Administration*, vol 80, no 1, pp 1-22.

Scottish Parliament Finance Committee (2000) *The finance functions of the Scottish Executive*, 12th report, SP 167, Edinburgh: The Stationery Office.

Talbot, C. (2000) 'Performing "performance" – a comedy in five acts', *Public Money and Management*, vol 20, no 4, pp 63-8.

THREE

Who choosing what? The evolution of the use of 'choice' in the NHS, and its importance for New Labour

Ian Greener

Introduction

"Choice is an important principle for our reform programme" (Tony Blair, 2002, p 28).

> Choice is very, very important, for two reasons. First, because it is absolutely in accord with the sort of society in which we live. People make choices in their lives continually. Second, because I think choice is the primary means by which you can drive the NHS to better focus on the needs of its individual patients. (Alan Milburn, Secretary of State for Health, interviewed by Nicholas Timmins, 2002, p 132)

This chapter considers the role of 'choice' in UK health policy documents, examining the remarkable changes over who is meant to make choices in the National Health Service and what sort of choices they are supposed to be making, especially with regard to New Labour's health policy since 1997. 'Choice' is a key aspect of consumerism in contemporary welfare policy; indeed "the maximization of patient choice" is at the top of Nettleton's (1995, p 249) list of what consumerism means in the context of the NHS. But 'choice' has meant different things at different times. Given New Labour's recent attempt to place patient choice at the heart of driving reform in the NHS, it is especially salient to compare this initiative with attempts to utilise choice as a policy instrument in the past, and consider what it might mean for the future.

The evolution of the health consumer

In crude, but essentially accurate, terms we can periodise the 1970s as being a time in which we can discern a mounting criticism of public services both from the public and media. This criticism became more vocal during the

1980s amid a move towards a more individualist model of society (Walsh, 1994; Beardwood et al, 1999), paralleled by the resurgence of neo-conservatism and a populist shift from the collectivist ideals of the post-war consensus to a free-market, individualised ideal to self-care, individual responsibility and the decline of the state (Mishra, 1990). The NHS managerial reforms of the early 1980s were made in the name of providing better 'customer service', with the vocabulary of private sector business enthusiastically imported to that end (Meerabeau, 1998). Patient 'choice' then assumed centre stage in the 1989 White Paper, *Working for patients* (Secretary of State for Health, 1989) and was further embedded in the NHS with the publication of *The Citizen's Charter* in 1991, which committed health workers to clear standards in public services, so introducing a 'mimic consumerism' into health services (Klein, 2000).

The movement towards offering greater consumer choice in healthcare has therefore come alongside wider societal changes that have resulted in patients becoming more confident in challenging physician authority (Haug and Lavin, 1983), and calling into question the producer-led service of 1948 (Klein, 2000) by requiring clinicians to respond to patient complaints and to demonstrate far greater accountability.

Hugman (1994) differentiates between 'market consumerism', in which the consumer is purchaser and the state regulator, and 'democratic consumerism' in which the consumer is not the purchaser, but is involved in defining the service, and argues that the internal market introduced by the Conservatives in 1991 contains elements of both models. According to Hugman, the internal market is a clear example of a consumerist policy as patients were now meant to take responsibility for making provision to meet their own needs where possible. Abercrombie (1994) appears to endorse this, noting that authority had shifted from the producer of public services, to the consumer.

Scepticism with the health consumer project, however, appears in the work of other commentators. Stacey (1976) makes the crucial point that the patient's body is the work object for treatment, raising a series of underlying tensions concerning medical knowledge and power, and the ability of the patient to act as a consumer in the same way as in other arenas where such information asymmetries and potential for self-damage exist. Toth (1996) claims that many of the prerequisites in neo-classical theory for the functioning of a market do not exist in healthcare; we do not have a range of competing goods or high quality information, and so not much of a market. Lupton et al (1991) make similar points, noting that patients do not have the bargaining power, freedom of choice, knowledge or the motivation to choose, and also lack the power to challenge medical authority. Gabbott and Hogg (1994) question the extent to which patients are able to assess their doctor's ability to cure, and so make evaluations about the type of treatment they are receiving, and Shackley and Ryan (1994), while acknowledging that patients appear to want more information concerning their treatment, do not necessarily want to make treatment choices, with there being considerable barriers to consumer sovereignty in healthcare.

The notion of the health consumer then, is subject to considerable contest. Shackley and Ryan (1994, p 518) define the concept in neo-classical economic terms as "someone who can adequately assimilate information on the costs and quality of health care, and on the basis of such information, has an ability and a desire to make health care choices...". This definition, however, appears extremely rationalistic, with contemporary scholarship questioning the extent of reflexivity and subjectivity present within it (Hoggett, 2001; Greener, 2002b).

It is possible to locate the confusion over choice as a part of the project of 'reflexive modernity' (Beck et al, 1994) in which contemporary society is increasingly characterised by individuals having no choice but expected to make choices – perhaps we are being coerced into making healthcare choices because we feel we have no alternative. In this context, healthcare becomes another life area in which risk appears to have moved from being the collective responsibility of society to an individual risk, with an associated hatred of the dependency that the doctor–patient relationship conventionally represents (Hoggett, 2000).

Equally, there is some confusion between the terms 'consumer' and 'customer' (Pickard, 1998). Here, we will define them in line with Mullen (1990). Type I markets, in which individual users are purchasers, we will call 'consumer' markets. Type II markets, where an intermediary such as a doctor works on behalf of the ultimate user, we will call 'customer' markets.

As we saw above, there are serious questions about the ability of NHS patients to become consumers and make choices for themselves, a declared aim that is central to New Labour's health policy. In the conclusion of this chapter we will consider the possibility that it might be more appropriate to view patients as 'customers' instead.

We now consider in greater depth the evolution of choice in the NHS through an analysis of its usage in policy documents.

Choice in health policy documents

The health policy of governments in the 1960s and 1970s appears, in many respects, to be remarkably continuous. Both Labour and Conservative governments appear to have based their approach upon implicitly Fabian assumptions in which the NHS was perceived as an organisation where professionals made choices on behalf of patients, with the mode of behaviour expected resembling a visit to a 'church', with the sick as passive recipients of wisdom from superiors (Klein, 1993). Mention of 'choice' is most striking by its absence in the White and Green papers leading up to the first reform of the NHS in 1974 (Ministry of Health, 1968; Department of Health and Social Security, 1970, 1971). In those years it appears only in the context of choices from the centre concerning the allocation of capital monies and details concerning local authority membership. This is clearly the paternalistic model of healthcare prominent at that time (Hewitt, 1992).

We can see the beginnings of a new approach, however, in the White Paper that precedes the 1974 reforms (Secretary of State for Health and Social Services, 1972). Keith Joseph suggests that "users will be able, as now, to cross boundaries without hindrance or formality, to get the services best suited to his needs, his convenience, and, as far as practicable, his choice" (1972, p 11). The health service in 1972 was clearly a very different organisation, with a discourse in place carrying a set of very different assumptions. Then, the NHS was dominated by health professionals, with patient choice only being admitted "as far as practicable". Patients (who were obviously all male), far from driving the service, should only have their wishes taken into account where it was straightforward for health professionals to do so. This is perhaps entirely what we would expect in a document from that time period; but a second usage of 'choice' in the document is far more prophetic:

> The Government recognises the contribution made by the private sector of medicine to the sum of health care, through a wide variety of private hospitals, nursing homes and other institutions and through individual practitioners. It thinks it right for people to have an opportunity to exercise a personal choice to seek treatment privately. The existence of facilities for private treatment, both within and outside the NHS, provides this opportunity. The private sector can also act as a stimulus to enterprise, development and high standards of service.... (Secretary of State for Health and Social Services, 1972, p 42)

This is a remarkable statement, at least ten years ahead of its time, bearing some resemblance to the discourse of Conservatives during the 1980s. While many conventional accounts of health policy present the election of Thatcher as Prime Minister in 1979 as a 'cut-off' with the preceding 'golden age' of policy (Lowe, 1993), this gives us a glimpse of what was to come later.

The Thatcher government's first significant health policy document came in 1983 (DHSS, 1983), with Roy Griffiths' inquiry into Health Service Management. The Griffiths model of healthcare reorganisation, radically different from what had gone before in terms of content and presentation, is important because it marks the beginning of the process of the introduction of the 'new public management' (Hood, 1991) into health policy. The word 'choice' does not appear at all in the text, signalling a very different view of health services in which responsive managers acted to make sure that their customers were satisfied, rather than attempting to convert them into Type II consumers, hence Griffiths' lament that:

> Businessmen have a keen sense of how well they are looking after their customers. Whether the NHS is meeting the needs of the patient, and the community, and can prove that it is doing so, is open to question. (Department of Health and Social Security, 1983, p 10)

The internal market

The word 'choice' has strong ideological associations with the Thatcherite reforms of public services in the 1980s. An explicit goal of Thatcherism was to produce a radical cultural change in British society (Phillips, 1996, 1998). The supporters of the project described it as a break from the weaknesses of the previous policy consensus, and sought to replace it with an anti-collectivist, pro-individualist and pro-market value system (Ranalegh, 1992). We can see immediately how a more consumerist notion of the patient is a development entirely in concert with the Thatcherite agenda, placing 'choice' almost dogmatically at the heart of public sector reform.

The exact timing of the internal market reforms, located towards the end of Thatcher's time as Prime Minister rather than the beginning, is a complex affair, demonstrating the difficulty of securing significant reform in the politically sensitive area of health, even for a government with a significant parliamentary majority (Greener, 2002a). The movement towards a market-driven organisation for healthcare was perhaps predictable in direction, however, if not in actual content; the Conservatives had made clear that they expected public services to be more responsive, more like private sector business, and the introduction of the 'contracting out' of ancillary and cleaning services during the first half of the decade introduced the idea that it was possible to introduce sub-contracting into health organisation in the name of efficiency and cost reduction. The internal market separation of purchaser and provider was meant to make consumerism implicit in the health service, driving change, and the improvements in healthcare that the government demanded in the face of increasing criticism from all sides after the 1987 General Election (Klein, 2000).

'Choice', unsurprisingly, appears repeatedly in the Conservative 1989 White Paper, *Working for patients* (Secretary of State for Health, 1989) (there are at least 40 instances). The introduction of the document explicitly describes one of the aims of the document as being "to extend patient choice" (Foreword, p 3), and the justification for its use comes most prominently in the section examining NHS Trusts:

> The Government proposes to give NHS Hospital Trusts a range of powers and freedoms that are not, and will not be, available to health authorities generally. Greater freedom will stimulate greater enterprise and commitment, which will in turn improve services for patients. NHS Hospital Trusts will be a novel part of a system of hospital care alongside health authority-managed and private sector hospitals, and will increase the range of choice available to patients and their GPs. (Secretary of State for Health, 1989, p 25)

The identity of the agents making choices in the 1989-model NHS, however, is a little unclear; at some times it is clearly GPs – "Offering choice to patients means involving GPs far more in key decisions" (Secretary of State for Health, 1989, p 36) – but at others it is patients and doctors – "The first change is to give patients the opportunity to make a better informed choice ... and place more choice in the hands of individual patients and to shift responsibility, as far as possible, to those who are in the position directly to satisfy the needs of patients" (Secretary of State for Health, 1989, p 55). But patients actually had very little ability to exercise choice in the internal market. They could choose their GP, but it was not clear on what basis (Salisbury, 1989); they could also choose whether or not to take out private health insurance – a choice severely constrained by income. When in hospital, patients had an additional choice of whether they wished to pay extra for amenities such as a side room, but that choice was always compromised by a lack of availability. Choice then, as now, was crucially constrained by a lack of capacity to cope with it.

Instead, it was doctors and district health authorities that were meant to make choices through contracting with efficient providers, and making sure their services were responsive to patients. This is a 'customer' or Type II market, despite its pretences at consumerism and Type I status. In 1989, GPs especially were meant to treat their patients as customers, driving improvement in healthcare on their behalf. As such, the internal market was an extension of the earlier managerial reforms, an attempt to get health professionals and managers to adopt a greater customer focus, but in the name of a consumerism that the reforms did not deliver.

But even this rather compromised internal market framework of the 1989 White Paper did not come into practice quite as its architects envisaged. In November 1990, William Waldegrave replaced Kenneth Clarke as Secretary of State for Health, beginning a more conciliatory period in which the government, instead of imposing more reform, tried to get its existing legislation to work (Ham, 2000, p 14). When Virginia Bottomley took over from Waldegrave in 1992, her ambitions were similarly limited to "ensure that the reforms were so well established ... that they would no longer be a part of the party political debate" (quoted in Ham, 2000, p 19). From 1990 onwards, then, there was a period of attempting to calm down the health policy arena in the UK from the storm whipped up by Clarke's internal market proposals. But this calmness came at a price; it became increasingly clear that the reforms were never going to work in the radical way imagined by Clarke at their onset (West, 1998). The state found it impossible not to meddle in the day-to-day running of the service (Lapsley, 1994), a problem it still faces today (Halpern, 2001). Through the 1990s we can see an assumption that doctors would drive markets in response to their patients' needs, but practice indicates that this did not occur. Instead of health providers behaving in a competitive way, they appear to have been far happier to maintain the status quo (Walsh, 1995; Bennett and Ferlie, 1996).

By 1996, under another Secretary of State for Health, Stephen Dorrell, the Conservatives released another NHS White Paper, *A service with ambitions* (Secretary of State for Health, 1996). 'Choice' appears to have once again almost disappeared completely from view. This document built on *The health of the nation* (Secretary of State for Health, 1992) in presenting a view of the health service in a wider context than simply an organisation designed to cure illness. It described how the government will provide advice on "how to stay healthy and choose healthy options" (p 27) and promised "to provide information to patients and the public so they can make informed choices about their own lives, know what action to take to help themselves, know when and how to seek help, and so they can take part in decisions and choices about care and treatment" (p 42). This is the Conservatives' most radical public health statement.

Alongside the reduction in ambition attached to the internal market project, we can see an accompanying shift in the language of health policy. The discourse of the 1989 White Paper became diluted; with competition fading into contestability, purchasing turned into commissioning; and health service hospitals were urged to curtail radical change in their contracting habits as the market began (Sheldon, 1990). Reviews of the success or otherwise of the internal market in securing the changes the government required appear ambiguous to say the least (Ham, 1994; Robinson and Le Grand, 1994; Le Grand et al, 1998). Light (1997) suggests that the government's goals could have been achieved with far less organisational flux than that caused by the introduction of the internal market. The extent to which general practitioners and district health authorities could exercise choice between health trusts, even should they have wished to do so, was questionable. Local people for the most part wished to be treated locally, and the incentive for general practitioners to contract outside their normal patterns was not clear, except in the face of manifest failure of their usual provider of care. This ambivalence towards the contracting process led to a 'precautionary principle' (Wainwright, 1998) and conservatism.

The attempt to introduce customers, or Type II consumers, into health policy via the internal market, appears in retrospect rather unclear in result (Le Grand, 1999); Klein's comment, borrowing from Galbraith, is perhaps the most cutting, in stating that, in retrospect, the reforms were like the "bland leading the blind" (Klein, 1998, p 116). We should perhaps consider the internal market experiment as being a series of reforms more managerial than market based in nature, building on the earlier 'Griffiths' reforms to provide chief executives with additional powers over clinicians (Greener, 2002a).

Policy after the internal market

If the internal market was something of a red herring, perhaps being more a managerial reform than a market-based one, the recent return of 'choice' to the health policy agenda is a little perplexing, the resurrection of a dead policy that never had much life in the first place. It also marks a significant reversal of New Labour's health policy (Boyne et al, 2003).

In 1997 the 'internal market' introduced by their Conservative predecessors was referred to in almost totalitarian terms in which "The market *forced* NHS organisations to compete against each other..." (Secretary of State for Health, 1997, sec 2.14, italics added) and "Hospital clinicians ... have been deliberately pitted against each other" (2.12) in a "system in which individual organisations were *forced* to work to their own *agendas* rather than the need of individual patients" (2.10, italics added). The internal market fragmented health services (2.10), caused unfairness (2.12), distortion (2.14), inefficiency (2.16), bureaucracy (2.18) and instability (2.20). New Labour, upon coming to power, claimed quickly to have abolished the internal market (1.3), but at the same time to have retained "the separation between the planning of hospital care and its provision" (2.6), retaining the essential separation between purchaser and provider introduced by the Conservatives. The proposals introduced by New Labour in 1997, taken together, signify a period of significant change for the health service (Ham, 1999), with the introduction of primary care groups in place of GP fundholders, and an attempt to integrate care across professional groupings in a genuinely radical way.

What was also apparent in the 1997 White Paper, however, was a return to a more Fabian approach to health policy with an emphasis on the importance of medical expertise in the health service; "Local doctors and nurses, who best understand patients' needs" (1.4) and nurses and family doctors "are best placed to understand their patients' needs as a whole and to identify ways of making local services more responsive" (2.7). New Labour presented their policy as removing the 'obstacles' (2.2) of the internal market and instead reorganising health services so that health professionals would enter into partnerships and collaborations with one another, and with those working in social services, in order to provide an integrated, efficient and high quality health service. The group to be 'empowered' by reform was not patients, but the medical profession (see sections 2.6, 2.12 and 2.24). The election of New Labour appeared to have represented a move from Enthoven to Etzioni (Klein, 1998), a mix of the radical, but also the pragmatic and populist (Powell, 2000). This rather contradictory mix of the old and the new (Paton, 1999) was the favoured solution in 1997.

But impatience appears to have quickly undermined this first attempt at reform. By 2000, the consumerist discourse was once again making itself felt. The explicit 'vision' of the NHS plan (Secretary of State for Health, 2000) was to offer "people fast and convenient care" (1.1) with services available "when people require them, tailored to their individual needs" (1.1). Alongside this there is a marked reduction in faith in health professionals to deliver the change the government requires – "Too many patients feel talked at, rather than listened to" (10.1) – a remarkable turnaround in attitude towards health professionals from the position in 1997. The driver of change in the NHS plan is its performance measurement system, with the implicit trust in clinicians present in 1997 becoming less apparent as health trusts were told that they were to be publicly graded on a range of indicators, and the most successful performers given additional funding and freedoms (see also DoH, 2001c). But the government's frustrations with the health service still do not appear to have abated. By the end of 2001 they published a consultative document entitled *Extending choice for patients* (DoH, 2001a) that appears to show the reintroduction of a favouring of the market mechanism that the government spoke about so derogatorily in 1997. Under the proposed system, patients will be able to choose not only when, but also where and how they will be treated when referred from their GP surgeries, and 'patient advisors' will be employed to help patients to decide on the possible types of, and locations of, the treatment available. Once the choice has been made, GPs will then apparently book an appointment using NHSnet. Where before the internal market caused fragmentation, the Secretary of State for Health now speaks of "plurality in local services" and "diversity in provision", and, if we doubt New Labour's commitment to reinstating a market for health services, we are told that primary care trusts will have the explicit freedom to purchase care from the most appropriate provider and that resources will follow the choices that patients make so that hospitals who do more get more (Milburn, 2002, see also Blair, 2002; Boyne et al, 2003).

New Labour's frustration with the NHS has a number of sources. First, it appeared to believe that, by claiming to abolish the internal market in 1997 (although their reforms represent more a recasting of relationships within the market than an abolition), and modernising the service through the use of IT and evidence-based medicine, sufficient improvements would be achieved to secure its future. Equally, despite all of the waste they claimed that the internal market had caused, the problems of the health service in 1997 were "exaggerated" (1.19) – again indicating that the NHS could be easily fixed. By 2000, perhaps realising that there is no magical solution to swift organisational change in the NHS (Klein, 2000; Maynard, 2001), the government tried again, introducing penalties for those not wishing to comply in the government's modernisation programme, and putting in place a much tighter performance system to monitor this compliance. It seems that between 1997 and 2000 the government moved from an essentially organisational, medical-based solution to the health services' ills, to a more managerial, performance indicator-based system. But still the pace of change appears not to be fast enough, resulting in the 2001 consultative document on patient choice, and the threat that a failure to deliver improvements would result in less rather than more money being directed at the NHS, and an increase in individual rather than collective provision (Milburn, 2002).

The confusion over the presence of a 'new' internal market in the NHS was recently made even more apparent in *Delivering the NHS plan* (Secretary of State for Health, 2002), in which, it was argued, that NHS providers face only weak incentives to improve their performance, hence the need for continual central interference. It seems that prices, in the new market (in which the term 'competition' has now been replaced with the rather more clumsy "system to reward good performers" [Appleby, 2002, p 24]), will be determined centrally, so that purchasers can concentrate instead on negotiating deals on the basis of quality and volume (Douglas, 2002). This appears a far cry from the atomistic model of patient choice advocated a mere five months before, and it is unclear exactly how the two approaches to an internal market coexist.

Patient choice and consumerism

Public sector reforms based around markets and choice assume, entirely sensibly perhaps, that people, in an age associated with consumerism, want to choose their health providers, and the date and time they receive treatment (Blair, 2002). But this ignores a number of crucial factors that makes healthcare rather different from other consumer commodities. First, no matter how much information health services provide about governmental assessments of quality and performance, doctors will, for the vast majority of the time, know better than patients the most appropriate course of treatment. State-provided information is often rather contradictory in its rankings of providers (Street, 2000), and patients usually have only a fragmentary physiological and medical knowledge of their condition. This means there is considerable uncertainty and unpredictability in medical care systems (Titmuss, 1968) – hardly the ideal conditions for complex choices to be made by patients.

This problem is also apparent in another policy document published in 2001, *The expert patient* (DoH, 2001d), which develops the idea of 'self management' for sufferers of chronic diseases. In the terms of the new economic sociology (Callon, 1998), health markets are not 'calculable' by patients, they do not possess the necessary information or skills in order to make choices, or even a framework within which the decision might be organised. When we incorporate Stacey's (1976) insight about health consumers also having to make choices concerning their own bodies, choices that may be irreversible and potentially dangerous, the ability of healthcare ever to resemble a consumerist market carries considerable doubt. Second, patients often require a programme of care both before and after any hospital treatment. Offering services that fragment, rather than 'join-up' patterns of care, seem to fly in the face of this (Marmor, 2002). Third, the proposals would seem to be offering choices to people when they, incapacitated by illness or pain, are often least able to make them. It is easy to see how decisions may be made on the basis of waiting time rather than medical performance (even assuming this can be measured accurately), to attempt to simply get rid of hip pain. This also has implications for continuity of care, as we have mentioned above; if patients from Bristol have to go to Glasgow or even continental Europe for their operation, where are they to recover? Fourth, we are assuming that, even if health consumers exist, they know what it is they want, something not borne out by research in even simple consumer markets (Riquelme, 2001). Fifth, we must assume that the capacity exists for meaningful patient choice to take place – something that is far from clear (Le Grand, 2002; Greener, 2003: forthcoming).

Finally, we are assuming that patients actually want all these choices in the first place. Hoggett (2001) suggests that this is because New Labour (see for example, Segal, 1998) are acting on a model of agency for welfare recipients that is over-reflexive, being based around Giddens' theory of structuration (Giddens, 1979, 1984, see also Greener, 2002b). In such a model, agency is based on action, and there is a tendency to assume predominantly reflexive learning behaviour on the part of agents who are able to shape their environment. In the case of healthcare, patients are often at a substantial knowledge disadvantage, and not in the optimal state to make important decisions. Studies have shown that patients are even reluctant to exercise their choice of doctor (Salisbury, 1989), and that increased choice does not necessarily mean patients are more satisfied (Amyx et al, 2000). By way of a solution to this problem, we would suggest that New Labour appear to be muddling the notions of consumer and customer, and a resolution of this may provide a better answer than the one they are offering at the moment.

In 1989, as we have seen, neither patients nor healthcare purchasers appeared to especially want to create a healthcare market. There is, therefore, one would assume, little reason for assuming that patients would want to take the responsibility for becoming fully-fledged health consumers today. Equally, research appears to indicate that both the passive patient and dynamic healthcare consumer positions are unrealistic, with patients prone to moving between these two extreme positions depending on the circumstances and context of their medical encounter (Lupton, 1997; see also Hoggett, 2001). Even if patients want to reinvent themselves as health consumers, it is not clear on what they can base their newly granted choices; how are patients to make comparisons between potential providers of care, or types of treatment? It seems more likely that waiting times are meant to be the main criteria for patient choice, but this surely flies in the face of quality: proven providers are more likely to have established waiting lists, leaving only 'new entrants' who do not have the experience or reputation to provide a shorter wait. Even those patients taking a more active role in their health regime may not want to take over their own health diagnosis and management, and to assume this to be the case appears unrealistic.

A possible answer to these dilemmas, but which is still aligned with the government's apparent obsession with performance measurement is an old one. In 1983, as we have seen, there was an inquiry into the management of the NHS (DHSS, 1983). The emphasis of the Griffiths proposals was not one of healthcare *consumers*, but one of healthcare *customers* instead, and, as we have seen, there is an important difference. Consumers are active drivers of a process, reflexive and knowledgeable about the product on offer (Bell, 2001), and are willing and able to make choices. In Mullen's (1990) terms, they are Type I consumers. They are the New Labour model of agents, founded more in neo-classical economics than in healthcare experience (Warde, 1994). Even were health consumers to exist, it seems clear that such an over-reflexive model of health agency would discriminate across class boundaries in a similar way as it has in education policy; it is usually the middle classes that gain most by being offered the chance to 'play' the system to their advantage (Ball et al, 1995).

A view of patients as customers, on the other hand, is based much more on a marketing model of behaviour, in which a service is provided by one party, and received and assessed by another. It is not necessary that such agents make choices, or that markets exist to accommodate them. Instead they are left to consider the quality of the service they receive (as in Gabbott and Hogg, 1994). If a customer is not happy with the service, and remedies that are adequate are on offer, then choice between services is not necessary. Where these remedies are clearly explained, and offered as a matter of course, they might offer a model for 'empowering' patients in a way that allows those who have the greatest knowledge about the most successful ways to treat them, the doctors, to make choices on their behalf. Patients can then monitor the performance of the system in a far less crude way than is presently enforced by the state. Patients as customers would be able to declare their satisfaction or otherwise with the treatment they have received, and, instead of driving health reform through making choices, drive reform through raising the quality of existing services.

The confusion evident in New Labour's policy is apparent in their vacillating between considering patients as customers and consumers, perhaps unsure of the implications of whether they place either at the heart of the health service. *Extending choice for patients* (DoH, 2001a) clearly uses the consumer model, but other documents, for example *Reforming our public services* (Office of Public Sector Reform, 2002) and *Shifting the balance of power: The next steps* (DoH, 2002) appear to use the customer metaphor more frequently. Confusingly, however, the original document, *Shifting the balance of power within the NHS: Securing delivery* (DoH, 2001b), moves freely between the two. On page 13 of the latter document, for example, primary care trusts appear to be making decisions on behalf of their patients (customer model), whereas on page 26, "the voice of the patient is heard through every level of the service, acting as a powerful lever for change and improvement" (consumer).

Customers in the NHS want low waiting times (New Labour at least have got this right [Lustegarten et al, 2002]) and to be reassured that they are receiving a high standard of treatment. It is the job of managers to ensure that, with reasonable levels of resources at their disposal, that these expectations are met. This would mean that the government live up to the rhetoric of the last 20 years, devolve management, and, perhaps even more importantly in the context of New Labour, leave those running the health service to get on with their job without unnecessary interference and constant meddling from the Department of Health. The model of patient as customer is more realistic, and more flexible; it does not require an overactive consumer driving the whole process, but an individual who has needs to be satisfied, and is dependent on others to fulfil them. This more accurately describes the doctor–patient relationship than the over-reflexive model of the healthcare consumer, and is linked, perhaps, to a more appropriate solution for healthcare organisation than that offered by New Labour. It also demonstrates the need for healthcare decisions to take place predominantly at the local, and not national, level.

Conclusion

The changes in meaning of 'choice' in the NHS can be summarised through the use of a table. In Table 3.1 a textual analysis of policy documents from the dates listed in the table shows the words with the highest co-word coefficients alongside 'choice' in each case, alongside their coefficient. The higher the coefficient is to one, the more likely the word is to occur alongside 'choice'.

In 2002 'patient' is almost inextricably associated with 'choice', and we can also see the basis on which treatment will be chosen clearly, with strong mentions of both 'wait' and 'time'. The rather vague basis of choice in the internal market (1989) is apparent, with 'widen' being the most frequent co-word, but little to inform us of exactly what 'widened' choice might mean. In 2000, after the rather low coefficients of 1997, the return of patient choice occurs, as discussed above, with 'patients' being encouraged to 'exercise' choice, along with an association with waiting lists. The mention of 'refer' implies that, in 2000, the government, again as suggested above, appeared rather unclear whether it was doctors or patients who were meant to be making these choices. The low coefficients from the health reorganisation documents in the 1960s and 1970s also bear out the analysis, implying that choice is not being used systematically in those time periods.

By 2002 the Labour government's rhetoric concerning health service organisation has undergone a remarkable turnaround. Patient choice in a market environment under the internal market of the 1990s, caused 'fragmentation', 'split' responsibility and 'forced' clinicians to work to government-based agendas rather than those of patients. But by 2002, the very market mechanism so derided in 1997 was now complimented for its 'plurality' and 'diversity' and its ability to give clinicians 'freedom'. The government appears to wish to pass responsibility for the running of health services to subsidiary organisations and individuals, while retaining strong central control, effectively putting health policy on 'remote control' (Hoggett, 1994). Having set up an NHS inspectorate, and passed responsibility for driving reform through choice to patients, the state has perhaps divorced itself from having to take any further blame for the health service's problems. In the name of 'devolution' and 'delegation' the government has, at the same time as it continues to issue directives from the

Table 3.1: Highest ranking co-words with choice in policy documents

Word rank	1968-1972 word (coefficient)	1989	1997	2000	2002
1	Private sector (0.25)	Widen (0.61)	Budget (0.26)	Exercise (0.56)	Patient (0.99)
2	Suit (0.25)	Patient (0.48)	Count (0.26)	Patient (0.49)	Treatment (0.76)
3	Able (0.25)	Bed (0.37)	Admission (0.20)	Strengthen (0.47)	Wait (0.75)
4	Natural (0.25)	Place (0.35)	Maximum (0.20)	Refer (0.37)	NHS (0.71)
5	Cross (0.25)	Healthcare (0.33)	Barrier (0.20)	List (0.37)	Time (0.64)

centre, effectively removed itself from day-to-day responsibility for the health service. As politicians allow areas such as healthcare to be drawn into the consumerist discourse, there are increasing pressures to package the 'product' and sell it to 'consumers'. But the product in this case, healthcare, cannot be disembedded from time and space in the way required for smooth exchange in an economic market; the fact that the body operated on is our own, means that we literally have to live with mistakes in our choices that may have long-term consequences for our health.

Equally, it seems that the notion of what the healthcare consumer is meant to look like is a contested notion, even in literature sympathetic to its use (Telford et al, 2002). As well as this, and in common with other technically complex areas such as finance and banking, the nature of the 'goods' on offer in healthcare markets means that it is imperative that consumers' access to the product is controlled heavily by rules and safeguards (Fairclough, 1996). This leads in turn to the government's rather hybridised discourse, having to move between consumerism on the one hand and regulation and caution on the other (most manifest in the use of the word 'ensure' in its various forms in health documents) in order to demonstrate that such markets are, in fact, safe. This is what Winkler (1987) describes as the 'supermarket model' of consumption, where patients have a choice, but this choice has been limited by the providers and decision-makers in the healthcare system – in the case of the NHS this is perhaps for their own good.

New Labour's attempt to use patient choice as the driver of health reform is a mistake: it is unlikely to secure the changes that the government requires, and may instead be an attempt by the state to be less responsible for the NHS generally, passing the buck onto managers who can be 'franchised' if their performance is not up to the national standards set by the centre. Until we base health organisation around a form more likely to deal with the very real problems that the health service faces, and recognise that markets in healthcare did not work in the 1990s under the control of clinicians, and will not work now with patients driving them, then we will continue to miss the opportunity of finding a new organisational settlement for healthcare in the UK (Keaney, 1999).

Acknowledgements

Thanks to the editors and anonymous referees who improved this chapter considerably through their suggestions, to those that attended a staff seminar the author presented at the University of Bath in March 2002, where a number of ideas discussed in this chapter were discussed, and to the Centre for Economic and Social Research at the University of the West of England for the small grant that helped free the time to develop the chapter. The quantitative textual analysis in the chapter was performed using the excellent T-lab text analysis package available at www.t-lab.it/en.

References

Abercrombie, N. (1994) 'Authority and consumer society', in R. Keat, N. Whitely and N. Abercrombie (eds) *The authority of the consumer*, London: Routledge, pp 43-57.

Amyx, D., Mowen, J. and Hamm, R. (2000) 'Who really wants health-care choice', *Journal of Management in Medicine*, vol 14, no 5/6, pp 272-90.

Appleby, J. (2002) 'This little piggy…', *Health Service Journal*, 15 August, pp 24-9.

Ball, S., Bowe, R. and Gewirtz, S. (1995) 'Circuits of schooling: a sociological exploration of parental choice of school in social class contexts', *The Sociological Review*, vol 43, no 1, pp 52-78.

Beck, U., Giddens, A. and Lash, S. (1994) *Reflexive modernisation*, Cambridge: Polity Press.

Beardwood, B., Walters, V., Eyles, J. and French, S. (1999) 'Complaints about nurses: a reflection of "the new managerialism" and consumerism in health care?', *Social Science and Medicine*, vol 48, no 3, pp 363-74.

Bell, A. (2001) 'Patients: participants, proxies, power…', *British Journal of Healthcare Management*, vol 7, no 3, p 120.

Bennett, C. and Ferlie, E. (1996) 'Contracting in theory and in practice: some evidence from the NHS', *Public Administration*, vol 74, no 1, pp 49-66.

Blair, T. (2002) *The courage of our convictions*, London: Fabian Society.

Boyne, G., Farrell, C., Law, J., Powell, M. and Walker, R. (2003) *Evaluating public management reforms*, Buckingham: Open University Press.

Callon, M. (1998) 'Introduction', in M. Callon (ed) *The laws of the market*, London: Blackwells, pp 1-57.

DHSS (Department of Health and Social Security) (1970) *National Health Service: The future structure of the National Health Service*, London: HMSO.

DHSS (1971) *National Health Service reorganisation: consultative document*, London: HMSO.

DHSS (1983) *NHS management inquiry*, London: HMSO.

DoH (Department of Health) (2001a) *Extending choice for patients: A discussion document*, London: DoH.

DoH (2001b) *Shifting the balance of power within the NHS: Securing delivery*, London: DoH.

DoH (2001c) *NHS performance ratings: Acute trusts 2000/01*, London: DoH.

DoH (2001d) *The expert patient: A new approach to chronic disease management for the 21st century*, London: DoH.

DoH (2002) *Shifting the balance of power: The next steps*, London: DoH.

Douglas, R. (2002) Health select committee, 19 June 2002, uncorrected evidence, available at www.parliament.the-stationary-office.co.uk/pa/cm200102/cmselect/cmhealth/uc934i/uc93402.htm

Fairclough, N. (1996) *Discourse and social change*, Cambridge: Polity Press.

Gabbott, M. and Hogg, G. (1994) 'Competing for patients: understanding consumer evaluation of primary care', *Journal of Management in Medicine*, vol 8, no 1, pp 12-18.

Giddens, A. (1979) *Central problems in social theory*, London: Macmillan.

Giddens, A. (1984) *The constitution of society*, Cambridge: Polity Press.

Greener, I. (2002a) 'Understanding NHS reform: the policy-transfer, social-learning, and path dependency perspectives', *Governance*, vol 15, no 2, pp 25-47.

Greener, I. (2002b) 'Agency, social theory and social policy', *Critical Social Policy*, vol 22, no 4, pp 688-705.

Greener, I. (2003: forthcoming) 'Performance in the NHS: the insistence of measurement and the confusion of content', *Public Performance and Management Review*, vol 26, no 3, pp 237-50.

Halpern, S. (2001) 'Hunting out the government's centralising follies', *British Journal of Healthcare Management*, vol 7, no 1, p 8.

Haug, M. and Lavin, B. (1994) *Consumerism in medicine: Challenging physician authority*, Beverly Hills: Sage Publications.

Ham, C. (1996) 'Management markets in health care: the UK experiment', *Health Policy*, vol 35, no 3, pp 279-292.

Ham, C. (1999) *Health policy in Britain: The politics and organisation of the National Health Service*, Basingstoke: Macmillan.

Ham, C. (2000) *The politics of NHS reform: Metaphor or reality?*, London: Kings Fund.

Hewitt, M. (1992) *Welfare, ideology and need*, London: Harvester Wheatsheaf.

Hoggett, P. (1994) 'The politics of modernisation of the UK welfare state', in R. Burrows and B. Loader (eds) *Towards a post-Fordist welfare state?*, Routledge: London, pp 38-48.

Hoggett, P. (2000) *Emotional life and the politics of welfare*, Basingstoke: Macmillan.

Hoggett, P. (2001) 'Agency, rationality and social policy', *Journal of Social Policy*, vol 30, no 1, pp 37-56.

Hood, C. (1991) 'A public management for all seasons?', *Public Administration*, vol 69, no 1, pp 3-19.

Hugman, R. (1994) 'Consuming health and welfare', In R. Keat, N. Whiteley and N. Abercrombie (eds) *The authority of the consumer*, London: Routledge, pp 207-27.

Keaney, M. (1999) 'Are patients really consumers?', *International Journal of Social Economics*, vol 26, no 5, pp 695-706.

Klein, R. (1993) 'The goals of health policy: church or garage?', in *Health Care UK 1992/3*, London: Kings Fund.

Klein, R. (1998) 'Why Britain is reorganising its National Health Service – yet again', *Health Affairs*, vol 17, no 4, pp 111-25.

Klein, R. (2000) *The new politics of the NHS*, Harlow: Pearson.

Lapsley, I. (1994) 'Market mechanisms and the management of healthcare: the UK model and experience', *International Journal of Public Sector Management*, vol 7, no 6, pp 15-25.

Le Grand, J. (1997) 'Knights, knaves or pawns? Human behaviour and social policy', *Journal of Social Policy*, vol 26, no 2, pp 149-69.

Le Grand, J. (1999) 'Competition, cooperation, or control? Tales from the British National Health Service', *Health Affairs*, vol 18, no 3, pp 27-44.

Le Grand, J. (2002) 'Further tales from the British National Health Service', *Health Affairs*, vol 21, no 3, pp 116-28.

Le Grand, J., Mays, N. and Mulligan, J. (eds) (1998) *Learning from the NHS internal market*, London: Kings Fund.

Light, D. (1997) 'From managed competition to managed co-operation: theory and lessons from the British experience', *Milbank Quarterly*, vol 75, no 3, pp 297-34.

Lowe, R. (1993) *The welfare state in Britain since 1945*, London: Macmillan.

Lupton, D., Donaldson, C. and Lloyd, P. (1991) 'Caveat emptor or blissful ignorance? Patients and the consumerist ethos', *Social Science and Medicine*, vol 33, no 5, pp 559-68.

Lupton, D. (1997) 'Consumerism, reflexivity and the medical encounter', *Social Science and Medicine*, vol 45, no 3, pp 373-81.

Lustgarten, H., Cowley, C. and Scobie, S. (2002) 'Benefits of the doubt', *Health Service Journal*, 8 August, pp 28-30.

Maynard, A. (2001) 'Izzy whizzy, let's get busy! Is Sooty alive and well in the NHS?', *British Journal of Healthcare Management*, vol 8, no 10, p 422.

Marmor, T. (2002) 'Policy and political fads: the rhetoric and reality of managerialism', *British Journal of Healthcare Management*, vol 8, no 1, p 16.

Meerabeau, L. (1998) 'Consumerism and health care: the example of fertility treatment', *Journal of Advanced Nursing*, vol 27, no 4, pp 721-29.

Milburn, A. (2002) 'Diversity and choice within the NHS', speech given to *NHS Confederation*, 24 May.

Ministry of Health (1968) *National Health Service: The administrative structure of the medical and related services in England and Wales*, London: HMSO.

Mishra, R. (1990) *The welfare state in crisis*, Brighton: Wheatsheaf Books.

Mullen, P. (1990) 'Which internal market? The NHS White Paper and internal markets', *Financial Accountability and Management*, vol 6, no 1, pp 33-50.

Nettleton, S. (1995) *The sociology of health and illness*, Cambridge: Polity Press.

Office of Public Sector Reform (2002) *Reforming our public services: Principles into practice*, London: Office of Public Sector Reform.

Paton, C. (1999) 'New Labour's health policy: the new healthcare state', in M. Powell (ed) *New Labour, new welfare state?*, Bristol: The Policy Press, pp 127-44.

Phillips, L. (1996) 'Rhetoric and the spread of the discourse of Thatcherism', *Discourse and Society*, vol 7, no 2, pp 209-41.

Phillips, L. (1998) 'Hegemony and political discourse: the lasting impact of Thatcherism', *Sociology*, vol 32, no 4, pp 847-67.

Pickard, S. (1998) 'Citizenship and consumerism in health care: a critique of citizen's juries', *Social Policy and Administration*, vol 32, no 3, pp 226-44.

Powell, M. (2000) 'New Labour and the third way in the British welfare state: a new and distinctive approach?', *Critical Social Policy*, vol 20, no 1, pp 39-60.

Ranalagh, J. (1992) *Thatcher's people: An insider's account of the politics, the power and personalities*, London: Fontana.

Robinson, R. and Le Grand, J. (1994) (eds) *Evaluating the NHS reforms*, London: Kings Fund.

Riquelme, H. (2001) 'Do consumers know what they want?', *Journal of Consumer Marketing*, vol 15, no 5, pp 437-48.

Roth, A. (2001) 'Milburn's next-stage permanent revolution', *British Journal of Healthcare Management*, vol 7, no 5, p 178.

Salisbury, C. (1989) 'How do people choose their doctor?', *British Medical Journal*, vol 299, 2 September, pp 608-10.

Secretary of State for Health and Social Services (1972) *The National Health Service reorganisation: England*, London: HMSO.

Secretary of State for Health (1989) *Working for patients*, Cm 555, London: HMSO.

Secretary of State for Health (1992) *The health of the nation: A strategy for health in England*, Cm 1986, London: HMSO.

Secretary of State for Health (1996) *The NHS: A service with ambitions*, London: The Stationery Office.

Secretary of State for Health (1997) *The new NHS: Modern, dependable*, Cm 3807, London: The Stationery Office.

Secretary of State for Health (2000) *The NHS plan: A plan for investment, a plan for reform*, Cm 4818-I, London: The Stationery Office.

Secretary of State for Health (2002) *Delivering the NHS plan: Next steps on investment and reform*, Cm 5503, London: The Stationery Office.

Segal, L. (1998) 'The importance of patient empowerment in health system reform', *Health Policy*, vol 44, no 1, pp 31-44.

Shackley, P. and Ryan, M. (1994) 'What is the role of the consumer in health care?', *Journal of Social Policy*, vol 23, no 4, pp 517-41.

Sheldon, T. (1990) 'When it makes sense to mince your words', *Health Service Journal*, 16 August, p 1211.

Stacey, M (1998) 'The health service consumer: a sociological misconception', in L. Mackay, L. Soothill and K. Melia (eds) *Classic texts in health care*, Oxford: Butterworth-Heinemann, pp 54-9.

Street, A. (2000) 'Confident about efficiency measurement in the NHS?', *Health Care UK*, spring, pp 47-52.

Telford, R., Beverly, C., Cooper, C. and Boote, J. (2002) 'Consumer involvement in health research: fact or fiction?', *British Journal of Clinical Governance*, vol 7, no 2, pp 92-103.

Timmins, N. (2002) 'A time for change in the British NHS: an interview with Alan Milburn', *Health Affairs*, vol 21, no 3, pp 129-35.

Titmuss, R. (1968) 'Choice and "the welfare state"', in R. Titmuss (ed) *Commitment to welfare*, London: George Allen and Unwin, pp 138-52.

Toth, B. (1996) 'Public participation: an historical perspective', in J. Coast, J. Donovan and S. Frankel (eds) *Priority setting: The health care debate*, Chichester: John Wiley, pp 169-202.

Wainwright, D. (1998) 'Disenchantment, ambivalence and the precautionary principle: the becalming of British health policy', *International Journal of Health Services*, vol 28, no 3, pp 407-26.

Walsh, K. (1994) 'Citizens, charters and contracts', in R. Keat, N. Whiteley and N. Abercrombie (eds) *The authority of the consumer*, London: Routledge, pp 189-206.

Walsh, K. (1995) *Public services and market mechanisms: Competition, contracting and the new public management*, London: Macmillan.

Warde, A. (1994) 'Consumers, identity and belonging: reflections on some theses of Zygmunt Bauman', in R. Keat, N. Whiteley and N. Abercrombie (eds) *The authority of the consumer*, London: Routledge, pp 58-74.

West, P. (1998) 'Market—what market? A review of health authority purchasing in the NHS internal market', *Health Policy*, vol 44, pp 167-93.

Winkler, F. (1987) 'Consumerism in health care: beyond the supermarket model', *Policy & Politics*, vol 15, no 1, pp 1-8.

Part Two:
International issues

Five chapters make up the middle section of this *Review*, their contents ranging from theoretical assessments of the relationship between 'globalisation' and welfare regime change, to accounts of changes and challenges to welfare systems in specific countries. Herman Schwartz begins with a penetrating exploration of the connections between global economic pressures and ongoing change in the nature of 'social protection'. Marketisation has certainly transformed welfare provision not least because far-reaching labour market changes have effectively ended men's privileged access to employment. Nevertheless, all mature welfare systems continue to provide social protection: the difference is that welfare provision has become a matter of (regulated) individual, rather than collective, responsibility.

Denis Bouget continues the 'globalization' theme through an exploration of the meaning of 'convergence' in the European context. This term often stands as short-hand for a 'race to the bottom' as governments cut social spending in their quest for economic 'efficiency'. In fact, as Bouget explains, economic theories provide only a limited account of the full picture. For one thing, they ignore additional pressures *for* convergence in the form of EU treaties, directives and so on, but also disregard counter-tendencies *against* convergence – the embedded, institutional characteristics of welfare regimes, being an example of the latter. Bouget argues that the relationship between convergence and divergence is inevitably complex, and that it does not lead in any simple manner to rapid cost-cutting and other market-pleasing actions of this kind.

The following three chapters are country-specific and concerned with the current state of social policy and the impact of ongoing change in Greece, the US and East Asia. Mick Carpenter asks why Greece has enjoyed such remarkable success in public health improvements and suggests that reasons can be found in both 'lifestyle' and 'structural' explanations of Greek health trends over the past 50 years. The real challenge lies in the future, however, because further progress will depend on the shift to better systems of primary care and a welfare system which sustains increased longevity by virtue of greater equality – and quality – of social provision. For their part, Pamela Holcomb and Karin Martinson examine the changes made to US welfare policy in the wake of the 1996 Personal Responsibility and Work Opportunity Reconciliation Act (PRWORA). They describe how the legislation has been interpreted by different states and also report on their research into the implementation of PRWORA at local level. As the chapter demonstrates, there has clearly been a radical shift in US welfare provision, the impact of which has been mixed. Holcomb and Martinson point out that welfare spending has fallen dramatically – but many of those on employment programmes do not find permanent employment and a sizeable minority appear to drop out of the system altogether. The future, in their opinion, looks even bleaker.

The final chapter in Part Two focuses on the Asian tigers – Hong Kong, Singapore, South Korea and Taiwan. Ian Holliday and Paul Wilding explore the similarities and differences in welfare provision among these welfare systems and ask whether the 'common orientation' of their welfare systems is likely to be sustained in an increasingly challenging economic and political environment. While the impact of the Asian financial crisis is well known, changes in family structure, rising demands for greater democracy and an enhanced role for social movements threaten each of these regimes – the likely outcome being that the East Asian welfare 'model' will lose its tenuous coherence as Taiwan and South Korea take a more democratic path to welfare reform than the two more 'authoritarian' tiger economies.

FOUR

Globalisation/welfare: what's the preposition? And, or, versus, with?

Herman M. Schwartz

Introduction

What, if anything, is the relationship between globalisation as a process and the welfare state as a set of institutions and political relationships? Does globalisation imply an end to the welfare state and its use as an instrument of social policy? Or is globalisation perfectly compatible with stable or expanded welfare spending? Are the major threats to the welfare state domestic, rather than global, in nature, like the ageing of society? Are the politics and substance of welfare state reorganisation in rich countries uniform?

Although the cottage industry devoted to answering these questions has grown into an impressive, almost industrial edifice, many of the products are marred by poor conceptualisation. Conceptual confusions abound in the equation linking globalisation to welfare. This no doubt explains the variety of causal effects on the welfare state attributed to globalisation, and the desire of many analysts to (unnecessarily) oppose 'domestic' and 'global' causes for welfare state change. After all, not everyone sees globalisation as ineluctably compromising the welfare state. Some analysts believe globalisation will provoke political cries for more welfare while others see welfare not only as a necessary political price to be paid for more globalisation, but one which is perfectly compatible with continued globalisation. Furthermore, this latter argument is deployed not only by Washington DC based apologists for free trade like Dani Rodrik (1997), but also is explicit in the debate David Cameron (1979) started about the political exchange of welfare for trade exposure in corporatist welfare states.

This chapter addresses some of the usual arguments and confusions about globalisation and the welfare state by focusing on three issues. First, I will make the case for looking broadly at social protection, rather than narrowly at state tax, transfer and service organisations. Second, I will show how the use of a broader conception of social protection allows us to make a better causal argument about the connection between 'domestic' and 'non-domestic' causes of changes in the supply of and demand for welfare services or transfers, and changes in the role of women in the economy. Finally, I will suggest that globalisation has definitely transformed the post-war welfare state. After all, much of the economy is now exposed to market pressures, and the sizeable portion of the female population that formerly was excluded from labour markets now finds itself working for wages. So the formal welfare state of taxes, transfers, and services matters much more now than it ever did. At the same time, the welfare state's internal administration and its organising rationales themselves reflect market logics more than ever. In this light, the post-war system of social protection is as much responsible for the phenomena known as 'globalisation', as globalisation is responsible for changes to that post-war system. Globalisation and an expansion of the visible welfare state go hand-in-hand.

Globalisation or markets?

The globalisation side of the globalisation and welfare debate contains a profusion of alleged causes for changes in the welfare state, as well as conflicting predictions about those changes. Globalisation is variously understood to encompass one or all of the spread of US cultural norms, financial integration, increased trade penetration, rising rates of immigration (and their associated transnational communities), rising market power for multinational companies (and their associated transnational communities), and the emergence of a transnational community of capitalists (Hay and Marsh, 2000). These processes are held to compromise fiscal and monetary policy, the equalisation of income, efforts to boost employment, public ownership of firms, efforts at setting minimum wages, and efforts to spend more on social services and transfers. And these processes are often seen as exogenous to the welfare state itself.

Much of this confusion stems from the apparent novelty of 'globalisation'. If welfare states preceded globalisation, then logically it is possible that globalisation might conflict with those welfare states by undermining their economic or social preconditions. But if globalisation is an old phenomenon, the logical force of this argument dissipates. There are good reasons to believe that most of the phenomena grouped under the globalisation rubric have been around for centuries, because they represent nothing more that the market's typical process of self-expansion (Schwartz, 2000). Even if we put Marx aside, little in today's globalisation debate was not already present in Georg Simmel's *Philosophy of money* (1900), or Walter Benjamin's 'The work of art in the age of mechanical reproduction' (1935). Globalisation is the steady expansion of market forces and market relations into more and more aspects of life. But understood this way, there can be no opposition between global and domestic markets as sources of change for the welfare state. Indeed, depending on how we understand the 'welfare state', the welfare state itself can be understood as a source of continued marketisation.

Welfare or social protection?

The welfare state side of the equation is meanwhile no less confused. Academic and popular understandings of what the welfare state was and is profoundly misinterpret the post-Second World War period. First, most academic research has conceptualised the welfare state as a system of tax-funded transfers and state-provided or funded social services that ameliorated life and economic risks for workers. Naturally most 'globalisation and welfare' research clusters around this conceptual lamppost, asking how globalisation has affected those programmes, but ignoring areas of darkness away from the lamp. As Richard Titmuss (1958, p 41) had already noted, important social policies that did not work through inward revenue flows, outward direct transfers, and public or publicly funded services were not recognised as inherent parts of the welfare state. Meanwhile, some tax-funded social policy, like education, is also not seen as part of the welfare state. So the confusion produced by a focus on nominal categories persists, despite the revival of Karl Polanyi's (1944) work.

Second, most welfare state research is animated by a profound normative bias that both favours social policy that protects workers and/or the poor, while also only identifying as social policy those policies that protect workers and the poor. This animation flows from T. H. Marshall's (1963) arguments about social citizenship, and Richard Titmuss' (1958) arguments about the importance of universality. But this bias obscures the fact that not all social policy or social protection is for workers, that the welfare state was never simply an instrumental tool for advancing labour's interests, and that 'welfare' – understood much more broadly as 'social protection' – was about sheltering all income streams, not simply wages, from market pressures. Similarly, much of the social policy directed at ameliorating poverty could also be understood as an effort to contain the poor.[1] In short, people's beliefs about what the welfare state *ought* to have been doing sometimes interfered with their analysis of what welfare states *were* doing.

These conceptual confusions make a proper analysis of globalisation and welfare nearly impossible, because they automatically rule out some important causes for the kinds of stresses contemporary welfare states face, while limiting our vision of the kinds of political dynamics leading to changes in the welfare state. In a narrow sense, looking only at taxes as a source of revenue to fund services and transfers, for example, obscures the size and effects of other instruments for redistribution, like tax expenditures, and the ways that regulation of product and services markets created lifetime employment for male breadwinners. This matters because a look at the distribution of tax expenditures in the US shows that the state provides substantial social protection, but that this protection is largely skewed towards the top six income deciles (Howard, 1997). Similarly, substantive regulation of goods and services markets shelters owners of profit streams as well as workers. This form of 'decommodification' affected about one quarter of most OECD economies in the 1990s. Thinking about welfare this way highlights the importance of looking at political efforts aiming at administrative and regulatory change rather than those to reduce taxes and spending in core welfare areas.

Social protection and markets

A better entry point into the globalisation–welfare debate is thus to start with Karl Polanyi's notion of 'social protection' (Polanyi, 1944). He elaborated the notion of 'social protection' in 1944 to encompass states' pervasive sheltering of workers *and* owners from the catastrophes that stretched from the international market's apogee in 1914 through to the Depression era market collapse. Social protection after the Depression and Second World War rested on three legs: the overt welfare state of the tax-funded transfers and services; the sheltering of the service sector (including and especially firms, and through them, workers) from competition; and the creation of tight labour markets through policies that reinforced a male breadwinner wage and thus low labour market participation by *married* females.

Relatively speaking the overt welfare state played the smallest role in this institutionalised sheltering, even for workers. Instead, tight labour markets and regulation assured most workers of employment at breadwinner wage rates, relieving the state of the need to make good on welfare state spending promises except at the margin. State control over domestic and international financial markets and over domestic service sector markets limited the full impact of markets on firms and employees; both thus could safely be inserted into these cosseted markets. Paradoxically workers did not need to rely on the decommodifying effects of welfare programmes because most labour markets themselves were already partly decommodified. This is evident in the fact that the 'crisis of the welfare state' and the coterminous 'fiscal crisis of the state' emerged not when programme expansion occurred, but rather when substantial labour market (re-)entry by married women and the deregulation of the service sector led to massive citizen uptake of existing programmes.[2] The removal of two of the pillars constituting post-war social protection shifted all the weight onto the remaining pillar, throwing it into a financial crisis.

Casting the dependent variable as social protection also makes it possible to sketch out the causal chains leading to stress on and thus changes to the overt welfare state, and to more precisely attribute causal force to components of the globalisation and domestic forces arguments. Progressive deregulation and marketisation of the service sector undermined the male breadwinner model, transforming what had been well paying and – perhaps more important – stable jobs into less stable and predictable forms of employment. At the same time, rising low wage competition from Asian producers and rising inward foreign direct investment had similar effects, displacing male employees from stable breadwinner jobs in manufacturing. Both of these in turn increased the incentives for married women to re-enter labour markets. Massive labour market re-entry by married women in turn put downward pressure on service sector wages, most notably for men, reinforcing male labour and marriage market exit, and further undermining the breadwinner model. These trends created more demands on the overt welfare state, particularly in the areas of unemployment insurance, early retirement programmes, childcare, and tertiary education.

However, neither of the two changes noted above should be seen only as the outcome of changes exogenous to institutions for social protection. Though it is not counted as such in the OECD social expenditure database, education is a major form of social protection because it provides generic skills that permit employability, as well as specific skills that create claims to above average rates of pay. The post-war inclusion of women in tertiary education motivated and equipped women for employment in an economy increasingly based on services. Married women's re-entry generated a self-sustaining process of service sector expansion because re-entering women needed to replace their own childcare and home maintenance services with purchases from the market or access to state services. These services in turn employed yet more women, and increased female demand for access to higher education. At the same time, the increasing fragility of marriage and male breadwinner employment raised the returns on education for employed married women, propelling yet more women into the market.

Similarly, Asian competition and inward foreign direct investment (FDI) also had endogenous causes in the pervasive social protection offered by rich countries after the war. By raising wages to breadwinner levels and removing women from the labour market, social protection expanded the gap between relative unit labour costs in rich and poor countries. This in turn motivated some firms with labour-intensive production processes to shift production to cheaper 'southern' locations. So, just as the post-war welfare state endogenously generated a supply of women unhappy with its breadwinner model, it also generated a supply of imports that also undermined the breadwinner model.

The discussion above suggests uniform trends in rich country welfare states. But the discussion conceals substantial divergence among those welfare states. Welfare states started from different initial conditions, experienced the changes sketched above in different ways, and responded in different ways. Post-war welfare states sheltered the service sector using different kinds of property rights: some regulated prices and profits, others used state ownership, while still others used producer self-governance backed up by state control over credit or market entry. Similarly, welfare state incentives for female labour market participation ranged from outright discouragement to active facilitation by some in the 1960s. Welfare states thus created diverging incentives for firms to move offshore, and diverging rates of female labour market participation. Consequently these welfare states experienced globalisation in different ways, producing divergent outcomes.

The rest of this chapter thus addresses three issues that arise from looking at social protection rather than the welfare state more narrowly. First, I will flesh out the case for looking broadly at social protection, rather than narrowly at state tax, transfer and service organisations. Second, I will assess some of the usual arguments about globalisation and the welfare state, showing how the use of a broader conception of social protection allows us to make a better causal argument about the connection between 'domestic' and 'non-domestic' causes of changes in the supply of and demand for welfare services or transfers. Finally, I will suggest that globalisation has definitely transformed the post-war welfare state.

What was the post-war welfare state?

Two academic deformations of reality create problems sorting out the ways that globalisation translates into policy choices about the welfare state and then identifying the specific causal mechanisms that link changes in the international economy to actors' interests, actors' policy preferences and, finally, to policy outcomes. First, academic work on social protection focuses unnecessarily narrowly on the formal welfare state and typically only as an instrument of redistribution towards workers. The conventional wisdom about the politics of the welfare state is that capital firmly opposes welfare and redistribution while workers equally tenaciously favour welfare and redistribution, and that the welfare state is the only mechanism for redistribution. Second, academic work on the welfare state historically focused unnecessarily narrowly on men, or, more precisely, subsumed women's interests into that of households headed by breadwinner males (Orloff, 1993). Both deformations blurred academic understandings of the relationship between social protection and the phenomena grouped under the concept of globalisation.

Start with the first deformation. Why should capital automatically favour market allocation and the labour movement redistribution? Why see the formal welfare state as the only mechanism for redistribution? The interesting thing about the so-called golden era of the Keynesian welfare state, after all, was not widespread recourse to formal welfare by those in the labour market or even the deliberate (if only occasional) use of expansionist monetary policy. The astounding thing about the golden era was stable employment, wages and investment across all sectors, and predictable access to deferred wages after retirement. Political movements forced states to create this stability in reaction to the exposure of virtually all life chances and income streams to the logic and volatility of the market in the long 19th century (Polanyi, 1944). Workers were not the only actors who benefited from and campaigned for redistribution and stability (Baldwin, 1990).

Polanyi's counter-movement after all was about sheltering 'productive organisation' from the market. The welfare state is a visible and fiscally expensive modality for providing social protection. But budget financed services and transfers are not the only modality for social protection. After the 1930s states provided social protection – and achieved redistribution – through a wide variety of instruments: trade protection, minimum wages, centralised collective bargaining, product market regulation, the allocation of investment capital, the delegated control over markets to producer groups, and, of course, formal welfare states. All these instruments disconnect or buffer income streams from market outcomes, whether those incomes take the form of wages, employment, or profits. Analysts of the formal welfare state have traditionally preferred to view welfare entitlements as 'social' rights, and there are important reasons for doing so (Klausen, 1995). But the streams of income the state created through regulation and the welfare state are also *property rights* and share important similarities as such. Welfare state socialisation of various life and economic risks created property rights to streams of income from the state, as in the case of defined benefit pensions or disability pensions; by the same token, tax sheltered defined contribution pensions can create a property right if the tax expenditure is linked to the contribution. Workers with varying degrees of job tenure also had a legally enforceable property right in their job.

These property rights took different forms. The service sector, the source of most post-war employment and employment growth, contained the most expensive and important property rights related to social protection, whether expressed as public ownership or regulation of the service sector. These property rights guaranteed workers stable wages and employment while guaranteeing for regulated private owners steady revenue and profit streams. State regulation dampened or eliminated competition by segmenting markets for services like telecommunications, road, rail and air transport, power and water generation and distribution, and retail distribution. These four sectors amount to a fifth of most OECD economies and a significant source of producer costs in the manufacturing sector.

Consider how investor-owned, power-generation utilities in the US were sheltered from the market. The state offered firms territorial monopolies, access to tax privileged equity capital and bond finance, and regulated rates of return in order to induce firms to make highly asset specific investments. In turn firms offered workers stable employment at predictably rising wages linked to the utility's equally predictable expansion of its assets in an environment in which the price of electricity was also predictable. Workers for state-owned utilities in Europe often got the even greater stability of civil service status.

The degree to which this regulation sheltered services from market pressures can be seen in the relatively greater dispersion of productivity levels for services production in the 19 OECD economies in 1990, as compared with manufacturing, which faced world market competition. While the standard deviation of productivity levels in manufacturing was 16.1, it was 15.8 for telecommunications, 21.1 for retail distribution, 26.8 for electricity generation and 57.1 for air transport (Pilat, 1996). The larger dispersion of productivity levels around the mean (the larger standard deviation) indicates that historically there was much less market pressure to conform to best practice production norms. The obvious exception is telecommunications, where progressive deregulation and privatisation had already unleashed market pressures before 1990 that reduced the dispersion around the mean to a level similar to that in manufacturing. But in the other three sectors considerable divergences remained.

Most productivity studies attribute this divergence to government ownership and regulation of labour and product markets (McKinsey, 1992; Pilat, 1996).

Deregulation of the service began in the late 1970s in the US and exposed substantial numbers of workers to market forces. Successive administrations deregulated transportation, telecommunications, finance, and energy transmission and generation services, producing novel ways to cause market catastrophes, as in the collapse of the savings and loan (cooperative savings banks) industry and firms like Enron. Although in many instances the total headcount of jobs in a given sector increased, these jobs were characterised by weaker employment guarantees and a tighter connection between productivity and wages. In short, many breadwinner jobs disappeared.

This is where the second academic deformation comes into view. These breadwinner jobs mattered because a second unseen pillar of post-war social protection was the forced or voluntary withdrawal of many married women from the labour market. Consider the US. There, although women's participation in open labour markets had risen steadily, if slowly, from about 18 per cent in 1890 to about 26 per cent in 1930, married women's participation had actually fallen slightly over the same period, once unpaid household workers are accounted for (Goldin, 1990; Costa, 2000). The Second World War brought a doubling in married women's participation from around 10 to 20 per cent between 1940 and 1950; a second doubling occurred 1950 to 1970; and a final near-doubling appears to have occurred through 1990 (Goldin, 1977, 2002).

Yet the relative withdrawal of female workers can be seen in the decline in their share of the US civilian workforce from its 1945 high of 36.1 per cent to about 29.1 per cent in 1950. The female share did not recover until the late 1960s (Maret, 1983). Similarly, women's wages relative to men actually fell roughly 10 percentage points and did not recover until roughly 1990 (Goldin, 2002, p 36). Outright expulsion from certain types of employment, marriage bars, short and dead-end career tracks, and pure gender discrimination all contributed to this drop in relative wages. The US was not an isolated example and in fact represented in most periods a society with relatively high levels of labour force participation by married women. In Australia and New Zealand, an explicit breadwinner orientation in wage regulation initially set women's wages at between 40 per cent and 75 per cent of male wages in similar occupations, discouraging married women's participation. In other societies, married women's retreat from the labour market was seen as a positive sign of a society healthy and wealthy enough to afford non-participation (Bussemaker, 1998).

Married women's withdrawal from labour markets made four significant contributions to the structure of social protection in the post-war period by tightening up labour markets. Withdrawal directly reduced the volume of labour at a time when the market had to absorb demobilised soldiers and the men who had been unemployed in the 1930s. This directly prevented wages from falling. This effect was particularly strong at the bottom of the labour market, where women, whose education levels almost everywhere were lower than for men, competed for unskilled/low-skilled jobs. So it helped extend the breadwinner effect down into the lower reaches of the income distribution. Withdrawal occurred at a time when manual farm labour was giving way to office work, which presumably should have strongly favoured increased female employment. Withdrawal also indirectly boosted male wages by contributing to a tighter labour market, stronger unions and thus higher wages. And withdrawal probably boosted fertility, contributing to sustained demand for housing and consumer durables at the same time that it secured the viability of pay-as-you-go pension systems. But withdrawal would not have made sense if stable breadwinner jobs for men were absent, or if the formal welfare state and tax system distributed benefits to individuals rather than households.

With this more complete view of the operation of social protection in the post-war period we can now understand not only the relative balance of endogenous and exogenous shocks on post-war social protection, but also how these shocks interacted to put more pressure on the formal welfare state. Essentially, three things occurred: first, male breadwinner wages priced labour at the bottom end of the manufacturing market out of world markets once firms had access to low-wage labour governed by a variety of Asian military or authoritarian governments. Second, female access to formal welfare, education, and the birth control pill reduced fertility and created the ability to enter labour markets once dominated by men. Finally, a cross-class coalition in parts of the economy exposed to world market competition tried to maintain competitiveness by reducing costs in the non-traded part of the economy (Schwartz, 2001).

What went wrong with post-war social protection?

Asian competition

The post-war system of social protection eventually priced low-skilled male labour out of both manufacturing and service sector markets. Unionisation and tight labour markets raised wages above the levels that prevailed in many Asian and Latin American economies characterised by overt repression of labour unions. It is important not to overstate the wage gap, because lower rates of productivity in most of newly industrialising Asia meant that the relative gap in *unit costs* is not as large as the absolute wage gap indicates. Nonetheless, even by 2000, manufacturing wage costs in the richest Asian economies only stood at about 40 per cent of the US level, while wages in the poorest were less than 10 per cent. This provided a huge incentive to relocate production away from OECD economies.

The gradual reduction in tariffs, telecommunications and transportation costs made this labour accessible to multinational and other firms in labour intensive, loosely coupled industries. Highly labour intense industries characterised by batch production at individual workstations, like garment assembly, shoes, toys, luggage, and cheap lighting, all gradually went offshore to Asia. In turn, the supply industries for these sectors also migrated to collocate with their sources of final demand. Thus, even capital-intensive industries like fibre production and textiles weaving eventually relocated to Asia. From 1980 to 2000 industrialising Asia more than doubled its share of total world trade from roughly 8 per cent to nearly 20 per cent, reflecting even larger shares (circa 40 per cent) of industries like woven clothing. All this put downward pressure on wages and employment at the bottom end of the labour market.

There are different ways to measure this pressure, because it could take the form of lost jobs, falling wages, fewer hours of work, or substitution of capital for labour. Adrian Wood argues that this sort of southern competition alone accounts for a loss of at least 9 million OECD manufacturing jobs, equivalent to about two thirds of Euroland's total unemployment in 1998 (Wood, 1994). Similarly, William Cline argues that trade and immigration together account for between 20 and 25 per cent of the observed increase in US wage inequality (Cline, 1996). In the US median weekly earnings for full-time male production workers fell 13 per cent from 1973 to 1995. This reflects a sharper fall in both hours and wages for the bottom decile of male wage earners (Freedman, 1999). In almost every OECD economy both the number of manufacturing jobs and the number of hours in manufacturing has fallen since 1990, and in many employment has fallen by about 1 per cent per year since 1979 (BLS, 2002).

This low-wage competition generated two natural, market-based responses. First, falling prices for increasingly commoditised manufactures increased disposable income in the economy as a whole, shifting demand towards services and better quality manufactures. Second, this shift permitted firms that had been labour-intense to respond to low-wage competition by moving upmarket and substituting capital for labour, in what Adrian Wood (Wood, 1994) calls 'defensive innovation'. This can be seen clearly in the US, where the share of non-production workers in manufacturing rose from 1970 to 1990 (Jensen and Troske, 1999). While these shifts helped GDP to grow, they also exacerbated the wage/employment problem at the bottom of the labour market.

Any argument about the effects of capital fleeing high-wage economies for low-wage economies has to also account for the fact that most capital flows among rich countries. But this movement had the same effects in terms of the reduction of breadwinner male manufacturing employment, because this investment almost always involved displacement of lower productivity firms in the host (recipient) economy. Successful multinational firms uniformly had higher productivity than firms in their host economy. In the six largest OECD economies, on an unweighted basis, the ratio between assets and employment for inwardly investing manufacturing firms at the beginning of the 1990s was 1.6 (versus a nominal economy-wide ratio of 1), suggesting higher capital intensity and lower than average direct employment from FDI (UNCTAD, 1993, p 5).

FDI thus carried more efficient production norms from each OECD economy into the others, causing job losses as domestic firms adapted to higher productivity levels or simply exited the market. Consider how Japanese investment reduced the number of automobile jobs in North America. Put differently, because FDI accounts for 20 per cent of manufacturing capital stock, manufacturing employment is roughly 7.5 per cent lower in these OECD countries, an effect similar in magnitude – 7 million breadwinner jobs – to the losses that Wood identifies. While FDI largely leaves wage rates for these kinds of jobs unaffected (in contrast to low-wage competition), it does reduce the overall volume of manufacturing jobs. Technological change thus led to greater productivity on the one hand, but declining breadwinner employment on the other.

The weakening of the bottom of the labour market introduced some, but not all, of the fiscal stress felt by OECD welfare states, because active and passive unemployment expenditures rose. But absolutely these cannot account for the increase in public sector deficits in the last 10 years or the 20 years before that. From 1980 to 1996 active and passive unemployment outlays for the 18 rich OECD countries rose on average by only 1.2 percentage points to 3 per cent of GDP (OECD, 1998). But fiscal deficits rose by considerably more than that, driven by an increase of 1.9 percentage points of GDP in spending for old public debt, and an increase of 4.8 percentage points for social expenditures unrelated to unemployment. Health and old age pensions thus were the major cause for increased deficits, reflecting that in most economies the cost of these deferred wages runs at roughly five times the cost of unemployment insurance and early retirement schemes.

Marketisation of the service sector

The deregulation and commercialisation of the service sector introduced a second major source of stress on the post-war system of social protection. States had either regulated or owned large swathes of the service sector after the war, particularly those involving reticulation networks in power generation, transportation, and other utilities. Regulation of prices and profits in nominally privately owned utilities firms had the indirect effect of guaranteeing stable wages and employment for relatively unskilled workers. Pervasive public ownership in Europe often carried with it civil service status for these workers. And, as noted above, the absence of competitive pressures meant that large disparities in productivity could emerge. These disparities in productivity could only persist in the absence of market competition, sheltering roughly a quarter of OECD workers.

Two developments in the US unleashed competition in the regulated service sector and thus removed social protection for these workers. First, in the 1970s, an endogenous political dynamic produced internal demands for deregulation of the US service sector. Unlike most European states, the US had largely opted for substantive regulation of infrastructure and public services rather than state ownership. The absence of state monopolies and the inability to perfectly regulate any given market meant that new forms of competition were always emerging at the margin of regulated businesses.

By the 1970s a series of court decisions had considerably widened the size of this margin, permitting, for example, non-bank financial firms to take deposits and offer loans, private (non-public utility) telephone companies to offer long-distance service, and courier services to offer shipment of things that formerly had travelled through the post. Regulation created costs for regulated firms that unregulated firms did not have to carry. Thus banks were hobbled with reserve requirements and the cost of deposit insurance, unlike non-bank financial firms. Public utility phone companies were forced to cross-subsidise local phone services with expensive long distance charges, while private telephone firms could charge marginal cost for long distance.

Regulated firms in these sectors thus faced a dilemma. If they demanded more intrusive regulation of their own sector, they would face rising costs, yet some firms might still find ways to evade regulations and pose a competitive threat. On the other hand, if they did not get regulation of these unregulated firms, they would have to compete while carrying all the costs of regulation. Consequently many firms in regulated sectors opted to press for deregulation, so as to level the playing field. Deregulation began under the Democratic Carter administration and continued under the Republican Reagan and the first Bush administrations. Deregulation permitted all the normal market processes to work. It led to market entry, mergers, bankruptcies and, most important for the globalisation part of the story, rising productivity and falling prices.

Second, by the 1980s declining US competitiveness in manufacturing provoked the US state into a variety of policy responses to restore equilibrium in its current account. The most important of these was a conscious decision to expand the market opening operations of the General Agreement on Tariffs and Trade (GATT) to encompass the service sector and agriculture. This eventually culminated in the launching of the World Trade Organization (WTO) and its General Agreement on Trade in Services (GATS). One by one finance, transportation, the post and power generation and distribution were opened to foreign and domestic competition.

The first development partly drove the emergence of the second development, because the relative competitiveness of US firms in the newly deregulated service sectors was high. By 1999 the US was running a $72 billion trade surplus in services that reflected equally large deficits in countries with weaker services sectors, like Japan (a $49 billion deficit) and Germany (a $46 billion deficit).

But the second development – successful US pressure to open up public sector monopolies in Europe and elsewhere – created conditions leading to a rerun of the US deregulation dynamic in those newly opened markets. For how could a public firm with obligations to cross-subsidise various activities for social welfare purposes, with an inability to impose wage discipline on its civil service employees, let alone to fire them, and with constant political pressure to buy from local suppliers rather than seek global standard equipment, ever hope to compete with private firms that had shed these various restraints?

Somewhat like regulated US firms, these state-owned firms faced a 'trilemma':

they could continue to price at a level that included their 'regulatory' costs, and thus lose market share; they could price at market levels, run at a loss and try to balance their books by seeking subsidies from the finance ministry; or they could opt for privatisation. Even when these state-owned firms preferred some combination of the first two options to the third, deficit-minded finance ministries and local consumers of services pushed for deregulation and if not privatisation, at least commercialisation. The European Union's single integrated market reinforced these trends. Consequently the security of breadwinner male employment in the service sector evaporated in ever-hotter competition in service sector markets.

Just as Asian competition destroyed male breadwinner employment in the bottom half of the manufacturing market, deregulation destroyed breadwinner employment in much of the service sector. But as with Asian competition, disentangling 'domestic' and 'global' causes for the erosion of social protection is impossible. Similarly, the collapse of the US version of service sector regulation had endogenous causes. Deregulation in the US arose in part from the weakness or incompleteness of its form of post-war social protection – publicly regulated but privately owned utilities created a space in which unregulated competition could emerge. In this sense deregulation was a purely domestic affair. But the export of US deregulation owed much to declining US competitiveness in global manufacturing markets, and did much to bring down service sector-based social protection in other economies.

Bringing women back in

The third source of stress on post-war welfare states was a once-only reintegration of married women, and especially married women with children, into formal labour markets. The reintegration of national markets through increased FDI and trade (globalisation) increased the returns to education in ways that favoured labour market re-entry by married women at the same time that they began to desire employment. Voluntarily or involuntarily, women surrendered the social protection afforded them by breadwinner male wages and exposed themselves directly to labour markets. From 1970 to 1996, the average rate of female labour market participation in the OECD rose 15 percentage points to 63 per cent.[3] There was of course substantial variation, with the Scandinavian and Anglo economies seeing 22 percentage point rises off already high bases, while the continental economies saw roughly 10 percentage point rises off lower participation rates. Meanwhile, the average level of male labour force participation in the OECD fell from about 90 per cent to 83 per cent from 1970-96.

One understanding of the effects of rising participation by married women is that it pushed men out of breadwinner occupations at the top of the income ladder, for example as families composed of two doctors replaced two families headed by male doctors. From 1970 to 1990 women's share of enrolments in US professional schools rose from 10 per cent to over 40 per cent (Goldin and

Katz, 2000), and from 1970 to 1993 the share of dual-income US families rose from 39 per cent to 61 per cent (Winkler, 1998). But this understanding clearly is wrong. First, the aggregate weight of these professions is too small to account for the prolonged and substantial fall in wages, employment, and hours for US males in the bottom two or three income deciles. Second, female penetration of the manufacturing sector, particularly the unionised assembly line parts of manufacturing, was limited in relation to the more substantial contraction of manufacturing jobs that occurred in this period. Finally, most of the professions experienced substantial growth as the economy shifted away from manufacturing and agriculture and towards services.

In fact, an analysis of the American labour market shows that women in dual-income marriages or relationships at the top of the income ladder typically work fewer hours per week than those at the bottom (Winkler, 1998). Coupled women at the bottom of the income distribution are not only more likely to be working full time than their counterparts at the top of the income distribution, but also more likely to be working more hours than their male partners. Thus, in the US, 57 per cent of working women married to men whose wage was in the first quintile earned an hourly wage higher than their husband's, as compared to only 7 per cent of women married to men with wages in the fifth quintile, and 31 per cent of the women in the first group earned 50 per cent more than their husband (Winkler, 1998). On an annual basis − a necessary adjustment given how many women work part time − the disparity is much the same, reflecting the reduction in working hours for men in the bottom quintile.

What do these trends mean? Two things are relevant to the argument about globalisation. First, the destruction of male breadwinner jobs in the bottom half of the income distribution through increased trade and increased inward FDI coincided with a shift of employment away from manufacturing and towards services. But men did not benefit much from this shift. Rather, women did. We may speculate that the higher emotional and social intensity of many service jobs favoured female job seekers, and it is also certainly true that the part-time and 'flexitime' nature of much service sector employment comports better both with some women's needs and with the gendered image of women as secondary income earners in families. Whatever the reason, the market for service sector employment favoured women, allowing the huge increase in would-be working married women to find jobs.

The second factor relevant to the discussion of globalisation concerns the returns to education. On the demand side, women had to confront the fact that they could no longer depend on men as reliable wage earners or marriage partners. But it is also true that their own increased rate of higher education not only permitted them access to a much broader range of jobs than before, but also at much better rates of pay than before. Competition with imports manufactured with low-wage labour, and the increased salience of inward FDI in all OECD economies, shifted the demand for skilled and credentialed labour upwards. Women were well positioned to take advantage of this shift in demand, because their rates of higher education had not only equalised with those of men in most OECD countries by the 1980s, but by the 1990s substantially exceeded those for men in many countries (Jönsson, 1999). In the US at least, increased higher education for women translated into substantially higher pay. Female college graduates saw their earnings increase by 20 per cent during 1979-95, in contrast to the 17 per cent decline for male high school graduates (Freeman, 1999). Female high school graduates meanwhile saw only a 4 per cent decline in earnings.

Although there are no comparable data for European trends, I will note two conflicting trends. First, women in female-dominated occupations in Europe tend to be more highly educated than men in those same occupations, and in general in Europe the proportion of university educated employed women aged 25-39 was higher at 26.0 per cent than for men, at 22.5 per cent (Jönsson, 1999). Female rates of higher education are lowest in some continental European countries with the lowest female labour market participation, and highest in the Scandinavian countries, where robust public service sectors and resistance to foreign guest workers mobilised women early. This suggests that rising returns to education caused in part by 'globalisation' trends have pulled women into the market everywhere in the OECD. On the other hand, during the 1990s public sector pay was stagnant or declining in real terms in most OECD countries, including some with the fastest rates of growth of female labour market participation, like Australia and the Netherlands. At the same time that 'globalisation' pulled or pushed women into work, it generated a politics that drove privatisation of public sector utilities and the effort to introduce market and wage disciplines into the rest of the public sector in the 1990s (Schwartz, 2001). So globalisation conceivably had contradictory effects on labour market re-entry by married women.

Finally, women's labour market entry was a self-sustaining process. Not only did one part of the welfare state – education – assist it, but it also created demands for expansion of other public and publicly subsidised parts of the welfare state like child and elder care. It also created demand for more private services. And these services were typically staffed by more women. In this sense, globalisation – the expansion of labour markets into part of the female population – created demand for an expansion of the formal welfare state, and indeed could not have occurred in the absence of the formal welfare state.

Conclusion

Thinking about the welfare state more broadly, as social protection, and thinking about globalisation as the age-old process by which markets based on competition and accumulation have come to dominate more and more facets of life and more and more economic activities, allows us to recast the debate about globalisation and the welfare state. Rather than seeing globalisation and welfare state change as separate phenomena that are necessarily opposed, we can see the ways in which the older round of globalisation before the First World War triggered demands for social protection when markets collapsed. We can also see how dynamics endogenous to the provision of post-Second World War social protection created some of the processes later perceived as a new round of globalisation. Put simply, the system of social protection in which risks were socialised through the maze of cross-subsidies embedded in public ownership of services and breadwinner male employment has given way to a system of social protection in which risks and cash flows are transparent, and in it is easier to individuate risks.

The post-war system of social protection rested on three fundamental restrictions on markets: women were restrained from labour market entry; markets were banished from much of the service sector, particularly infrastructure services; and international trade in services was highly regulated, and trade in manufactures liberalised only gradually. All three constraints on the market created breadwinner employment for males. To these, states certainly added large measures of social assistance and public health and education services. But breadwinner wages in the bottom half of the male labour market created enormous incentives to go to low-wage manufacturing sites. Limits on trade in manufactures encouraged competitive OECD firms to invest in target OECD markets. And the very liberality of education provision created a new generation of women whose potential earning power was very high, and who would not tolerate exclusion from work life. The system of post-war social protection thus ironically undermined itself in various ways.

By definition, once those restraints on the market began to break down, social protection began to dissipate. States made markets in what had been regulated or publicly owned services, privatised and commercialised public firms, and permitted or encouraged female labour market entry. Breadwinner male employment thus shrank, and with it both old style social protection and its associated, historically unusual, flat distribution of income. I leave it to the reader to assess whether the benefits of Asian industrialisation for Asian workers and more labour market participation for married women offset the costs associated with the loss of breadwinner employment.

But none of this implies any necessary opposition between globalisation and the formal welfare state. First, and most important, the breakdown of the old system of social protection not only partly arose endogenously from the provision of higher education to women, but also created demands for new forms of social services. Female labour market participation could not have increased without an expansion of direct and indirect public financial support for childcare, as well as reductions in the gender bias of employment protections and tax laws. Second, the startling rise in male unemployment and male employment insecurity brought with it a marked shift in funding away from passive income support and towards active labour market policies. Third, while there have been massive changes in the administration of welfare, and in the administration and organisation of public sector services, there have not been deep cuts in core social transfers or public services. Pension, healthcare and education spending continue to rise in most places, driven both by demographic shifts and substitution effects. But the organising principle has changed from one of collective responsibility to one of individual responsibility. As Thatcher might have said, 'from each according to their insurance premia, to each as they individually encounter life and market risks'.

Some, like Jessop (2002), might read this as the emergence of some new sort of welfare state, oriented towards Schumpeterian growth or the enhancement of the competitiveness of national economies, and contrast it with the competition (and innovation) stifling nature of post-war social protection. Others see the post-war welfare state as possessing a highly decommodifying orientation that is now lost. While both views are partly correct, they also misread the nature of the change. First, some of the most highly thought of and redistributive welfare states of the post-war period were already Schumpeterian by Jessop's criteria. The golden age Swedish welfare state made strenuous use of the *Arbetsmarknadsstyrelsen* to retrain and replace the unemployed in jobs requiring higher levels of skill, thus facilitating a shift in the industrial structure away from labour-intense sectors. Meanwhile, until the late 1970s, Swedish public sector infrastructure firms were compelled to run in business-like fashion. Thus the expansion of that model to other public services is just that – an expansion rather than a revolution. Second, despite academic rhetoric about decommodification, Swedish firms, unions and the state cooperated in the *commodification* of women by bringing them into the labour market, at the same time that the unemployment insurance system motivated labour market re-entry for male workers.

This suggests that welfare is not only compatible with globalisation, but also part of the process of globalisation. Thus the various levels of formal welfare state-based social protection and informal social protection on display in Europe and elsewhere are reasonably viable in the current global environment. The volume of social protection in any given society remains a political question, still largely settled at the national level, and based on local norms about the 'proper' level for government budget deficits, women's 'proper' role in the household and labour market, and the 'proper' degree of redistribution. The state is necessarily involved in translating these normative beliefs into real programmes. Globalisation – the relentless expansion of markets – will continue as a phenomenon, but is both caused by and causes further expansion of formal welfare and the regulation of people's lives by the state. The answer to the question posed in the title is thus globalisation with welfare.

Notes

[1] One salient exception to both biases is Abram De Swaan (1988), who defines old age pensions as a form of politically created property right, and provides an analysis of the emergence of social assistance that has nothing to do with concerns for the poor per se. Because of its origins in work by Tawny and Titmuss, British analyses of welfare tend to focus strongly on poverty alleviation.

[2] The ambiguity of women's labour market entry is that the majority of unmarried women work for some time and then drop out subsequent to marriage and, more important, childbirth. So married women are rarely entering the labour market for the first time.

[3] Separate data for married women only are not available. So the figures here and below understate the shift in married women's labour market behaviour, as does the fact that the average is unweighted, and thus understates the significance of the 22 percentage point shift in the US, which accounts for about 40 per cent of the OECD's population.

References

Baldwin, P. (1990) *Politics of social solidarity*, Cambridge: Cambridge University Press.

Benjamin, W. (1935) 'The work of art in the age of mechanical reproduction', in H. Arendt (ed) *Illuminations* (1969), New York: Schocken Books, pp 217-51.

BLS (Department of Labor, Bureau of Labor Statistics) (2002) *Foreign labor statistics homepage*, www.bls.gov/fls/home.htm.

Bussemaker, J. (1998) 'Rationales of care in contemporary welfare states: the case of childcare in the Netherlands', *Social Politics*, vol 5, no 1, pp 70-96.

Cameron, D. (1978) 'The expansion of the public economy: a comparative analysis', *American Political Science Review*, vol 72, pp 1243-61.

Cline, W. (1996) *Trade and income distribution*, Washington DC: Institute for International Economics.

De Swaan, A. (1988) *In care of the state*, New York: Oxford University Press.

Freeman, R. (1999) 'The new inequality in the United States', in A. Fishlow and K. Parker (eds) *Growing apart: The causes and consequences of global wage inequality*, New York: Council on Foreign Relations, pp 21-66.

Goldin, C. and Katz, L. F. (2002) 'The power of the pill: oral contraceptives and women's career and marriage decisions', *Journal of Political Economy*, vol 110, no 4, pp 730-71.

Goldin, C. (2002) 'The rising (and then declining) significance of gender', NBER Working Paper no 8915.

Hay, C. and Marsh, D. (2000) 'Introduction: demystifying globalization', in C. Hay and D. Marsh (eds) *Demystifying globalization*, New York: St. Martin's Press, pp 1-17.

Howard, C. (1997) *The hidden welfare state*, Princeton: Princeton University Press.

Jensen, J. and Troske, K. (1999) 'Increasing wage dispersion in U.S. manufacturing: plant level evidence on the role of trade and technology', in A. Fishlow and K. Parker (eds) *Growing apart: The causes and consequences of global wage inequality*, New York: Council on Foreign Relations, pp 118-48.

Jessop, B. (2002) *The future of the capitalist state*, Cambridge: Polity Press.

Jönsson, I. (1999) 'Women and education in Europe', *International Journal of Contemporary Sociology*, vol 36, no 2, pp 145-62.

Klausen, J. (1995) 'Social rights advocacy and state building: T.H. Marshall in the hands of social reformers', *World Politics*, vol 47, no 2, pp 244-68.

Maret, E. (1983) *Women's career patterns*, New York: University Press of America.

Marshall, T. H. (1963) *Sociology at the crossroads*, London: Heinemann.

McKinsey Global Institute (1992) *Service sector productivity*, Washington DC: McKinsey Global Institute.

OECD (Organisation for Economic Co-operation and Development) (1998) *Economic survey: Australia 1998*, Paris: OECD.

Orloff, A. (1993) 'Gender and the social rights of citizenship: the comparative analysis of state policies and gender relations', *American Sociological Review*, vol 58, no 3, pp 303-28.

Pilat, D. (1996) 'Competition, productivity and efficiency', *OECD Economic Studies*, vol II, no 27, pp 107-46.

Polanyi, K. (1944) *The great transformation*, New York: Beacon Press.

Rodrik, D. (1997) *Has globalization gone too far?*, Washington, DC: Institute for International Economics.

Schwartz, H. (2000) *States versus markets: The emergence of a global economy*, London: Macmillan.

Schwartz, H. (2001) 'Round up the usual suspects! Globalization, domestic politics and welfare state change', in P. Pierson (ed) *New politics of the welfare state*, Oxford: Oxford University Press, pp 17-44.

Simmel, G. (1900) *Philosophy of money*, London: Routledge.

Titmuss, R. (1958) *Essays on the 'welfare state'*, London: George Allen and Unwin.

UNCTAD (1993) *World investment directory 1992: Developed countries*, New York: United Nations.

Winkler, A. (1998) 'Earnings of husbands and wives in dual-earner families', Department of Labor, *Monthly Labor Review*, April, pp 42-8.

Wood, A. (1994) *North-South trade, employment, and inequality*, New York: Oxford University Press.

FIVE

Convergence in social welfare systems: what does it mean?

Denis Bouget

Introduction

Convergence has been defined in the social sciences as "the tendency of societies to grow more alike, to develop similarities in structures, processes, and performance" (Kerr et al, 1973, p 3). The term is also described as a process in which one unit becomes increasingly similar to other units facing the same environment – what is called 'institutional isomorphism' by DiMaggio and Powell (1991) and Lodge (2000), or 'conditional convergence' in economic literature. Convergence simultaneously refers to a process and to a final stage. Generally speaking, the final stage is conceived as a stable one, static or dynamic, and without uncertainty. Furthermore, the word is often axiomatically positive because the ultimate objective is widely accepted as enhancing 'social quality'. After the Second World War, the judgement that the populations of each nation would be entitled to experience rising living standards has pervaded all corners of the globe (Adams and Pigliaru, 1999). Facilitated by modernisation and technical progress as well as the extension of education and so on, 'convergence' was conceived as a positive way of evolving towards a golden age, a society of 'goodness', and a peaceful and affluent utopia. The idea that societies move towards a condition of similarity is a common feature in a number of academic debates and discussions – for instance, within the various theories governing social change (for example, pre-revolutionary French philosophers and the Scottish moral philosophers, as well as de Tocqueville and others), studies of industrial (Kerr et al, 1973) and 'post-industrial' societies, as well as in debates about the 'post-modernist aspects of contemporary society' (Coughlin, 2001) and 'the end of history' (Fukuyama, 1989). This is fundamentally based on a Darwinian evolutionary perspective of society, because those societies which do not adopt the rules of universalist liberal democratic values are not meant to survive in competition with the liberal model.

Within this general scheme, convergence is often perceived as a more or less long-term trend. Even when divergent features can be noted, the net result or the dominant trend is supposed to be convergent. A supposedly steady evolution also means the denial of any dramatic break in the trend (for example, a revolution, a war or an economic crisis) and hence an essentially unbroken or continual historical process towards peaceful societies, while convergence implies a reduction of uncertainty in daily life. Conversely, divergence suggests a risk of crisis, impoverishment and increasing uncertainty. However, the emphasis on convergence leads to the underestimation, and sometimes overlooking, of the simultaneous counter-movement towards divergence.

Within this general evolution of societies, we will restrict the analysis to convergence in social welfare systems in developed societies. Empirical studies on convergence in social welfare systems of the developed countries show that the trajectories of the systems lead to a convergence of the statistical data (per capita social expenditure, percentage of social expenditure in GDP, financing schemes). The convergence of benefits and financing is often conceived as a causal convergence, resulting from internal mechanisms of social welfare systems and socioeconomic factors largely linked to globalisation and Europeanisation. As we shall see in this chapter, those empirical results can be explained by two main types of theoretical arguments: the economic theory of convergence on the one hand, and theories of law on the other.

The main concern in this chapter is to show that the theoretical explanations of convergence are insufficient, fragile or contradictory. We shall see that both often disregard the contradictions in trajectories and the power of certain divergent forces in the evolution of the social welfare systems. For instance, many authors note that national social welfare institutions experienced few changes throughout the 1980s and 1990s. This means that even in a process of convergence, the typologies of the systems appear quite unchanged (Kautto, 2001).

Convergence in social welfare systems and economic development

Convergence among social welfare systems is often supposed to stem from a more general economic convergence (Powell and Hewitt, 2002). Certain empirical studies show that the cross-section observation of the increasing relationship between the share of social expenditure and per capita GDP is largely related to a country's evolution. Indeed, despite the period of economic crisis or recession in the 1980s and 1990s, the long-term extension in social expenditure remains largely linked to economic development. In addition, there exists a clear relationship, which links the level of social benefit per head, the share of social expenditure in GDP and per capita GDP. This relationship simultaneously shows the different dimensions of the convergence, but also highlights the difficulty in interpretation.

The convergence of GDP per head, for example, has an automatic effect on the convergence of social benefit per head. In this case, any economic catch-up entails a degree of social convergence. This effect can be reinforced by the cross-national increasing relationship between GDP and the extension of social protection. Both types of convergence are in fact interrelated.

The limited explanatory power of economic theories

A large amount of literature on economic convergence focuses on the empirical tests of convergence in GDP per capita. The conclusions are not always very clear because the results are sensitive to the periods, to the number and the types of countries, to the type and normalisation of data (for example, real domestic trends and purchasing power parity) as well as to the statistical methods (s-convergence, b-convergence, various econometric methods) employed. However, the general conclusion is that there actually has been a long-term economic convergence among the developed countries, with a convergence boom in the 1950s and the 1960s, which faded in the 1990s.

Two main traditional economic theories explain economic convergence: economic growth theory and international trade theory in a process of international openness. International trade theory (ITT) anticipates convergence through market forces, trade and competition, not least because two thirds of international trade is trade managed by and within multinationals with the great bulk of foreign direct investment being carried out by multinational enterprises. This development of multinational and transnational firms reduces any room for manoeuvre for national governments (Unger and van Waarden, 1995). The competition between national governments for the location of such multinational firms could also produce a convergence of industrial policies. Pan (1999), argues that trade openness and capital freedom are positively associated with growth prospects which produce a convergence in the conditional sense.

In fact, the relationship between internationalisation, openness and social welfare systems is contradictory (Mishra, 1999; Sharpf and Smith, 2000). Social welfare systems create a distortion in prices in the 'generous' social welfare countries in the name of competitiveness, thus convergence stems from a dismantlement of social welfare systems within the developed countries. Internationalisation without a high level of regulation produces a 'race to the bottom' (Unger and van Waarden, 1995). According to Kitzmantel and Moser (1995), internationalisation is likely to produce a 'convergence for the worse'; Engbersen expects and fears convergence towards a 'residual model'; Keller (1995) finds some convergence to the bottom and towards minimal standards of welfare. These challenges exert irresistible pressures on the welfare state and echo older functionalist arguments from neo-Marxists (O'Connor, 1973; Gough, 1979; Offe, 1984) and the logic of industrialism proponents (see for example, Wilensky, 1975). They tend to argue that current types of welfare states will not make it far into the 21st century. They frequently argue that these pressures will lead to a negative convergence of welfare states.

We can nevertheless consider that as emerging markets grow in an increasingly globalised competitive environment, the protection of property rights, which requires an effective judicial system and the respect of civil rights, also becomes a criterion for convergence. New social protection policies can also protect people from the production of inequalities, new social risks, and so on. Therefore, social welfare systems are correlated to openness because they become an instrument for sustainable economic development and for protecting people from the economic consequences of business cycles and impoverishment. Social protection systems in open countries become a factor in economic development (Hagen, 1999).

The reference to ITT leads to another discourse on the supposed upper-limits of social expenditure in the most developed countries. Several approaches are often used to explain that the recent trend towards convergence comes from stabilisation and from a stricter control of national social expenditure. This perspective is based on the idea that the most developed countries have reached a kind of saturation point in social expenditure because basic needs are largely covered by the provision of social benefits (Cornelisse and Goudswaard, 2002). In fact, the stabilisation of any aggregated social benefit signifies more a process of rationing than any 'real' saturation point in an affluent society. The idea of a saturation point is more often used by governments to justify macroeconomic decisions based on rationing and containment, to limit fiscal deficits (Pierson, 2001).

In the late 1980s and early 1990s, the sudden increase in the percentage of social expenditure in GDP was frequently conceived explicitly or implicitly as a catastrophe because it was often correlated to a budgetary deficit. The stabilisation of social expenditure thus stemmed from a rationing process on the financing side (Pierson, 1996, 2001). Therefore European integration, driven by its key engines, the European Commission, EMU, the single market and tax policy coordination, is pushing member states' financing solutions in a similar direction (Hout, 1998; Kautto, 2001).

Evenly developed convergence via international trade is strongly contested by a large number of authors. For instance, Kitschelt et al (1999) link the convergence process to a wider analysis of the evolution of capitalist societies. They reject the idea of a convergence on a 'uniquely superior model of markets' for several reasons: the imperfect international competition, the different sensitivity of domestic economies according to the type of country, the degree of political agreement in favour of liberalisation, the strength and organisational capacity of producer groups, the configuration of political parties and the role of intermediate bodies. Even if some of the convergence comes from the decline in the traditional patterns of inequality, it remains embedded in a mixture of convergent and divergent evolutionary pathways. Furthermore, this convergence is located in different types of economies, namely 'business coordinated market economies' (CMEs) and 'liberal market economies' (LMEs). Diverse forms of the welfare state and systems of organising social inequality are associated with each form of capitalism. For instance, national CMEs are now moving towards certain similar features: business–labour cooperation, comprehensive welfare states, business relationships and powerful unions. Finally, the trend towards convergence largely depends on the weight of path dependency (Kitschelt et al, 1999). Particular forms of divergence are strengthened by political and institutional dimensions. In a world where social welfare arrangements have been institutionalised at the national level and where local actors have adopted strategies that succeed in local or national terms, there is no automatic or necessary movement towards any particular definition of efficiency-market – dictated or otherwise.

According to the neoclassical models of economic growth (Solow, 1956; Swan, 1956; Koopmans, 1965), diminishing returns on capital, implicit in the neoclassical production function, forecast that the rate of return on capital (and therefore its growth rate) will be very large when the stock of capital is small and vice versa. If the only difference among countries is their initial levels of capital, then the forecast in the neoclassical growth model is that countries with little capital will be poor and will grow faster than rich countries with large capital stocks, so there will be cross-country b-convergence. Another explanation of the catch-up in economic growth theory is based on the contagion model, that is a catch-up based on technological imitation compared to innovation. Knowledge and technology are transferable from the innovative countries to the less developed countries at a lower cost than innovation. In the long run, the world growth rate would be driven by discoveries in the state-of-the-art economies. Followers converge towards the leaders because imitation is cheaper than innovation. A part of the contagion is seemingly explained by the presence of the 'imitative entrepreneur' (Baumol, 1994). This economic thesis has also been reinforced by the standard historical analysis of 'Americanisation' as a process of imitation in technology.

However, a tendency for imitation costs to increase reduces the follower's growth rate and thereby generates a pattern of conditional convergence. Initial differences could grow boundlessly over time due to spillover effects that generate increasing social returns that can prevent any convergence. In some cases, firms in the richest countries are capable of preventing a situation in which the new knowledge diffuses so quickly that they would not be able to cover their initial outlays. In other cases, countries are so poor that they cannot allocate sufficient resources to innovation for a catch-up process. Zeitlin and Herrigel (1999) also contest the simplistic trajectory of 'Americanisation'. They refute the argument that during the post-war reconstruction the US succeeded in exporting a unitary and coherent 'American model' to western Europe and Japan. In fact, their study clearly shows that the process is not unilateral but cross-mixed – a hybridisation process that maintains the heterogeneity of societies, which remain largely based on their own cultural values and ways of life (Zeitlin and Herrigel, 1999).

Certain economic analyses on convergence identify several 'convergence clubs' that display a simultaneous process of convergence within certain groups of countries (and sometimes a divergent – or a non-convergent – trend among the clusters of countries). The debate on clubs of convergence especially highlights the evolution of societies between the developing and developed countries. Convergence is very often positively conceived as a reduction in income differences among nations. In fact, a large number of comparisons focus on the developed countries while lower territorial tiers, as well as the other factors of individual well-being, are ignored. In general terms, a large number of comparative studies on the trends of per capita GDP among the developed countries describe a slight convergence process as part of their conclusions. However, the findings of such studies, which comprise a larger number of countries, relate to club convergence – that is a double convergence *within* both the developing and the developed countries – and to a general pattern of divergence between both. In fact, such divergence constitutes a kind of bipolarisation between developing and developed countries.

The analysis of convergence in social welfare systems also shows this type of club convergence (Kautto, 2001), among, for example, the Nordic countries. Jordan (1996) also analyses the structure of the different social welfare systems as 'club goods'. A further type of divergence is the increase in income inequality and/or an ending of the decreasing pattern of inequality within many developed countries in the 1980s and the 1990s. This general increase is also linked to a process of social exclusion that affects certain vulnerable groups. Despite the different challenges that the European welfare states are facing today, one socio-economic group – the unskilled – is more likely to suffer from precarious jobs exposed to international low-wage competition, cuts in public service jobs and provision, changing family patterns, modest employment and income protection (Kvist, 2000). One possible trend is that of a dual society in each nation, with an increasingly marked division between those who are more mobile and skilled, and the less skilled. This would arise not only because of the difference in income (a well known fact today), but also because values diverge. Several studies show that structural unemployment increasingly focuses on unskilfulness, which creates a new type of social inequality. Estevez-Abe et al (2001, p 146) develop a new economic theory of social welfare based on skilfulness: "Firms are not free in their choice of product market strategies that may require highly specific skills. Firms' choices are constrained by the availability of necessary skills. Availability of specific skills, in turn, requires appropriate social protection". The result of this theory for an analysis of convergence is contradictory. On the one hand, the study points out that vocational training reduces domestic wage inequality but, on the other hand, skilled people are integrated into a new country, Europe, from which the non-skilled are more or less excluded. This divergent trend perhaps can explain the differences in voting behaviour and the increase in nationalistic ideology among the less skilled because they think that they will lose out as regards European development.

In addition, it is necessary to question the explanation of convergence through technical progress, which is seemingly a quasi-public good. We have already seen that societal convergence can be combined with divergent processes. Improvements in education can also contribute to improvements in innovation in many fields, which will not necessarily converge at the moment of their inception.

The diffusion of new types of communication, the use of new information technology, and access to globally distributed information privileges a minority of well-off people, but it simultaneously excludes others who do not use this dominant pattern in order to communicate. Access to, and benefits from, the new technologies appear to be disproportionately concentrated among the 'haves', while increasingly excluding the 'have-nots' from any participation whatsoever.

Finally, as seen above, the European dream of a knowledge-based society, which has become a kind of European banner, seems to ignore the potential consequence of divergence between and within countries, which will not be offset by a new type of social welfare system based on minimum social rights.

The role of structural and political convergence

Traditional economic analysis distinguishes several types of convergence (Baumol et al, 1994). One very important distinction is the structural convergence versus 'decisional' or 'induced' convergence. A structural convergence can be defined as an increasing similarity among the fundamental structures of the economies at work in domestic reactions to economic crises (Tavera, 1999). This approach (Solow, 1956) means that capital, demography and technology are among the most important factors in economic convergence or divergence. The long-term evolution would be fundamentally determined by the factors of the real domain, not by the monetary or budgetary domain. Consequently, the convergence of per capita GDP produces little information on real convergence because the aggregate is also manipulated by political decisions. Solow creates a distinction between the convergence created by specific policies and autonomous convergence due to the 'autonomous' mechanism of the economy.

A similar distinction can be made in the study of convergence in social protection defined in the following manner (Concialdi, 1999): for each type of social policy, the per capita social benefit depends on the social benefit per recipient and the percentage of recipients in the population. The social benefit per recipient is mainly defined by national rules and reflects the definition of social rights even if it depends on given economic and budgetary constraints. The second variable depends on demographic changes and other structural changes in society. Let us suppose that in all countries the criteria of eligibility to benefits were to remain unchanged. As a result, the unique factors of change in social expenditure would be the demography and structural foundations of the national economy. This approach makes it possible to indicate the nature of convergence within areas of social protection in a more accurate way. In the long term a relationship can be observed in all countries between the economic development of the countries and the development of social protection and suggests that this trend is mainly linked to the structural factors in society. However, there is no doubt that convergence in social protection is largely dependent on political decisions. The ratio of social expenditure to GDP is an indicator that has effectively become a political instrument. Furthermore, many political and legal decisions about the nature of social protection influence the real economy and demographic variables.

Finally, it is difficult to link convergence in GDP and convergence in social welfare systems because most of the benefits are non-tradable, while the convergence in GDP results from trade. Therefore, we have to seek the causes in another way, such as 'convergence' in law and common reference to doctrines of solidarity and doctrines of law.

Convergence and law

Some legal factors of convergence

In all the developed countries, social welfare systems are based on national legal schemes that change in accordance with different social reforms. For instance, the goal of 'Social Europe' is not only to imagine European solidarity, but also to build common social rights throughout Europe. Therefore, we can conceive that the convergence of social welfare systems is tied to, or at least a component of, a general process of convergence in law within the developed countries, and especially within Europe.

The 1980s and 1990s were characterised by a powerful movement towards legalism. Global integration, the Europeanisation of English law (the convergence between the Anglo-Saxon and the continental approach to the law) aided the general tendency towards systemic similarity (Markesinis, 1994; Teubner, 2001), through a wide range of European legal instruments and also by the use of policies of harmonisation or coordination in many fields. This trend is being reinforced by scholarly activity aimed at developing a European legal framework (Smits, 1999).

Concerning social rights, a type of convergence is directly linked to the development of the single market and this mainly comprises the rules connected with the protection of employees at work and of European citizens in that market (Smits, 1999). European law has, and is, eroding national regulations. Increasingly national regulations are becoming invalidated, and pressure has been mounting on the member states to replace such regulations with supranational ones. Sometimes, countries which themselves have high levels of protection, lobby for the adoption of their norms in the EU. Such political integration could fuel a counter-hypothesis, that of a 'race to the top', rather than to the bottom – that is to a convergence at a high level of protective regulation (Unger and van Waarden, 1995). For instance, Eichener (1995) finds that European occupational health and safety regulations provide a high level of protection and even develop innovative approaches. The forthcoming public health action (De la Porte, 2001) programme is designed to support the promotion of quality and best practice in healthcare systems, notably by supporting comparative analyses of them as well as of medical treatment (European Commission, 2001).

A second factor of convergence is the increasing references to human rights. To date, the most sizeable contribution of the European Court of Human Rights in Strasbourg has been in European family law; many discriminating national rules, for example, have been set aside on the grounds of Article 8, European Convention of Human Rights, and in civil procedure (Smits, 1999). In 2000, the EU passed two important directives on equal treatment and anti-discrimination. These directives stemmed from the active involvement of national and European anti-discrimination movements. The proposed legislation sought to both harmonise and extend many member states' existing legislation. Its efforts rested on the belief that the only legal solution to racism and discrimination across Europe was the harmonisation of legislation at the European level (Chopin, 1999).

A third factor is the European methods of harmonisation and coordination of policies, especially in social policies. Finally, the transplantation of policies from abroad is becoming increasingly frequent. In many countries, policy-makers who are preparing new reforms are taking foreign rules, policies or experiments into account and adapting them in their home countries. A fourth factor concerns the similarity of certain national social policies as a process, for example, hybridisation or welfare mixes of social policies. Theret (2001) notes that hybridisation between Bismarckian and Beveridgean rationales has also been a key factor in changing the French social protection system over the last 20 years. This apparent trend of convergence, which seems to dominate European history, has to be questioned, however.

Transplant versus mirror theory

The analysis of convergence in law, a part of the comparative analysis of law, is dominated today by a debate between the *transplant* theory (Watson, 1993) and the *mirror* theories (Kahn-Freund, 1976; Legrand, 1996). Watson's theory claims that there is no inherent relationship between law and the society in which it operates. He identifies transplants as the main source of legal change and states that law develops by transplantation, not as a consequence of social structure but because those who exert control over lawmaking are already familiar with foreign legislation and have observed the merits that could be derived from it (see also Mitselis, 2000). An extreme version of Watson's transplant thesis does not merely disregard political constraints on the adoption of legal models from other jurisdictions, but explicitly rejects this type of influence as irrelevant.

This theory is implicitly based on a Darwinian evolution of societies and, at the European level, we can find an example of this philosophy in the development of the notion of 'best practice' or 'good practice', officially promoted in the EU. One consequence is the supervision of each country and a kind of 'honours list' containing the results of reforms, evaluated as a success or a failure. Using this approach, the EU tries to promote 'good practice' – that is the reforms are regarded as successful in some countries – and to 'export' them. Multilateral surveillance procedures and convergence programmes have been implemented to facilitate progress towards a medium-term orientation of macroeconomic policy (De Macedo, 2000). These references to best practice have been reinforced and generalised in the 'Open method of co-ordination' (Chassard, 2001; De La Porte and Pochet, 2002).

The *mirror* theories oppose this transplantation thesis and claim that laws cannot be separated from their purpose or from the circumstances in which they are made. It is impossible to take for granted that rules or institutions are transplantable. According to Kahn-Freund, legal institutions may be more or less embedded in the nation's life. Therefore, the law must be observed in its social context and cannot be treated as a technical instrument for a group of lawyers and policy-makers in a society 'receiving' a foreign code, a foreign legal institution or a foreign legal principle (Gessner, 2001). Kahn-Freund (1974) identifies a two-step process to determine the viability of a proposed transplant: the first step is to determine the relationship between the legal rule to be transplanted and the socio-political structure of the donor state; the second step involves comparing the socio-political environment of the donor and host state.

Some authors try to define a middle ground between these two opposing theories. They refuse the idea of a total autonomy of law vis-à-vis society because it is difficult to conceive that a society can implement a legal framework that is totally cut off from the principles and the foundations of society itself. Yet they also refuse an oversimplistic idea of a systematic correlation or an 'embeddedness' between the development of law and the values in society – because this would be to ignore the inevitably contradictory decisions and trends that characterise any society, which can be expected to disrupt any easy consonance between legal principles and wider social norms. For instance, even in a nation state, the cultural and social values differ from one region to another whereas the law is a national one. This intermediate position is illustrated by Bradley (1999) in family law:

> Without denying the impact of industrialisation or the imitation of foreign models in law reform, political priorities and ideology exert a significant influence on transplantation and convergence in the field of family law. However, narrow versions of mirror theories must be qualified, in that a particular law can operate effectively in different environments. In addition, Kahn-Freund's assertion that knowledge of the 'power structure' of one jurisdiction, if a similar law is to be imitated or adapted elsewhere, also appears misconceived. (p 143)

Teubner (2001) has also proposed certain specific features pertaining to the link between law and society: the law's contemporary ties to societies are very selective, connected to specific fragments or groups of societies and evolve with conflictual trajectories including new divergences. Modernisation processes lead naturally to legal structures similar to those that can be observed in western societies and also to global structures which will emerge on the same model.

The globalisation of the economy, the modern technology and modern communication, urbanisation and the differentiation by society of the legal cultures of the world lead to convergence and to an exclusion of the non-modernised countries from this process (Gessner, 2001). Modernisation theorists observe the emergence of a cross-national legal culture (Friedman, 1996) based on the model of the historical experiences of the nation state (Gessner, 2001). Therefore, convergence is functional and legal transplants useful, if they are compatible with the rest of the legal body in the recipient country.

As states around the globe implement dramatic political and economic changes in response to external and internal developments, their legal systems become radically altered. In making these changes, legislators determine whether the borrowing of foreign law is feasible and if the international harmonisation of a particular set of laws is viable. This argument is further supported by the fact that states are under pressure in the increasing interdependent world to create uniformity in law (Mitselis, 2000). Institutional economics and transaction cost analysis explain that economic performance is largely dependent on efficient institutions and that markets have to be structured by rules (Gessner, 2001). This theory concludes that the main convergent trend in the legal framework is linked to the Europeanisation process, the development of the single market and the domestic application of international norms expressed by the European Court of Justice. According to Lodge (2001), the Europeanisation process is an institutional isomorphism that combines three factors: European coercive pressures (European Commission and the European Court of Justice), mimetic pressures (policy transfer, organisational learning) and normative pressures (increasing professionalisation leading to the establishment of particular rules).

In fact, the debate on convergence in law focuses largely on the need for a common commercial legal framework for the improvement of economic efficiency (contracts, property rights). In terms of commercial law, it is supposed that the stability in international commercial relations and the reduction in legal liability both strengthen national economies and create a healthy competitive environment (Gessner, 2001). It has rightly been observed that there is a direct relationship between the legal framework and the attitude of the foreign investors (Mitselis, 2000).

Weak convergence in social welfare systems and the internationalisation in law

Generally speaking, the debate on convergence in law focuses on private law and we need to address the issue concerning social rights defined in the social welfare systems. Let us quote Watson (1993, p 96): "Societies largely invent their constitutions, their political and administrative systems, even in these days their economies; but their private law is nearly always taken from others". In fact, whatever the theoretical point of view (transplant/mirror), the profound differences between the political environments of countries suggest that the rules of public law are the most resistant to transplantation. According to the culturalist point of view, even when the convergence of legal rules and institutions is observable, the social structures, legal cultures and mentalities as expressed in legal mythologies remain historically unique and cannot be bridged (Teubner, 2001). Legrand's starting point is that merely drafting uniform *rules* does not result in standard *law* because legal mentalities differ among the various cultures. These differences in democratic countries have shaped the national public institutions, such as legal systems and structures and traditions of public administration.

Convergence on any unique democratic political economic model is unlikely, both because there are strong theoretical reasons to doubt such convergence is even functionally dictated and because path-dependent cognitive, institutional, and political factors militate against it (Kitschelt et al, 1999; Palier, 2002). Furthermore, the pattern of convergence simultaneously becomes unstable because of the sensitiveness to the business cycle and also a "more volatile politics of representation" (Kitschelt et al, 1999). This trend creates a good deal of uncertainty over convergence, which can be understood as a current development that mixes both divergent and convergent processes as a transitional period, and could be conceived as a proto-society of a future and more stable system.

This perspective can explain the apparent non-convergence among social welfare systems that are national institutions based on a notion of solidarity (workers, citizens), and which are either public or quasi-public institutions. Social rights seem not to be affected by a trend towards convergence because they directly depend on national public institutions that do not experience the same pressure as private law. Furthermore, at least two obstacles prevent any European convergence in the social field. One obstacle to a jurisdictional convergence of social welfare systems is the principle of subsidiarity. This principle is coupled with the required unanimity in European decisions concerning social protection. Until the 1970s, the harmonisation project failed to produce anything of significance; the directives on coordination of social benefits in Europe did not change the national welfare systems and remained limited to migrants. In addition, the Council recommendation on the convergence of social protection objectives and policies in 1992 did not lead to any practical results (Quintin, 1999; Chassard, 2001; De la Porte and Pochet, 2002). Today, the transplanting of the open method of coordination from the economic and employment field into social protection is expected to produce a positive result but this system of soft law remains uncertain (De la Porte and Pochet, 2002). All these decisions or non-decisions at the European level have paved the way to the theory of path dependency, which explains the non- or limited convergence of social welfare systems in Europe (Pierson, 2001). Several authors also observe that convergence is not linear and unique and that the development of common rules and norms in Europe can also produce new divergences (Teubner, 2001; Guillen, 2001).

Comparative policy analysis stresses the importance of the distinction between policies and their outcomes. Policy goals are often similar, such as 'increasing the welfare of the nation', shared by all governments at a general level. Many countries recognise more or less the same risks: pensions, healthcare, unemployment and family policies. Nevertheless, these goals can turn out to be quite different when a concrete policy choice has to be made (Unger and van Waarden, 1995). Furthermore, the new social risks in society (lack of housing or opportunities in education, the quality of childcare, care for the frail elderly, low employability, indebtedness, social exclusion and racial discrimination), sometimes explained by the emergence of new types of economy (services, information), appear as factors of divergence in society because some countries implement new social policies, but others do not create any new social coverage in these areas of need. Despite the adoption of apparently similar welfare programmes in economically developed countries, there is a divergence in welfare policy (O'Connor, 1988; Hemerijck and Bakker, 1995; Hay et al, 1999), in the protection of workers (Mosley, 1995), and poverty regimes (Engbersen, 1995). The mirror theories also claim that the convergence process in certain areas is confused with the production of new forms of divergence (Gessner, 2001).

The resistance against the process of Americanisation is an example of a more general situation. In the words of De la Porte and Pochet (2002):

> the weakness of the approach of the social protection players is that there is no implicit or explicit model on which to converge, contrary to that of the economically-oriented players, looking to the EMU process to legitimise their policy prescriptions.... In contrast to the sphere of the monetary policy, where the model was the German one, in the area of pensions, there is no hegemon capable of enforcing a single vision of social objectives of social security system. (p 240)

In many European countries, the reforms have mainly been 'home grown'. Major reform initiatives are formulated by senior civil servants (Saari, 2001). It is possible to transfer certain foreign experiences *within* a national welfare system but it is not likely that any different *system* could be transferred to a nation. This interpretation of the recent development has gradually taken the place of papers whose conclusion had been to describe a kind of privatisation of the social welfare systems in western countries. The new interpretation seems to refer to Watson's (1993) theory of the transplantation of law. The accumulation of new social policies, new rules and norms do not yield any significant change in national institutions because many reforms are inspired by foreign experiences and decisions that look like good practices compatible with national institutions. National welfare systems are partly protected from European harmonisation by the principle of subsidiarity. The principle of coordination can be interpreted as the development of interdependence and connectivity between the different systems of social welfare states, but is restricted as regards social security for migrants (Pieters, 2001) and does not significantly affect national arrangements. Consequently, the reforms in each country often appear as domestic ones, more or less consistent with the national institutions, and look like institutional 'irritants' (Teubner, 2001).

For at least two decades, the gradual reforms of social welfare systems have also produced two main types of social rights: 'hard' social rights and 'soft' social rights. This development is linked to a more general trend in law that insists on the creation of a new paradigm in law foundation, which is called soft law, relative law, flexible law. Ost (2002) explains that post-modern societies experience a reduction in the power of the pyramidal or hierarchic law and a shift towards a concept of flexible law, which matches the development of post-modern society as a set of networks. The consequence in social welfare systems is the appearance of a split within the regulation of the systems themselves. On the one hand, 'hard' social rights refer to the quasi-constitutional status of those fundamental rights in democratic countries which are enforced by the constitution (or directives and charters) in order to safeguard vulnerable groups in circumstances of extreme poverty, severe discrimination and so on (Saari, 2000). Another section of social rights gradually becomes 'soft', which means that they are flexible, sensitive to economic and political changes, and potentially temporary. Access to benefits can be rationed, for example, with benefits being provided within the framework of an individual contract describing the rights and duties of every claimant. The most striking instance is probably labour market policy defined as a response to the business cycle or economic crises. Activation policies also try to escape the rigidity of traditional social rights. This general trend can be compatible with a certain amount of privatisation of the system particularly the tools of governance and regulatory regimes (Lodge, 2001). Consequently, convergence (fundamental social rights) and divergence (social policies) in the social welfare domain can work in the evolutionary process towards 'Social Europe'.

We can find a similar phenomenon in the extension of minimum standards in social policies, and the development of policies on minimum benefits against poverty and social exclusion in Europe. This convergence is justified not only by ethical values but also by economic reasons. Member states are most likely to be prevented by fiscal competition from achieving their objectives of anti-poverty policies by purely national policies. Therefore, the principle of subsidiarity would justify a European action (Atkinson et al, 2002). A generalisation of this doctrine over all national policies would lead to, and would be understood as, a negative convergence. However, such a general process would be complemented by other or new national policies reflecting the different national types of solidarity in each country. Therefore, convergent and divergent trends could be embedded simultaneously.

Finally, transplant theories can explain a part of convergence in law, while mirror theories largely explain national resistance against the threat of European uniformity. Is it possible in the long run to observe growing common social rules, norms and policies in Europe and the upholding of unchanged national institutions or unchanged welfare systems? Can we conceive of a Europe with convergent rules but divergent, or non-convergent, institutions? To date, there appears to be general agreement that, despite a plethora of reforms over the last two decades, national institutions of social protection have not radically been altered.

Conclusion

Convergence is often described as a combination of several trends such as the place accorded to the market, the administrative reorganisation of the state (decentralisation, regionalisation), convergent public interventions (regulations and norms, tax expenditure), constraints associated with the European Union, and the increasing hybridisation of social, economic and political systems (André, 2002). This chapter has noted a slight convergence of several socioeconomic indicators associated with the evolution of social welfare systems. Traditional economic theory is often used to explain (and to justify) this long-run convergent trend.

The 1980s and 1990s were characterised by a long list of new reforms and the emergence of new doctrines that appear as 'exogenous' insofar as they are formulated outside the recipient country. European treaties, directives and the decisions of the European Court also seemed to fuel a convergent process of norms, while theories and the comparative analysis of law attempt to explain this apparent process of convergence purely in terms of a convergence in law.

It has been suggested here that economic analysis hides the complexity of the process and underestimates or ignores the processes of divergence. Among the main roots of divergence can be seen the permanent nature of differences in the institutional foundations of welfare systems, whatever the type of reforms proposed and implemented. Furthermore, despite the supposed similarity of the difficulties, we also note that national reforms can lead to divergence among European member states. The principle of subsidiarity within the domain of social welfare systems can, for example, maintain differences among countries and fuel divergence. Furthermore, the complex trend of convergence and divergence among societies did not prevent the increase of inequalities among individuals in the 1980s and the 1990s.

References

Adams, J. and Pigliaru, F. (1999) *Economic growth and change, national and regional patterns of convergence and divergence*, Cheltenham: Edward Elgar.

André, C. (2002) 'Ten European systems of social protection: an ambiguous convergence', in D. Pieter (ed) *European social security and global politics*, The Hague: Kluwer Law International, pp 4-44.

Atkinson, A.B., Bourguignon, F., O'Donoghue, C., Sutherland, H. and Utilis, F. (2002) 'Microsimulation of social policy in the European Union: case study of a European minimum pension', *Economica*, vol 69, no 274, pp 229-43.

Baumol, W.J. (1994) 'Multivariate growth patterns: contagion and common forces as possible sources of convergence', in W.J. Baumol, R.R. Nelson and E.N. Wolff (eds) *Convergence of productivity*, Oxford: Oxford University Press, pp 62-85.

Bradley, D. (1999) 'Convergence in family law: mirrors, transplants and political economy', *Maastricht Journal of European and Comparative Law*, no 6, pp 3-19, pp 127-50.

Chassard, Y. (2001) 'European integration and social protection: from the Spaak Report to the open method of co-ordination', in D.G. Mayes, J. Berghman and R. Salais (eds) *Social exclusion and European policy*, Cheltenham: Edward Elgar, pp 277-305.

Chopin, I. (1999) *Campaigning against racism and xenophobia: From a legislative perspective at European level*, Brussels: European Network Against Racism.

Concialdi, P. (1999) 'Demography, employment and the future of social protection financing', in *Financing social protection in Europe*, Helsinki: Ministry of Social Affairs and Health Publications, vol 21, pp 91-116.

Cornelisse, P.A. and Goudswaard, K.P. (2002) 'On the convergence of social protection systems in the European Union', *International Social Security Review*, vol 5, July-September, pp 3-17.

Coughlin, R.M. (2001) 'Convergences theories', in E.F. Borgatta and M.L. Borgatta (eds) *Encyclopaedia of sociology*, New York: Macmillan, pp 295-303.

De la Porte, C. (2001) 'The soft open method of co-ordination in social protection 2001', Brussels: European Trade Union Yearbook 2001, pp 339-63.

De la Porte, C. and Pochet, P. (eds) (2002) *Building social Europe through the open method of co-ordination*, Brussels: Peter Lang.

DiMaggio, P. and Powell, W. (1991) 'The iron cage revisited: institutional isomorphism and collective rationality in organization fields', in W.W. Powell and P.J. DiMaggio (eds) *The new institutionalism in organizational analysis*, Chicago: Chicago University Press, pp 45-77.

Eichener, V. (1995) 'European health and safety regulation: no "race to the bottom"', in B. Unger and F. van Waarden (eds) *Convergence or diversity? Internationalisation and economic policy response*, Aldershot: Avebury, pp 229-51.

Engbersen, G. (1995) 'Poverty regimes and life chances: the road to anomia?', in B. Unger and F. van Waarden (eds) *Convergence or diversity? Internationalisation and economic policy response*, Aldershot: Avebury, pp 200-26.

Estevez-Abe, M., Iversen, T. and Soskice, D. (2001) 'Social protection and the formation of skills: a reinterpretation of the welfare state', in P.A. Hall and D. Soskice (eds) *Varieties of capitalism: The institutional foundations of comparative advantage*, Oxford: Oxford University Press, pp 145-83.

European Commission (2001) *The internal market and health services*, report of the High Level Committee on Health, December, Brussels: European Commission.

Friedman, L. (1996) 'Borders: on the emerging sociology of transnational law', *Stanford Journal of International Law*, vol 32, pp 65-90.

Fukuyama, F. (1989) 'The end of history', *The national interest*, summer, no 16, pp 3-18.

Gessner, V. (2001) 'Legalism in the era of globalisation', in R. Appelbaum, W. Felstiner and V. Gessner (eds) *Rules and networks: The legal culture of global business transactions*, Oxford: Hart Publishing, pp 55-76.

Gough, I. (1979) *The political economy of the welfare state*, Basingstoke: Macmillan.

Guillén, M. (2001) *The limits of convergence: Globalization and organizational change in Argentina, South Korea, and Spain*, New Jersey: Princeton University Press.

Hagen, K. (1999) 'Towards a Europeanisation of social policies? A Scandinavian perspective', in MIRE (ed) *Comparing social welfare systems in Nordic Europe and France*, Paris: DREES, Coll. MIRE, pp 661-90.

Hay, C., Watson, D. and Wincott, D. (1999) 'Globalisation, European integration and the persistence of European social models', POLSIS, Working Paper no 3, November.

Hemerijck, A. and Bakker, W. (1995) 'A pendulum swing in conceptions of the welfare state', in B. Unger and F. van Waarden (eds) *Convergence or diversity? Internationalisation and economic policy response*, Aldershot: Avebury, pp 144-81.

Hout, W. (1998) 'Globalisation and national policy autonomy: the case of the Netherlands', in P.K. Madsen (ed) *Work and welfare*, COST A7, London, final conference, Luxembourg: European Commission, pp 1-18.

Jordan, B. (1996) *A theory of poverty and social exclusion*, London: Polity Press.

Kahn-Freund, O. (1974) 'On the uses and misuses of comparative law', *The Modern Law Review*, vol 37, no 1, pp 6-27.

Kautto, M. (2001) 'Moving closer? Diversity and convergence in financing of welfare states', in M. Kautto, J. Fritzell, B. Hvinden, J. Kvist and H. Uusitalo (eds) *Nordic welfare states in the European context*, London: Routledge, pp 232-61.

Keller, B. (1995) 'European integration, workers' participation, and collective bargaining: a Euro-pessimistic view', in B. Unger and F. van Waarden (eds) *Convergence or diversity? Internationalisation and economic policy response*, Aldershot: Avebury, pp 252-77.

Kerr, C., Dunlop, J.T., Harbison, F. and Myers, C.A. (1973) *Industrialism and industrial man: The problems of labour and the management of economic growth* Cambridge, MA: Harvard University Press.

Kitschelt, H., Lange, P., Marks, G. and Stephens, J.D. (eds) (1999) *Continuity and change in contemporary capitalism*, Cambridge: Cambridge University Press.

Kitzmantel, E. and Moser, E. (1995) 'State competition with tax policy', in B. Unger and F. van Waarden (eds) *Convergence or diversity? Internationalisation and economic policy response*, Aldershot: Avebury, pp 135-43.

Koopmans, T. (1965) 'On the concept of optimal economic growth', in *The econometric approach to development planning*, Amsterdam: North-Holland, pp 225-87.

Kvist, J. (2000) *Activating welfare states: Scandinavian experiences in the 1990s*, research programme on comparative welfare state research, The Danish National Institute of Social Research, Working Paper, no 7.

Legrand, P. (1996) 'European legal systems are not converging', *International and Comparative Law Quarterly*, vol 45, no 1, pp 52-81.

Liebfreid, S. (1993) 'Towards a European welfare state? On integrating poverty regimes into the European community', in C. Jones (ed) *New perspectives on the welfare state in Europe*, London: Routledge, pp 133-56.

Lodge, M. (2000) 'Isomorphism of national policies? The 'Europeanisation' of German competition law and public procurement law', *West European Politics*, vol 23, no 4, pp 89-101.

Lodge, M. (2001) *Varieties of the welfare state to convergence of the regulatory state? The 'Europeanisation' of regulatory transparency*, Queen's Papers on Europeanisation, no 10.

Macedo, J.B. (ed) (2000) *Converging European transitions*, technical paper no 159, OECD development centre: unclassified, CD/DOC(00)3.

Markesinis, B.S. (1994) 'Learning from Europe and learning in Europe', in B.S. Markesinis (ed) *The gradual convergence: Foreign ideas, foreign influences, and English law on the eve of the 21st century*, Oxford: Oxford University Press, pp 1-14.

Markesinis, B.S. (1994) *The gradual convergence: Foreign ideas, foreign influences, and English law on the eve of the 21st century*, Oxford: Oxford University Press.

Mishra, R. (1999) *Globalization and the welfare state*, Cheltenham: Edward Elgar.

Mitselis, L.A. (2000) 'Regulatory aspects: globalisation, harmonisation, legal transplants, and law reform; some fundamental observations', *International Lawyer*, vol 34, pp 1055-69.

Mosley, H. (1995) 'The 'social dumping' threat of European integration: a critique', in B. Unger and F. van Waarden (eds) *Convergence or diversity? Internationalisation and economic policy response*, Aldershot: Avebury, pp 182-99.

Mueller, D. (1999) 'On the economic decline and decline of nations', in F. Pigliaru and J. Adams (eds) *Economic growth and change, national and regional patterns of convergence and divergence*, Cheltenham: Edward Elgar, pp 15-45.

O'Connor, J.S. (1973) *The fiscal crisis of the state*, New York: St Martin's Press.

Offe, C. (1984) *The contradictions of the welfare state*, London: Hutchinson.

Ost, F. and van de Kerchove, M. (2002) *De la pyramide au réseau? Pour une théorie dialectique du droit*, Brussels: Publications des Facultés Universitaires Saint Louis.

Palier, B. (2002) 'Europeanising welfare states: from the failure of legislative and institutional harmonisation of the systems to the cognitive and normative harmonisation of the reforms', Paper presented at the 'Ideas, Discourse and European Integration' conference, Center for European Studies: Harvard University.

Pan, H. (1999) 'Openness, capital mobility and global convergence', in G. Pigliaru and J. Adams (eds) *Economic growth and change, national and regional patterns of convergence and divergence*, Cheltenham: Edward Elgar, pp 102-26.

Pierson, P. (ed) (2001) *The new politics of the welfare state*, Oxford: Oxford University Press.

Pierson, P. (ed) (1996) 'The new politics of the welfare state', *World Politics*, vol 48, no 2, pp 143-79.

Pieters, D. (2001) *Final report concerning the seminars organised in the member states concerning the application of co-ordination regulation*, (EC) no 1408/71, Leuven: European Institute of Social Security.

Powell, M. and Hewitt, M. (2002) *Welfare state and welfare change*, Buckingham: Open University Press.

Quintin, O. and Favarel-Dapas, B. (1999) *L'Europe sociale: Enjeux et réalités*, Paris: La Documentation Française.

Saari, J. (2001) *Reforming social policy: A study on institutional change in Finland during the 1990s*, Social Policy Association, no 56, University of Turku: Department of Social Policy.

Sharpf, F. and Schmidt, V.A. (eds) (2000) *Welfare and work in the open economy: vol 1: From vulnerability to competitiveness*, Oxford: Oxford University Press.

Smits, J. (1999) 'How to take the road untravelled? European private law in the making', *Maastricht Journal of European and Comparative Law*, vol 6, pp 25-46.

Solow, R.M. (1956) 'A contribution to the theory of economic growth', *Quarterly Journal of Economics*, vol 70, no 1, pp 65-94.

Swan, T.W. (1956) 'Economic growth and capital accumulation', *Economic Records*, vol 32, November, pp 334-61.

Tavera, C. (1999) 'La convergence des economies Européennes: un réexamen à partir du concept de convergence structurelle', in C. Tavera (coordinator), *La convergence des economies Européennes*, Paris: Economica, pp 1-18.

Teubner, G. (2001) 'Legal irritants: how unifying law ends up in new divergences', in P.A. Hall and D. Soskice (eds) *Varieties of capitalism: The institutional foundations of comparative advantage*, Oxford: Oxford University Press, pp 417-41.

Théret, B. (2001) *Changes in the French social protection system: Path dependencies, timing, and international challenges*, CNRS, IRIS: Université Paris Dauphine.

Unger, B. and van Waarden, F. (1995) 'Introduction: an interdisciplinary approach to convergence', in B. Unger and F. van Waarden (eds) *Convergence or diversity? Internationalisation and economic policy response*, Aldershot: Avebury, pp 1-36.

Watson, A. (1993) *Legal transplants: An approach to comparative law*, Atlanta: University of Georgia Press.

Wilenski, H. (1975) *The welfare state and equality: Structural and ideological roots of public expenditure*, Los Angeles: University of California Press.

Zeitlin, J. and Herrigel, G. (1999) *Americanisation and its limits: Reworking US technology and management in postwar Europe and Japan*, Oxford: Oxford University Press.

SIX

Analysing the health transition: what the Greek case tells us about the social determinants of health

Mick Carpenter

Introduction

Most research into and discussion of the social determinants of health inequalities has tended to generalise from the experience of advanced capitalist countries. As a counterpoint, this chapter focuses on Greece as a southern European society that took a distinct route to modernity, and along the way radically improved the health status of its people.[1] This is an interesting topic in its own right but may also shed light on wider debates about the social influences on health and their relationship to capitalist modernity. My central question is whether Greece has achieved its impressive health gains despite or because of remaining an economic laggard, being subject to authoritarian government from the 1930s until 1976, maintaining a distinct culture and 'lifestyle', and developing less extensive systems of state health and welfare than countries in northern Europe. Do Greek similarities or differences from other forms of capitalist modernity account for improvements in health, and what does the future hold?

There are of course good foundational reasons for seeing universal processes at work in human health. First, people are biologically and psychologically similar everywhere and health is a basic social need for self-realisation across the lifespan (Doyal and Gough, 1992). Second, capitalist modernisation involves similar processes closely associated with health improvement and change: in other words both *advances* in health and *shifts* in its patterning. Yet against this convergent trend there are significant national variants in the nature of capitalist modernity, with associated health differences, influenced by distinct cultural values, institutional structures and social mobilisations. In social policy generally these persistent variations in the nature and effects of 'welfare capitalisms' since 1945 have underpinned regime theory's assertion of three distinct 'worlds' of welfare capitalism, with differential impacts on class inequalities in living standards (Esping-Andersen, 1990). Independently Wilkinson (1996) showed that while the economic growth associated with capitalist modernity led to health gains, beyond a certain point distributional inequalities in income had the greatest impact on health variations within and between countries. One purpose of this chapter, therefore, through examination of the Greek case, is to bring these two 'paradigms' closer together, drawing attention to parallel strengths but also weaknesses, some of which are illustrated by the fact that countries like Greece cannot be easily accommodated within their frameworks.

The problems with regime theory have been exhaustively discussed, so I will only focus on those most relevant to this chapter, arguing that it remains a viable paradigm even if one in need of substantial revision. First, there is a need to analyse, rather than take for granted, the broader global geopolitical and economic context in which 'three worlds of welfare capitalism' were able to flourish up to 1981, the period accounted for by Esping-Andersen's 'classic' narrative. At the same time the global perspective needs to be complemented by a greater emphasis on locally distinct pathways. Thus, while Greece shares characteristics with other southern European countries like Spain and Portugal, it also has features of its own. Second, as many have mentioned, the focus on class inequality needs broadening to examine processes and effects associated with gender, and also 'race' and ethnicity (Williams, 1995). Third, the notion of effects needs broadening as Esping-Andersen's distributional emphasis on 'decommodification' – money sufficient to live outside the labour market for pensioners, sick people, and so on – is too limited, tending to obscure analysis of deeper effects (Gough, 2000). One of these is the actual linkage of welfare regimes to health, but so is the more general need to examine the impact of welfare regimes on *social relations* of power and subordination associated with divisions of class, gender, 'race', ethnicity and age.

Wilkinson's (1996) extensive work on the relation between income inequality and health has resulted in a 'paradigm shift' of similar proportions for analysis of health inequalities in modern societies, as regime theory has for comparative social policy. It should not in principle be difficult to integrate it with regime theory as Wilkinson has a similar consumptionist and distributional view of the social order. While there is a risk of oversimplification, his essential argument is that 'relative deprivation' associated with widening income inequality intensifies resentment of the losers, and raises social tensions which corrode 'social capital' and damage social cohesion. Thus the emotional features of unequal societies impact most on health, rather than the direct effects of deprivation, by their variable impact on people's sense of 'fairness' or injustice and the way that these tighten or loosen bonds between social groups. Wilkinson shows that the countries with narrowest income inequalities and most well-developed forms of social support had up to 1981 the best records on improved life expectancy (Wilkinson, 1996). In many instances these could be mapped against welfare regimes: Scandinavian or social democratic regimes have better records than liberal regimes such as the US, with 'continental' or 'Conservative' European countries like Germany somewhere in the middle. However, some countries baulk the trend: Japan, with compressed income inequalities and a highly cohesive society, but a 'liberal' welfare regime, is a country that has made impressive gains in life expectancy characterised by high GDP. Greece is even more surprising as it has achieved an impressive advance in life expectancy against only a modest increase in GDP, the wide income inequalities associated with southern European countries, and an underdeveloped welfare state. It is also characterised – though I will argue this needs some qualification – by a high degree of social cohesion, and patterns of consumption that differ from more 'advanced' countries.

Why then has Greece done so well and what are the broader theoretical implications for explanations of social variations in health? I will suggest that Wilkinson's (1996) explanation of Greece exceptionalism, that the health effects of reduction in absolute rather than relative poverty were the chief cause up to 1981, is only partially adequate. Rather the Greek case illustrates a number of important points. First, that not only living standards, but also *patterns* of consumption – diet, smoking and other 'lifestyle' influences – are significant influences on health in Greece and other southern European countries. Second, Wilkinson is correct about social bonds being significant to health and Greece provides additional evidence for the importance of social connections and integration for health. In the Greek case, however, these are rather different to those found in northern European countries linked to variations in associational life and the strength of civil society, as pictured by Putnam (1993) and identified as health protective by the Californian Alemeda County study (Berkman and Syme, 1979). Additionally, both Wilkinson and Putnam fail to specify the gendered nature of 'social capital', which in the Greek case is particularly pronounced. This apart, the strong body of evidence on the role of social capital in health protection indicates that we need to qualify the one-sided emphasis placed on personal autonomy within the 'theory of human need' developed by Doyal and Gough (1992), though I will argue that Greece does also illustrate its health benefits through resistance to the state and modern capitalist social relations. A final point is the role of access to modern health and welfare services. Given the poor access, unequal distribution and generally problematic quality of Greek healthcare (see Carpenter, 2003), Greece provides further evidence of the importance of non-medical influences on health gain. Thus, although modernisation and convergence, as measured by economic growth and rising living standards had some health benefits, much of Greece's impressive record is due to its retention of distinct social and cultural features. Their current erosion due to accelerating convergence to northern European patterns of consumption, work and political–economic governance therefore potentially threatens the impressive gains that have been made. This means that a somewhat 'different' form of analysis has to be developed to account for health trends in Greece and other southern European countries (Ramis-Juan and Sokou, 1989).

In substantiating these arguments, this chapter first briefly reviews theoretical accounts of the 'health transition' and seeks to adapt these to variations in policy regimes. It then focuses directly on Greece as a health and welfare regime, analysing its record on health outcomes up to 1981, before extending this to the present day. The conclusion then pulls the threads together and returns to the question of whether accelerating convergence to northern European social patterns will have happy or unhappy consequences for Greek people's health.

Theoretical debates on the health of nations and groups

The chief scientific and political dispute about the association between health gain and modernity is whether capitalism alone or 'welfare capitalism' has been responsible for improvements in health. The classic debate focused on the case of England and Wales, seeking to explain the declining death rate from infectious disease and the rise of life expectancy since the 19th century. While both McKeown (1976) and Szreter (1988, 1992) agree that improvements in medical care were not the main cause, they dispute the extent to which the decline in mortality was the spontaneous result of agricultural productivity and capitalist economic growth, leading to improvements in per capita income and associated nutrition, or whether political pressures and state regulatory interventions made a difference. McKeown argued that 'host' resistance to infection, resulting from improved nutrition rather than reduction to exposure to pathogens or allopathic treatment, was mainly responsible. However, Szreter sought to qualify this by arguing that public health medicine secured reductions in exposure through improved sanitation, clean water supplies and other public health measures. Political pressures were also important, including agitation for social reform and trade union action to raise income levels higher than capitalist interests would otherwise have conceded. Household decisions to restrict numbers of children also contributed greatly to improved health. While many social scientists support Szreter, a recent contribution has sought to turn the advantage back to McKeown's 'autonomous' model (Guha, 1994).

While this debate focused solely on the British case (itself subject to significant local variations), McKeown (1976) drew evidence from developing countries that malnutrition increased vulnerability to infectious disease, and research has now confirmed the centrality of nutrition to health throughout history, particularly for young children (Newman, 1990). Nevertheless, caution should be exercised in applying the model elsewhere where climactic and agricultural conditions may differ and where the nature and the timing of the transition to capitalist modernity may vary from the British case. There is evidence across northern Europe that the end of absolute food scarcity influenced the decline in infant mortality, although infant feeding practices checked further progress until the early 20th century, when improved milk supplies and infant welfare programmes led to more hygienic artificial feeding and weaning practices (Corsini and Viazzo, 1993). After infant mortality started to fall a decline in the mortality of young adults followed, particularly from tuberculosis, throughout the first half of the 20th century (Rothenbacher, 2000).

Nevertheless, despite this general trend, there were significant differences in timing of what Omran (1971) called the 'epidemiological transition'. Omran believed that capitalist modernisation rescued humanity from the high mortality from infectious disease, which had been its lot for thousands of years. However, this had been succeeded by an 'age of degenerative and manmade diseases', from circulatory disease, cancers and diabetes, as well as accidents and stress-related ill-health. However, Omran recognised two departures from the 'classical' or 'western' 'accelerated' model in which modernisation and mortality decline occur within a relatively short period – which fits Greece after 1950 – and a 'delayed' model involving less spectacular advance in developing countries (Omran, 1983).

Despite broad recognition of exceptions, traditional health transition theory did not sufficiently account for differences between modern societies, and tended to picture 'degenerative' disease as products of affluence. Wilkinson's (1996) reformulation of the 'epidemiological transition' shows convincingly that income inequalities and relative poverty are key influences on mortality risk from modern degenerative disease. Because its chief policy recommendation is political action to redistribute income to reduce health inequalities and repair the damaged social fabric, it has been studiously ignored by the 'modernising' centre-left. However, his framework has also been criticised from further left by 'neo-materialist' approaches that argue that the direct 'hazards' and social relations of contemporary capitalist society still pose a substantial direct risk (Muntaner and Lynch, 1999). There is no doubt that Wilkinson's work has served to connect epidemiology, social theory and social policy in promising directions. As he has recently put it: "Research into population health provides a re-socialized view of our humanity" (Wilkinson, 2000, p 8). Since much of this argument has been rather general or focused on the most advanced capitalist countries, this chapter now examines the Greek health transition in detail. It seeks to develop a 'situated' and holistic account of interactions between consumption patterns, cultural traditions and ways of life, and broader political–economic pressures.

Greek progress on health from independence to 'democratic consolidation' in 1981

Modern Greek history has been strongly shaped by external forces. Greek national 'independence' was achieved early in the 1830s but was constrained by the Great Powers who sponsored it as a way of undermining the Ottoman Empire. Although Greece sided with the Allies in the First World War, the victors decided not to help it in its war with Turkey in 1922, in which Greece was heavily defeated. The resulting exchange of populations led to a massive refugee problem that sorely taxed Greece's limited resources. The Second World War and communist uprising led to millions of deaths and severe starvation and by 1950 Greece was an exhausted and isolated outpost of western Europe, ruled by a rightwing client government of the US (see Clogg, 1992; Gallant, 2001).

Health and social conditions were poor, and drove millions of Greeks to emigrate at the end of the 19th century. Infant mortality was very high, and infectious disease including malaria was rife. The refugee crisis in large cities like Athens and Salonika led to threats of epidemic disease and the spread of communist support among the urban population. The Liberal government, aided by the Rockefeller Foundation and the International Labour Organization (ILO), sought in the late 1920s to create a national health service, centralised public health system, and rudimentary system of social security. These reforms were blunted by medical resistance, the 1930s Depression, and the onset of dictatorship (Liakos, 1997; Venieris, 1997; Gianulli, 1998).

There is some evidence from the statistics in Table 6.1 that the limited economic modernisation, rising living standards and social improvements made during the interwar period were beginning to bear fruit. In 1928 it was estimated that life expectancy was 40.9 years for males and 50.9 for females, somewhat higher than elsewhere in the Balkans (NID, 1944b, p 29). However, League of Nations data showed that child deaths from typhoid, dysentery and abnormalities were higher in 1936 than for any other European country (NID, 1944a, p 269). Therefore, most of the health improvements that had been made by 1981 occurred after 1950, when Greece was a country under US 'protection', with a variety of governments, none of which initiated significant social reforms. Greece was a recipient of Marshall Aid, mostly for military or infrastructure purposes, and only some was used to improve sanitation and water supply and clear the swamps where malaria was rife.

On the face of it, Greece's accelerated health transition was thus 'autonomously' generated by economic growth from the mid-1950s. This was aided by the United States' dollar standard which underwrote an expanding world capitalism, and whose military intervention in 1949 ensured Greece was a part of it. The weak power of labour and puppet trade unions enabled a rapid expansion of the economy and a degree of industrialisation occurred, leading to claims of a Greek 'economic miracle' along the lines of Germany, Italy and Japan, as the country achieved one of the highest rates of economic growth in the OECD.

Table 6.1: Infant mortality rate per 1,000 live births in Europe in selected countries, including Greece, from 1850-1940

	1850	1900	1930	1940
England and Wales	145.6	154.0	60.0	57.4
Hungarian Republic	–	225.1	152.5	130.1
Germany	–	206.8	84.6	59.8
Greece	–	–	133.8	118.2
Spain	170.9	185.9	117.1	108.7
Sweden	146.2	98.5	54.7	39.2

Source: Rothenbacher (2000, p 7)

Tables 6.2: Trends in life expectancy in selected countries from around 1950 to the early 1970s

	Around 1950		Early 1970s	
	Male	**Female**	**Male**	**Female**
Greece	63.4	66.7	70.1	73.6
England and Wales	67.1	72.3	69.6	75.8
Scotland	65.0	69.5	67.4	73.9
Spain	58.8	63.5	69.7	75.0
Sweden	69.0	71.6	72.1	77.9
USA	65.9	71.7	69.0	76.7

Source: United Nations figures, cited in Ramis-Juan and Sokou (1989, p 305)

However, Greece only partially industrialised (Pettifor, 1994, p 12), and both the middle classes and working classes resisted an industrialising mentality. Greek people chiefly benefited from capitalism's 'golden age' via 'trickledown' effects from the growth of its merchant fleet, expansion of tourism, and renewed migration which resulted in remittances home. All this undoubtedly led to absolute reductions in poverty, as Wilkinson (1996) shows, but with only modest reductions in income inequality (Katrougalos, 1996).

Against this background, the improvements in health up to 1981 were arguably a 'health miracle' of greater substance than the rather shadowy economic one. Tables 6.2 and 6.3 show that on key indicators of infant mortality and particularly life expectancy Greece had significantly closed the gap with wealthier countries, and male life expectancy was actually higher than in England and Wales. A major reason for this impressive performance was the low rates of mortality from 'degenerative' diseases common in northern countries. During this period Greece became a predominantly urban country, concentrated in Athens and one or two other cities. Much of this was unplanned, and gave rise to problems of pollution. Housing improved through unregulated and often illegal building to which authorities turned a blind eye, and public provision was minimal (Leontidou, 1990).

One of the few general surveys into health and living standards in this era found more ill-health among poorer children in 1975 in working-class Piraeus than generally in Athens. Respiratory and digestive disease, arthritis, rheumatism and heart and circulatory disease were common causes, linked to pollution of air and water, and lower quality community services. More women reported health problems than men (Iatridis, 1980). However, the survey found less association between child ill-health and poverty in Piraeus than a comparable survey in the US conducted in Boston in 1976, in terms of haemoglobin levels, and height and head circumference:

> The socio-cultural condition in Greece, and the dietary habits of the Greeks may have reduced the impact of deprivation. For example, the highly

Table 6.3: Trends in infant mortality rate per 1,000 live births in selected countries, including Greece, from 1960-80

	1960	1980
Greece	40.1	17.9
United Kingdom	22.5	12.11
Spain	43.7	12.3
Sweden	16.6	6.9
USA	26.0	12.6

Source: Apostolides (1992, p 7)

nutritious olive oil is extensively used, even among the poorest families. Moreover, social relations and ties within the extensive family system, and in local neighbourhoods, are still strong and effective in Greece, contrasted to some other more advanced industrialized countries like the USA. Such informal or formal, mutual aid networks may, at times, provide adequate prenatal and infant or child diet and care in early childhood. Responsible adults in Greek families are usually willing to undergo unusual sacrifices on behalf of their children's well-being. (Iatridis, 1980, p 188)

Health and social welfare since 1981: the PASOK era

The Greek Socialist (PASOK) government elected in 1981 launched itself on a Keynesian and social democratic road, as did other southern European countries, only to come unstuck. The oil recessions of the 1970s had severe effects, and it joined the European Union in 1981 at a time when Reagan and Thatcher had propelled the world economy in neo-liberal directions, exposing the Greek economy to strong international competition. PASOK did initiate a spate of social reforms, including the 1983 National Health Service, labour laws appeared, and wages were indexed to prices. While living standards rose rapidly ahead of productivity levels, inflation accelerated way above the European average. The growth rate, which had been 7 per cent in the 1960s, fell to 1.6 per cent in the 1980s, substantially below the European average (Thomadakis, 1995).

PASOK changed direction dramatically in 1985, described by Woodhouse (1991, p 333) as "the eclipse of socialism". As a condition for providing loans, the EU imposed an austerity programme that led to falling living standards in the 1990s, and eroded PASOK's electoral support. After a brief Conservative government in the early 1990s PASOK regained power, but maintained Greece's obligations under the 1991 Maastricht Treaty to reduce public borrowing and encourage 'flexibility'. The GNP increased from $3,070 per capita 1970–75 to $11,640 per capita by 1992–97, but still was only around half the EU average according to World Bank figures. *The European health report 2002*, enables more up-to-date comparisons to be drawn on the European countries surveyed earlier in this chapter and these figures are presented in Table 6.4. They confirm that Greece has made significant strides on health, with some further improvement in national wealth. A further comparison with Albania is included as an example of a Balkan country that from an even lower economic base made impressive health gains, which also appear to be strongly linked to dietary improvements.

How do these changes map onto trends in health since the 1970s? Basically the story is one of continuing improvements in mortality since 1970, but at a slower rate, and men have done relatively better than women. Life expectancy at birth for men rose to around 75 years by 1993, which in the rest of Europe was only bettered by Sweden, while for women it rose to around 80 years, close to the EU average (WHO Europe, 1998, 2002). However these general trends obscure the fact that formerly low rates of cardiovascular disease (CHD) and cancers have converged towards the European average, while Greece has the third highest mortality from strokes and road traffic accidents. Infant mortality rates fell rapidly during the 1980s, but remained higher than the EU average at around 8.4 per 1,000, particularly in urban areas (WHO Europe, 1998).

An urban–rural differential in health status is a distinct feature of Greek health patterning. Migration to the big cities such as the Greater Athens Area (GAA), Thessaloniki and Patras has been extremely rapid since 1950, where 65 per cent of people now live. The 1983 NHS reform introduced health centres to rural areas, but failed to create a primary care system in the cities. The shift to cities has been associated with shifts away from traditional diet and lifestyle, and there are also socioeconomic inequalities among urban people. We therefore need to assess the relative contributions of consumption and lifestyle, social cohesiveness and broader economic and environmental influences on health.

Table 6.4: Health and other social indicators in 2001 for selected European countries, including Greece

	GDP per person (PPP$)	Income inequality (Gini index)	Health expenditure per head ($)	Life expectancy in years Male Female		Perinatal mortality/ 1,000
Albania	3,189	–	79.18	72.0	78.0	11.50
Hungary	12,213	32.7	2,287	67.2	75.8	10.4
Germany	24,951	30.0	2,476	74.9	81.0	6.07
Greece	16,058	32.7	1,397	75.8	80.8	8.77
Spain	19,263	32.5	1,194	75.2	82.3	5.57
Sweden	24,402	25.0	1,732	77.0	82.3	4.67
UK	24,135	36.1	1,569	75.1	80.0	8.23

Consumption: the role of diet, alcohol consumption and tobacco

Evidence from Greece shows that 'modernisation' of diet can damage as well as advance health. The Seven Countries Study, which followed cohorts of middle-aged men from 1958 to 1989, showed a distinct coronary heart disease (CHD) advantage for Greek men compared to those in the US, Finland, the Netherlands, Italy, Croatia, Serbia, and Japan. The Cretan diet of low meat, high vegetable, fruit and cereals, and modest wine drinking with meals, was seen as the main reason. Elsewhere consumption of animal and dairy foods strongly correlated with CHD. Only Japan had comparable low rates of mortality (Menotti et al, 1999). There is also accumulating evidence that a diet rich in vegetables and fruit protects against intestinal cancer, while vitamin C may also mitigate the effects of air pollution (Kromhout and Bloemberg, 1997, Levi et al, 1999).

International consumption patterns are not, however, immutable and the North Karelia Project in Finland showed reduction in cholesterol and associated reductions of mortality from CHD, and the Cretan diet has been tried with some success in France, with positive effects on all-cause mortality (Menotti et al, 1999). In the opposite direction, the renowned Cretan diet is also becoming less common in Crete, and as we have seen is becoming less typical of the urbanised majority of Greeks. Rising living standards, allied to a traditional Greek culture emphasising family and public celebration has led to growing obesity, making Greeks the heaviest people in Europe. Greeks eat out more than most other nations and fast-food outlets have mushroomed in big cities as working lives have become more pressurised, and women enter the workforce (Greece Now, 2002).

The growth in smoking is undoubtedly one of the greatest contemporary threats to Greece's health achievements, particularly for women. In contrast to most EU countries cigarette consumption has risen steadily since the 1970s, and while the percentage of male smokers declined from 61 per cent to 46 per cent, female smokers increased from 25 per cent to 28 per cent. At 17 per cent, Greece has by far the highest proportion of heavy smokers of any EU country and in 1992 Greek people smoked more cigarettes per head (WHO, 1997). As far as women are concerned, research in northern Europe suggests that smoking functions as a 'coping mechanism' in relation to family and work pressures (Graham, 1987). In a Greek context, it perhaps also helps them to deal with the conflicts of being, as Kyriazis (1995, p 267) puts it, "caught between the forces of modernisation and tradition and modernity". It is true that the government takes these trends seriously and has sought to develop tax and health promotion policies to combat smoking (Petridou et al, 1999).

Social capital

Wilkinson's (1996) resocialised view of influences on health rightly draws attention to the role of social networks and social cohesiveness as influences on health. Therefore, the traditional Greek 'way of life', and not diet alone, may enhance health. Although something of a stereotype, Greek village life was characterised by an unrushed pace of life (siestas and a *siga-siga* or slowly-slowly approach), public sociability (*parea*), and dense family networks serviced by women. For men, the *kafenio* provided a reference point for sociability, although women were often isolated. While social networks survived the journey to the cities through chain migration, the unhurried way of life has been increasingly eroded in a pressured, noisy and polluted urban environment. Policies aiming at higher productivity and flexible working associated with meeting EU convergence rules, have accelerated these trends.

In any case, Greek familialism does not have entirely positive effects as it helps to reproduce the problematic relationship between civil society, the market and the state inherited from Ottoman days (Tsoukalas, 1995), and it of course also involves considerable costs for women. In many western countries new social movements have revitalised the political culture, even if participation in political parties has declined. In Greece political parties remain the focus for clientelist favours. Voluntary organisations are also weak or are often subservient to the state, although this may be changing (Robins, 1991; Harvey, 1995). Thus the Greek stock of social capital differs substantially from Putnam's associational ideal (Putnam, 1993). In addition, women's participation in the workforce and raised aspirations will lessen their ability to service familial social capital, exposing the weaknesses in southern welfare states.

Since Durkheim, suicide rates have often been seen as a marker of social cohesiveness, and (with the usual male–female differences) these remain consistently low in Greece, at 3.0 per 100,000 in 1993, compared with the highest European case of Finland at 22.8 per 100,000 (Morrison and Stone, 2000). Putnam sees social 'trust' as the glue binding social capital, which traditionally could be seen as high in Greece, at least as far as crimes against the person (theft and violence) are concerned (rather than swindling and corruption). With modernisation since the 1950s crime is rising but rates remain below those of other European societies. Gallant (1995) suggests that this may partly be caused by survival of the 'urban village', but also high emigration in the 1960s removed men of the age most prone to crime from the population. He suggests the increasing rates among women and juveniles since the late 1970s is a response to economic modernisation magnifying their sense of 'relative deprivation'. This high degree of trust must also be linked to ethnic cohesiveness, which is being tested by the influx of East European migrants, some of whom may be drawn into criminal activities and prostitution, linked to their impoverished condition (Baldwin-Edwards, 2001).

One of the few commentators to comment on social capital as a significant influence on Greek health, and particularly the beneficial effects of the Greek 'health miracle' for men, is Hollis-Triantafillou, a GP in Athens. She points out in a semi-joking fashion that the adulation of the male child, the low divorce rate, employment opportunities and respected old age all help as does a Greek tradition of male 'expressiveness':

Throughout his life he is expected and encouraged to express strong emotions by singing, dancing, shouting, laughing and weeping and through constant physical contact; hugging, kissing, holding hands, and caressing are normal components of everyday human contact for both men and women, as is constant, eloquent verbal communication. Being alone is equated with loneliness and is considered the worst of human afflictions, whereas good company, together with food and wine, is the elixir of life. (Hollis-Triantafillou, 1995, p 1474)

Socioeconomic inequalities in health

We move now from 'lifestyle' and 'cultural' to consider 'structural' influences on health, which unlike in Britain have been given little prominence in either research or policy debates (Tountas et al, 2002). A survey of 11 European countries, excluding Greece but including Italy, Spain and Portugal, found that inequalities of mortality and morbidity among men were widespread and broadly similar, though there were variations in risk factors (Kunst et al, 1998). While aspects of Greek life may mitigate the impact of health inequalities, it is likely that, as elsewhere, poverty, inequality and social exclusion will have strong effects on mortality and morbidity.

Although fully reliable national statistics do not exist, poverty levels in Greece remain among the highest in the EU, making its record on health even more impressive. Projections from the European Community Household Panel (ECHP) survey suggest that in 1993 2.25 million Greek people or 22 per cent of the population, including 380,000 children, were living below the average income or expenditure, an increase from just over 2 million in 1988, in all probability showing that the austerity programmes from 1985 onwards were starting to bite (Eurostat, 1997). The UK is the only northern European country with a similarly high rate of poverty. Research into the distribution of this poverty by Tsaklogou and Panopoulou (1998) through analysis of a national household budget survey carried out in 1987/88, looked not just at income but also access to basic 'necessities'. They found poverty concentrated among elderly people, often exacerbated by the highly inequitable pension system. Rural people were also often 'extremely' or 'precariously poor' despite EU subsidies. In urban areas, families with children and a growing number of long-term unemployed, due to economic restructuring, had a higher risk of poverty. These are two groups who are poorly served by the Greek social security system (Marinakou, 1998). The survey also underlined the close association between social position, poverty and educational qualifications in Greece. It thus showed that both 'old' and 'new' forms of poverty are to be found in Greece, though the low levels of single parenthood meant that this does not feature prominently as a cause.

In northern Europe the 'new poverty' is often associated with disadvantage linked to 'race' and ethnicity. Traditionally 'social capital' and cohesion in

Greece has been associated with ethnic similarity, which was demographically generated by the crisis of 1922, reinforced by Greek orthodox religion, and cemented by hostility to a perceived external (Turkish) threat. However, Greece is increasingly characterised by growing ethnic diversity associated with poverty and discrimination. Human rights groups have particularly criticised the prison conditions for migrants (see www.hrw.org). As well as the 1 million legal migrants, there are an estimated half a million 'undocumented' illegals, mainly from Albania and other East European countries. They are in low-waged, insecure work, not protected by labour legislation and the social security system. Illegal migrants were allowed to register with a Green Card in 1998, not for completely altruistic reasons but also to gather in tax revenues and social security contributions, and to conduct a police crackdown on remaining illegals. Debate about their presence includes awareness of their positive economic contribution, but increasing 'moral panic' about crime and prostitution (Fakiolas, 1999; Lazaridis, 2001). Human rights groups have also criticised the treatment of ethnic Turks who, until a law prohibiting it in 1998, were often deprived of Greek citizenship and continue to experience discrimination (www.hrw.org). Also present in Greece are Roma people, who have been traditionally discriminated against across Europe and who suffered from the recent resurgence of nationalist sentiment. These issues have led some to express concern at the ethnic exclusivity of the Greek state, illustrating that social capital can have its 'downside' (see Portes and Landolt, 1996).

The evidence on socioeconomic inequalities of health in Greece is patchy given the lack of a strong public health tradition of social epidemiology. What exists shows that they map onto poverty and social exclusion in complex ways. The evidence reviewed by Sissouras (1993) suggests that while poverty may be most common in rural areas, health statistics show that health tends to be worse in the urban centres of Greece. The higher infant mortality rate in urban areas indicates that this particularly affects women and young babies, and is linked to other significant issues for women and their relatively poor health indicators: pollution, access to health services, high smoking rates, low contraception and high resort to abortion (Matsaganis, 1991, 1992). This confirms the general point made by Wilkinson (1996) and others that capitalist economic growth and health are not always correlated, and in this instance the particularly poor quality of the urban environment in Greece is implicated.

There is thus suggestive evidence that socioeconomic inequalities of health are particularly a feature of urban life, due to both structural and behavioural influences. The review showed associations between the growth of industrial employment and higher risks of mortality, and associations between perinatal mortality, poverty and access to health services. The only national study of self-reported health, conducted by the National Centre for Social Research (EKKE) in 1988, showed that people in lower socioeconomic groups living in poor housing in urban areas, with few educational qualifications, were more likely to report negative health experiences. A more recent study of hospital admissions of school accidents to children in Athens showed a marked socioeconomic gradient, with children from single-parent families particularly at risk (Petridou et al, 1994).

The evidence on links between industrial employment and ill-health must however bear in mind that the formal wage earning class is still relatively small in Greece. Figures for the late 1980s showed only half were employees compared to the EU average of 82 per cent, while 31 per cent were self employed, often in shops or tourism, and 15 per cent were unpaid family workers. Those who were waged typically worked in small enterprises (Kritsantonis, 1992). While this low level of 'urban industrialism' may result in low productivity and levels of efficiency, it may in fact have some beneficial health effects. Evidence from more 'advanced' industrial capitalist countries shows that the psychosocial effects of subordinated mass work conducted under pressure (low control–high demand) are linked to high rates of all-cause mortality and CHD in particular (Marmot et al, 1991). Though this is now changing, traditionally in Greece employed work has mostly not been subject to high degrees of rationalisation, and the self-employed and agricultural sectors are associated with high degrees of occupational control, mitigating the effects of high demands on health.

Recent research on the effects of the transition to work insecurity and privatisation in northern Europe has shown that it results in deterioration in psychological and physical health (Ferrie et al, 2001). Greece has always had a large informal/underground economy, which as indicated above has been expanded as a result of migration from Eastern Europe. Efforts to restructure the Greek economy to meet EU convergence criteria have led to privatisation and increased emphasis on flexible labour practices, which emerging evidence suggests has negative health effects. This is confirmed by the results of the Second European Survey of Working Conditions (Walters, 1998; Benavides et al, 2000), which includes Greece and show that precarious employment is associated with high job dissatisfaction, stress, fatigue, backache and muscular pains. Many workers feel constrained and suffer the effects of intensified work (Walters, 1998; Benavides et al, 2000). These rapid changes in the traditional Greek way of life are leading to exceptionally high levels of perceived stress: 72 per cent state that they are regularly stressed, with the nearest other EU country in this regard being Belgium at 48 per cent (Eurostat, 2001).

In addition to these socioeconomic influences, two aspects of the urban environment that deserve mention are traffic accidents and pollution. Greece has one of the highest mortality rates from traffic accidents in the industrialised world, most of which occur in the Greater Athens Area. While this is partly due to the structural weaknesses of poor urban infrastructure and low investment in public transport, it is also linked to cultural-behavioural issues associated with Greek individualism, aggressive driving and unwillingness to wear seat belts (Petridou, 1998; Balourdos, 1999). Traffic congestion is a cause of ill-health from air pollution, which adversely affects children's growth and morbidity, and is directly implicated in higher deaths among older people. Urban pollution and traffic congestion affect all classes, but it is worse in overcrowded working-class districts with little vegetation and few parks (Kafourou et al, 1997; Touloumi et al, 1997). There are improvements, some of these being made with the help of EU structural funds, but there is still a long way to go. Both these environmental features serve to interact with economic/employment influences on health, involving direct exposure to hazards but also through stress to lowered levels of host resistance.

Conclusion

The Greek 'health miracle' may be fraying at the edges, but Greece's experience shows that improvements in GDP and poverty reduction alone may not be sufficient explanations of health gain. Greece made impressive health gains from 1950 to 1981 when the population's access to modern healthcare remained limited, patchy and highly inequitable. It thus confirms the primacy of non-medical influences on health. In Greece's case, the American influence through Marshall Aid in the 1950s confirms the role of public health improvements identified by Szreter (1988, 1992), which led to reduced exposure to risks. However, the health and welfare services in general, and the public health system in particular, remained rudimentary. Does the Greek experience then confirm the emphasis of McKeown (1976) and Omran (1971, 1983) on the autonomous effects of economic growth and rising living standards, as means of improving access to good nutrition and housing? Up to a point, but they also indicate that culturally variable patterns of consumption and forms of social support also play a significant role, delaying the onset of 'modern' patterns of degenerative circulatory disease and cancer. In Greece's case, too, modernisation with only a limited degree of 'Fordist' industrialisation may be one factor behind the health miracle: capitalist modernity was adapted along a particular social pathway.

In the case of Greece the 'power-resources' model associated with Esping-Andersen (1990) does help to explain the relative underdevelopment of social policy and its corporatist biases from the 1950s until 1981, at a time when economic growth potentially provided resources for institutional welfare. The fact that democracy and the labour movement only came of age at a time when the world economy had turned in a Washington-imposed neo-liberal direction shows how the global context yet again played a key role in Greek affairs. The role of the EU as an influence on Greek health trends is something which has had mixed effects. On the one hand, it soon curtailed PASOK's efforts to shift society's resources to the base of society, and generally imposed monetarist social policies and promoted increased flexibility of the economy. All this has put Greek people under stress and strain, with implications for their health and well-being. It has also reinforced tendencies towards unhealthy forms of consumption. On the other hand, however, Greece has been a beneficiary of resources redistributed to it as an agricultural country with high levels of poverty, which has particularly benefited rural areas. However, the sustainability of such policies in future is in doubt as enlargement of the EU beckons.

Overall, the analysis of the Greek case presented here qualifies rather than fundamentally undermines the 'paradigm shift' associated with Wilkinson (1996). It shows the importance of material influences to health: both distributional resources and living standards, and the effects of changing production relationships. It illustrates also that the nature and quality of socially patterned consumption must be considered. Not least it shows that people do not live by production and consumption alone, and confirms the significance of wider social networks and structures of 'belonging' to health. Finally, it suggests that the global context has *always* been important in shaping the choices that societies can make over their health, and not something that has just suddenly appeared on the historical horizon.

Note

[1] The research for this chapter was financed by a grant from the University of Warwick Research and Teaching Fund (RDTF), which enabled me to undertake a number of field trips to Greece. An earlier version of it was presented as a paper to the First Hellenic Social Policy Conference, Komotini, Greece, 10-13 May 2001.

References

Apostolides, A.D. (1992) 'The health care system in Greece since 1970: an assessment', *International Journal of Health Care Quality Assurance*, vol 5, no 5, pp 4-15.

Baldwin-Edwards, M. (2001) 'Crime and migrants: some myths and realities', unpublished paper, Greek Section International Police Association Conference, Samos.

Balourdos, D., Mouriki, A., Sakellaropoulosu, K., Theodoropoulos, K. and Tsakiris, K. (1999) *The prevailing car system in the Athens metropolitan area*, Athens: National Centre for Social Research (EKKE), Working Paper 6.

Benavides, F.G., Benach, J., Diez-Roux, A.V. and Roman, C. (2000) 'How do types of employment relate to health indicators? Findings from the second European survey on working conditions', *Journal of Epidemiology and Community Health*, vol 54, no 7, pp 494-501.

Berkman, L.F. and Syme, L.S. (1979) 'Social networks, host resistance and mortality: a nine-year follow-up study of Alemada County residents', *American Journal of Epidemiology*, vol 109, no 2, pp 186-204.

Carpenter, M. (2003) 'On the edge: the fate of progressive modernisation in Greek health policy', *International Political Science Review*, vol 24, no 2, pp 255-70.

Corsini, C.A. and Viazzo, P.P. (1993) *The decline of infant mortality in Europe – 1800-1950: four national case studies*, Florence: UNICEF.

Clogg, R. (1992) *A concise history of modern Greece*, Cambridge: Cambridge University Press.

Doyal, L. and Gough, I. (1992) *A theory of human need*, London: Macmillan.

Esping-Andersen, G. (1990) *The three worlds of welfare capitalism*, Cambridge: The Polity Press.

Eurostat (1997) 'Income distribution and poverty in EU12 – 1993', *Statistics in focus: Population and social conditions* series, report no 6, Luxembourg: Eurostat.

Eurostat (2001) *The social situation in the European Union 2001*, Luxembourg: Office for Official Publications of the European Communities.

Ferrie, J., Martikainene, P., Shipley, M., Marmot, M., Stansfeld, S. and Davey-Smith, G. (2001) 'Employment status and health after privatisation in white collar civil servants: prospective cohort study', *British Medical Journal*, vol 322, pp 1-7.

Fakiolas, R. (1999) 'Socioeconomic effects of immigration in Greece', *Journal of European Social Policy*, vol 9, no 3, pp 211-29.

Gallant, T.W. (1995) 'Collective action and atomistic actors: labor unions, strikes and crime in Greece in the postwar era', in D. Constas and T.G. Stavrou (eds) *Greece prepares for the twenty first century*, Washington DC: The Woodrow Wilson Centre Press, pp 149-90.

Gallant, T.W. (2001) *Modern Greece*, London: Arnold.

Gianulli, D. (1998) '"Repeated disappointment": the Rockefeller Foundation and the reform of the Greek public health system, 1929-1940', *Bulletin of the History of Medicine*, vol 72, no 1, pp 47-72.

Gough, I. (2000) 'Welfare regimes: on adapting the framework to developing countries', unpublished paper, University of Bath: Institute for International Policy Analysis.

Graham, H. (1987) 'Women's smoking and family health', *Social Science and Medicine*, vol 25, no 1, pp 47-56.

Greece Now (2002) 'Greek fat factor', www.greece.gr/LIFE/Lifestyle/greekfatfactor.htm, accessed 10/12/2002.

Guha, S. (1994) 'The importance of social intervention in England's mortality decline: the evidence reviewed', *Social History of Medicine*, vol 7, no 1, pp 89-114.

Harvey, B. (1995) *Networking in Europe: A guide to European voluntary organisations*, London: NCVO Publications.

Hollis-Triantafillou, J. (1995) 'Privileged men?', *British Medical Journal*, vol 310, p 1474.

Human Rights Watch (2001) *World report 2001: Greece: Human rights developments* (www.hrw.org, accessed 2 May 2003).

Iatridis, D.S. (1980) *Social planning and policy alternatives in Greece*, Athens: National Centre of Social Research.

Kafourou, A., Touloumi, G., Makroopoulos, V., Loutradi, A., Papanagiootou, A. and Hatzakis, A. (1997) 'Effects of lead on the somatic growth of children', *Archives of Environmental Health*, vol 52, no 5, pp 377-83.

Katrougalos, G.S. (1996) 'The south European welfare model: the Greek welfare state, in search of an identity', *Journal of European Social Policy*, vol 6, no 1, pp 39-60.

Kritsantonis, N.D. (1992) 'Greece: from state authoritarianism to modernization', in A. Ferner and R. Hyman (eds) *Industrial relations in the new Europe*, Oxford: Blackwell, pp 601-28.

Kromhout, D. and Bloemberg, B. (1997) 'Diet-related non-communicable diseases in Europe', in P.S. Shetty and K. McPherson (eds) *Diet, nutrition and chronic disease: Lessons from contrasting worlds*, Chichester: John Wiley and Sons, pp 1-9.

Kunst, A.E., Groenhof, F. and Mackenbach, J.P. (1998) 'Occupational class and cause specific mortality in middle aged men in eleven European countries: comparison of population based studies', *British Medical Journal*, vol 316, pp 1636-42.

Kyriazis, N. (1995) 'Feminism and the status of women in Greece', in D. Constas and T.G. Stavrou (eds) *Greece prepares for the twenty first century*, Washington DC: The Woodrow Wilson Centre Press, pp 267-301.

Lazaridis, G. (2001) 'Trafficking and prostitution: the growing exploitation of migrant women in Greece', *The European Journal of Women's Studies*, vol 8, no 1, pp 67-102.

Leibfried, S. (1993) 'Towards a European welfare state? On integrating poverty regimes in the European community', in C. Jones (ed) *New perspectives on the welfare state in Europe*, London and New York: Routledge, pp 133-56.

Leontidou, L. (1990) *The Mediterranean city in transition: Social change and urban development*, Cambridge: Cambridge University Press.

Levi, F., Lucchini, F., Negri, E. and La Vecchia, C. (1999) 'Worldwide patterns of cancer mortality 1990-1994', *European Journal of Cancer Prevention*, vol 8, no 5, pp 381-400.

Liakos, A. (1997) 'Welfare policy in Greece (1909-1940)', in B. Palier (ed) *Comparing social welfare systems in southern Europe*, vol 3, Paris: MIRE, pp 337-59.

Marinakou, M. (1998) 'Welfare states on the European periphery: the case of Greece', in R. Sykes and P. Alcock (eds) *Developments in European social policy: Convergence and diversity*, Bristol: The Policy Press, pp 231-47.

Marmot, M., Davey-Smith, G., Stansfeld, S., Patel, C., North, F. and Head, J. (1991) 'Health inequalities among British civil servants: the Whitehall II study', *Lancet*, vol 337, pp 1387-93.

Matsaganis, M. (1991) 'High infant mortality in the big cities of Greece', *Journal of Epidemiology and Community Health*, vol 45, no 2, pp 171-2.

Matsaganis, M. (1992) 'Maternal mobility and infant mortality in Greece: a regional analysis', *Social Science and Medicine*, vol 34, no 3, pp 317-23.

McKeown, T. (1976) *The modern rise of population*, London: Edward Arnold.

Menotti, A., Kromhout, D., Blackburn, H., Fidanza, F., Ratko, B. and Nissinen, A. (1999) 'Food intake patterns and 25-year mortality from coronary heart disease: cross cultural correlations in the Seven Countries study', *European Journal of Epidemiology*, vol 15, no 6, pp 507-15.

Mielck, A. and Giraldes, M. (1993) *Inequalites in health and health care: Review of selected publications from eighteen Western European countries*, Münster and New York: Waxman.

Morrison, A. and Stone, D.H. (2000) 'Injury mortality in the European Union 1984-1993', *European Journal of Public Health*, vol 10, pp 201-7.

Mutaner, C. and Lynch, J.W. (1999) 'Income inequality and social cohesion versus class relations: a critique of Wilkinson's neo-Durkheimian research program', *International Journal of Health Services*, vol 29, no 1, pp 59-81.

NID (Naval Intelligence Division of the Admiralty) (1944a) *Greece, volume I: Physical geography, history, administration and peoples*, London: NID.

NID (1944b) *Greece, volume II: Economic geography, ports and communications*, London: NID.

Newman, L.F. (ed) (1990) *Hunger in history: Food shortage, poverty and deprivation*, Oxford: Basil Blackwell.

Olshansky, S.J. and Ault, A.B. (1986) 'The fourth stage of the epidemiologic transition: the age of delayed degenerative diseases', *The Milbank Quarterly*, vol 64, no 3, pp 355-91.

Omran, A.R. (1971) 'The epidemiologic transition: a theory of the epidemiology of population change', *Milbank Memorial Quarterly*, vol 49, no 4, pp 509-38.

Omran, A.R. (1983) 'The epidemiologic transition theory: a preliminary update', *Journal of Tropical Pediatrics*, vol 29, pp 305-16.

Petridou, E., Kouri, N., Trichopoulos, D., Revinthi, K., Skalkidis, Y. and Tong, D. (1994) 'School injuries in Athens: socioeconomic and family risk factors', *Journal of Epidemiology and Community Health*, vol 48, no 5, pp 490-1.

Petridou, E. (1998) 'Person, time and place predictors of seat belt use in Athens – Greece', *Journal of Epidemiology and Community Health*, vol 52, no 8, pp 534-35.

Petridou, E., Mossialos, E., Papoutsakis, G., Skalkidis, Y., Tountas, Y., Velonaki, A. and Velonakis, E. (1999) 'Public health policies and priorities in Greece', in W. Holland and E. Mossialos (eds) *Public health policies in the European Union*, Aldershot: Ashgate, pp 127-47.

Pettifor, J. (1994) *The Greeks: The land and the people since the war*, Harmondsworth: Penguin.

Portes, A. and Landolt, P. (1996) 'The downside of social capital', *The American Prospect*, vol 7, no 6, pp 18-21.

Putnam, R.D. (1993) *Making democracy work: Civic traditions in modern Italy*, Princeton: Princeton University Press.

Ramis-Juan, O. and Sokou, K. (1989) 'Social health inequalities in south European countries: is it a different problem?', in J. Fox (ed) *Health inequalities in European countries*, Aldershot: Ashgate, pp 301-14.

Robins, D. (1991) 'Voluntary organisations and the social state in the European Community', *Voluntas*, vol 1, no 2, pp 98-128.

Rothenbacher, F. (2000) 'The European population: a historical data handbook for 21 European countries from 1850-1945', *Eurodata Newsletter*, vol 11, pp 1-10.

Sissouras, A. (1993) 'Reviews from Greece', in A. Mielck and M. Giraldes (eds) *Inequalities in health and health care: Review of selected publications from eighteen Western European countries*, Münster and New York: Waxman, pp 77-90.

Szreter, S. (1988) 'The importance of social intervention in Britain's mortality decline c. 1850-1914: a reinterpretation of the role of public health', *Social History of Medicine*, vol 1, no 1, pp 1-37.

Szreter, S. (1992) 'Mortality and public health, 1815-1914', *ReFresh*, no 14, pp 1-4.

Thomadakis, S.B. (1995) 'The Greek economy and European integration: prospects for development and threats of underdevelopment', in D. Constas and T.G. Stavrou (eds) *Greece prepares for the twenty first century*, Washington DC: The Woodrow Wilson Centre Press, pp 101-23.

Touloumi, G., Katsouyami, K., Zmirou, D., Scwartz, J., Spix, C., de Leon, A.P., Tobias, A., Quennel, P., Rabczenko, D., Bacharova, L., Basanti, L., Vonk, J.M. and Ponka, A. (1997) 'Short-term effects of ambient oxidant exposure on mortality: a combined analysis within the APHEA Project', *American Journal of Epidemiology*, vol 146, no 2, pp 177-85.

Tountas, Y., Karnaki, P. and Triantafyllou, D. (2002) 'Greece', in J. Mackenbach and M. Bakker (eds) *Reducing inequalities in health: A European perspective*, London and New York: Routledge, pp 223-28.

Tsaklogou, P. and Panopoulou, G. (1998) 'Who are the poor in Greece? Analysing poverty under alternative concepts of resources and equivalence scales', *Journal of European Social Policy*, vol 8, no 3, pp 213-36.

Tsoukalas, C. (1995) 'Free Riders in Wonderland; or, of Greeks in Greece', in D. Constas and T.G. Stavrou (eds) *Greece prepares for the twenty first century*, Washington DC: The Woodrow Wilson Centre Press, pp 191-219.

Venieris, D.N. (1997) *The history of health insurance in Greece: The nettle governments failed to grasp*, London: London School of Economics and Political Science.

Walters, D. (1998) 'Health and safety strategies in a changing Europe', *International Journal of Health Services*, vol 26, no 2, pp 305-31.

WHO (World Health Organisation) (1997) *Tobacco or health: A global status report*, Geneva: WHO.

WHO Europe (1998) *Highlights on health in Greece*, Copenhagen: WHO Regional Office for Europe.

WHO Europe (2002) *The European health report 2002*, Copenhagen: WHO Regional Office for Europe.

Wilkinson, R. (1996) *Unhealthy societies: The afflictions of inequality*, London: Routledge.

Wilkinson, R. (1997) 'Socioeconomic determinants of health: health inequalities: relative or absolute material standards', *British Medical Journal*, vol 314, p 591.

Wilkinson, R. (2000) *Mind the gap: Hierarchies, health and human evolution*, London: Weidenfeld and Nicolson.

Williams, F. (1995) 'Race/ethnicity, gender, and class in welfare states: a framework for comparative analysis', *Social Politics*, vol 2, no 1, pp 127-59.

Woodhouse, C.M. (1991) *Modern Greece: A short history*, London: Faber and Faber.

SEVEN

Welfare reform in the United States: the first five years of TANF

Pamela A. Holcomb and Karin Martinson[1]

Introduction

The welfare system in the United States was fundamentally altered in 1996 by the enactment of the Personal Responsibility and Work Opportunity Reconciliation Act (PRWORA). The centrepiece of the 1996 'welfare reform' law was a new block grant programme called Temporary Assistance for Needy Families (TANF), which replaced the cash assistance entitlement programme that had been in effect for over 60 years and explicitly gave welfare a time-limited and work-focused mission.[2] In addition to reducing dependency on welfare by increasing and supporting employment, other key objectives of the welfare reform law were to encourage two-parent families and stem the growth in non-marital births. PRWORA is by no means the first time that policy-makers have sought to reform the US welfare system.[3] Previous welfare reform efforts were shaped heavily by attempts to decrease poverty by increasing economic security for families while also reducing dependence on welfare. The most ambitious proposals to achieve this kind of comprehensive reform occurred in both the 1960s and 1970s but ultimately failed to be enacted. Meanwhile, widespread disenchantment with the welfare system, particularly with the cash assistance programme that primarily served poor single mothers with children, only deepened over time.

Whereas past large-scale structural reform failed, welfare reform efforts, focused on reducing welfare dependency by increasing recipients' work efforts, have met with greater success. In the late 1960s, Congress created a federally funded, state-administered employment and training programme for welfare mothers with children under the age of six. Legislative changes made in 1981 allowed states greater flexibility to design and operate their welfare-to-work programmes. National welfare reform legislation, enacted in 1988, built on the experiences of these state-administered welfare-to-work programmes and expanded funding for them, focusing heavily on providing education to welfare recipients as a pathway to self-sufficiency.

In response to an economic recession and record high welfare caseloads in the early 1990s, states increasingly sought federal waivers to support further welfare reform experimentation beyond what was permitted under existing federal legislation. The state waivers spanned a broad range of initiatives, including policies designed to mandate greater participation among adult cash assistance recipients in work activities. By the time PRWROA was enacted under the Clinton administration, almost all states had received federal approval for at least one welfare reform waiver demonstration.

PRWORA both built on past efforts to make welfare more work oriented and laid the groundwork for significant changes in welfare policy and operations at all levels of government. At the federal level, the law established important new principles and requirements for governing the cash assistance programme, primarily a strong emphasis of moving recipients into work and time limits on the length of assistance received. Within these parameters, the law created a largely devolved welfare system. States were given unprecedented authority to determine how best to meet the goals of PRWORA and set their own policies accordingly. Public agencies at both the state and local level faced the enormous and ongoing implementation challenge of developing system changes and organisational infrastructures needed to translate reform goals and policies into operational realities.

While the welfare reform law set the stage for genuine reform, it was not clear at the time of its passage how states would respond in a devolved welfare policy environment or even whether significant programmatic and institutional changes to the welfare system would really occur. Further, the likely impact of welfare reform on individuals and families was a matter of intense speculation and divergent opinion.

This chapter describes the most significant changes in welfare policy and programmes at the federal, state, and local level that occurred over the first five years since PRWORA's enactment. Such an assessment is particularly timely since the TANF programme is due for Congressional reauthorisation, the outcome of which could potentially change some of the key parameters of the law and have a significant impact on the future direction of welfare reform in the US.

Our review is divided into four parts. First, we highlight the key changes in federal welfare policy resulting from PRWORA, and then describe the range of policies states have established under the law. The implementation of welfare reform at the local level – based largely on in-depth interviews conducted in 17 cities – is discussed next, focusing on the most common strategies undertaken to move welfare clients to work and major institutional changes in the service delivery system. We conclude with a brief summary of research thus far on the effects of welfare reform on families and children and discuss issues for future consideration in light of the upcoming reauthorisation.

Key federal welfare policy reforms

Under PRWORA, federal welfare policy significantly changed along several dimensions. The major changes in federal policy – reduced federal control in favour of increased state flexibility, greater participation in required work activities, and the introduction of limits on the length of time individuals can receive cash assistance – are discussed in this section.[4]

A key aspect of welfare reform in the US is the changed nature of federal and state roles in welfare policy. Prior to welfare reform, the federal government was relatively prescriptive regarding rules for cash assistance programmes and states could only diverge from these rules if they obtained a 'waiver' from the federal requirements. State flexibility was deliberately and significantly expanded under PRWORA, with many of the rules concerning both eligibility and welfare-to-work programmes removed. States were given unprecedented authority to make their own policy choices, including setting the level of benefits, choosing what services they will provide and to whom, and what requirements they will impose on those receiving aid. In addition, some states chose to devolve programme responsibility a step further to the local or county level, providing new discretionary powers to local programme administrators.

PRWORA also eliminated the open-ended federal–state matching arrangement that required the federal government to match (at a specified level) each dollar spent by the state, and replaced it with a federal block grant allocation to each state. The new law uses pre-1996 welfare spending to fix the amount of federal spending available for TANF and to set a floor on states' spending.[5] States are still subject to contributing a certain level of their own resources, and must maintain 75 to 85 per cent of their prior spending levels.

The change in financing has important fiscal and programmatic implications for states. Prior to PRWORA, cash assistance was an entitlement programme – meaning states were required to provide benefits to all individuals who met the eligibility criteria. Under this arrangement, funding expanded or contracted depending on the number of people on welfare. However, under PRWORA, the programme is no longer an entitlement and each state is given a fixed block grant, regardless of whether the cash assistance caseload grows or declines.

Another significant change in the new welfare system resulting from PRWORA is its strong focus on work. The law requires states to place increasing percentages of cash assistance recipients in employment-related activities and requires all adult individuals that have received cash assistance for two years to participate in approved employment activities.[6] It also requires that a substantial number of hours per week are spent in these activities and limits the types of activities that can count towards the participation requirement to those that are focused on work – unsubsidised employment, job search, and work experience. In contrast, education and training count towards federal participation rates only in limited circumstances.[7] To ensure that families comply with the new work requirements, the federal law mandates states to reduce the level of cash benefits for families failing to follow programme rules, although states can determine the exact nature and severity of the sanction.

Finally, in a sharp departure from the previous cash assistance programme, PRWORA places limits on the amount of time individuals can receive assistance. Unlike sanctions, this cut-off is not tied to compliance with programme rules but rather sets a maximum deadline on benefit receipt among adult beneficiaries – no adult can receive federal welfare funds for more than five years over the course of his or her lifetime. At the same time, the law allows states broad flexibility in designing time-limit policies. States can opt to impose shorter time limits or they can choose to continue to pay benefits to someone who has hit the five-year federal time limit out of their own state revenues. They can also exempt certain categories of recipients from their time limits or can grant extensions to families who reach the limit.

Taken together, these changes in federal law fundamentally alter the federal–state partnership governing the operation of cash assistance programmes as well as the federal rules and requirements of the programme.

State policy responses

States moved quickly to put the new welfare reform law into place. Some were able to build on programmes they had established prior to the implementation of welfare reform – particularly those developed under federal waivers – while others developed new policies after the law was enacted. While there has been a diverse range of state policy responses to the new law, this section discusses a number of trends that have emerged regarding state policies and how states have implemented the new requirements – including stronger work requirements, policies to reward work, stricter sanctions, and time limits on cash assistance.

Reflecting the strong emphasis on work in the new law, states initially responded by designing welfare-to-work programmes and policies that emphasised rapid labour force attachment – focusing on job search and job readiness activities and placing less emphasis than in the past on skills development or education. States also increased programme coverage by permitting fewer exemptions from work requirements than had existed previously. Most states limited the exemption policy pertaining to the age of the youngest child to one year, while many states chose even shorter periods. Some retained exemptions for those with a disabling condition but others have narrowed these types of exemption policies as well. A few states provide no exemptions to participation in welfare-to-work programme activities (Thompson et al, 1998; Rowe, 2000).

The combination of stricter work requirements and narrower exemption policies has meant that more adult recipients are required to participate in work-related activities, with most states requiring individuals to spend a specified number of hours searching for a job after applying for welfare.

Another common policy change among the states was to modify programme rules to reward work. Thirty-one states quickly expanded earned income disregards, which allow welfare recipients to keep more of their cash benefits as they begin having earnings from work (Weil, 2002). The largest contribution to making work pay is the federal earned income tax credit, which was expanded in the 1990s prior to the enactment of PRWORA and can be obtained when individuals file their annual income taxes. A few states use TANF funds to support state-level earned income tax credits.

Financial sanctions have long been used to enforce work-related requirements for welfare recipients but, under TANF, states increased the severity of the penalties for non-compliance. Thirty-six states adopted full-family sanctions (that is, termination of the family's entire grant) and 18 of these impose full-family sanctions on the first instance of non-compliance. In the other states, a partial sanction is imposed first, but then it can escalate to a full-family sanction with repeated or continued sanctions (Rowe, 2000).

Although there is a five year maximum on federally funded cash assistance benefits, states have broad flexibility in designing time-limit policies and have also implemented a range of policies in this area. Currently, 40 states have time limits that can result in the termination of families' welfare benefits. Seventeen of these states have limits of fewer than 60 months. However, nearly half the national welfare caseload is in states that either have no time limit (two states) or a time limit that reduces or modifies benefits when the time limit is reached (eight states and the District of Columbia) (Bloom et al, 2002).

Finally, welfare reform has resulted in a dramatic shift in how states spend their resources – from systems that provide financial assistance to those that support efforts to engage in paid employment. For example, in 2000 only 41 per cent of TANF spending was on cash benefits – down from 76 per cent in 1996. Twenty-eight per cent of TANF funds were spent on childcare and work activities in 2000, up from just 9 per cent four years earlier (Zedlewski et al, 2002). The additional resources resulting from reduced cash assistance caseload (see below) and the flexibility provided under the block grant, gave states the ability to shift more resources into services.

Overall, TANF gave states unprecedented fiscal and policy authority to carry out the goals of welfare reform. States have taken advantage of this flexibility and used it to establish a mix of policies designed to promote and reinforce employment among welfare recipients. States have placed far less priority or resources on efforts to achieve welfare reform's family structure goals than they have to promote work (Weil and Finegold, 2002).[8]

Implementation of welfare reform at the local level

While the general policy framework set by federal legislation and state policy choices is important, at the heart of welfare reform is a complex, evolving and often unappreciated story of local efforts to translate welfare reform goals and policies into operational realities.[9] Even within the federal and state guidelines and rules that were established, many localities were generally given substantial discretion to design and operate their programmes.

Policy devolution combined with local level implementation differences has created a welfare reform experience, which varies tremendously within and across states. While acknowledging that this variation makes sweeping generalisations about welfare reform at the ground level difficult at best, case studies of welfare reform implementation reveal some common patterns and trends of significance. The remainder of this section draws heavily from locally based on-site visits to 17 cities in 13 states in 1999 and 2000, conducted as part of the Urban Institute's *Assessing the new federalism* (ANF) project.[10]

The development of work-first programmes

The primary implementation challenge confronting state and local welfare systems was to restructure welfare-to-work programmes and policies to better support the welfare reform legislation's goal of moving recipients off welfare and into employment. As described next, many states and localities initially responded by adopting a work-first programme model but, even in the short span of five years, many have subsequently sought to broaden welfare-to-work policy priorities and programmatic approaches within the wide parameters established by federal law.

The immediate period after PRWORA's enactment was marked by a programmatic shift in most states and localities from engaging a relatively small share of clients in education and training activities to aiming at moving many recipients quickly into employment. This 'work-first' approach is premised on the assumptions that any job is a good job and that simply joining the labour force is the first step towards getting a better job.

Work-first programmes typically require participation in job search, often combined with some job readiness skill building. Among the 17 case study sites, all moved towards adopting a work-first approach during the initial period of TANF implementation. As shown in Figure 7.1, in the period immediately after welfare reform was enacted (1996 to 1997), most implemented what we call a 'strictly' work-first model – that is, a programme with a strong emphasis on immediate employment and participation in job search for all clients and very little else by way of assessment, educational training case management, or services for the hard-to-employ.[11]

The widespread implementation of work-first programmes could not have occurred at a more propitious time. The economy was remarkably strong, with an unemployment rate below 4 per cent. Employers in need of low-wage workers did not have the luxury of picking and choosing from a broad cross-section of applicants and were willing to hire job candidates who lacked employment history, skills, or education – characteristics typically possessed by welfare recipients. Moreover, as the number of cash assistance recipients had grown considerably over time, the welfare caseload constituted a relatively untapped source of unskilled labour at a time when there was a surplus of low-wage, entry-level jobs. Thus, the attractiveness and effectiveness of the work-first approach was heightened by the prevailing economic conditions.

By the time most states and localities had fully implemented work-first programmes, some were finding that this approach was not effective for some clients – particularly those with multiple barriers who had not found jobs (known as 'hard-to-employ') and working individuals who had difficulty keeping their jobs or moving up to better ones. As a result, although employment remained the overarching goal of welfare reform, states and localities became increasingly concerned about a seemingly growing disconnection between the needs of some clients and their welfare-to-work programme capabilities. This led many to change and broaden the focus of their work-first programmes.

Hard-to-employ individuals still remaining on the caseload even after participation in a work-first programme generally have an array of diverse and complex barriers to employment, including physical disabilities, mental health or substance abuse issues, domestic violence issues, learning disabilities and limited English proficiency. To address the needs of this group, many states and localities modified their work-first approach to include a stronger programme focus on serving hard-to-employ welfare recipients and their families. As shown in Figure 7.1, several case study sites shifted from a strictly work-first or mixed services programme to an enhanced mixed services programme with a stronger focus on barrier reduction.

The case study sites that focused on barrier reduction usually added or redirected staff to specialise in addressing the needs of the hard-to-employ or contracted with organisations that had expertise in addressing specific barriers, such as substance abuse or domestic violence. Overall, the shift to programmes that better address the needs of the hard-to-employ has, to varying degrees, introduced some social work practices into an employment-oriented programme framework. For example, these programmes had incorporated a more in-

Figure 7.1: Shifts in service strategies

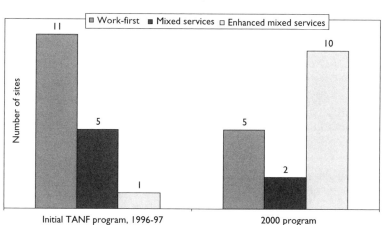

Source: Interviews with program staff conducted by the Urban Institute

depth assessment of individuals' barriers and provided more intensive, individualised case management to address client needs.

Another way that localities broadened their work-first approach was to include post-employment services, beyond traditional transitional supports such as childcare subsidies and medical assistance, for recipients who had found jobs. To address these issues, several case study sites made an explicit and systematic effort to design and implement services for welfare recipients who find jobs. These services often target those who are combining work and cash assistance, but can also include low-income families who have left TANF assistance. Post-employment services consist primarily of making regular contact with recipients to identify and resolve work or support service problems. A few sites used more innovative approaches such as offering financial incentives for finding and keeping a job.

The organisational dimension of welfare reform

Policy reform and organisational reform have been closely connected under PRWORA. Although PRWORA guided localities towards establishing a work-oriented welfare system, it did not specify how they should go about putting the necessary services and supports in place. Nevertheless, localities initiated institutional changes that resulted, to varying degrees, in a new organisational environment that often included greater involvement by other organisations *outside* the welfare agency as well as restructured staff responsibilities and services *within* the welfare agency.

The magnitude of institutional change occurring since PRWORA's enactment is larger than might have been expected, particularly because welfare agencies have been resistant to such change in past efforts to reform welfare (Meyers et al, 1998). PRWORA, however, combined three ingredients that had not been part of previous welfare reforms and help account for the greater level of institutional change experienced during this most recent round of reform: ample financial resources, more flexibility to spend those financial resources, and greater demands to deliver a broader range of work and supportive services to a larger pool of recipients.

The most striking institutional change is the development and expansion of organisational connections to fulfil new policy objectives and work programme requirements, although there is tremendous variation in what these systems look like at the local level. In particular, workforce development agencies[12] and non-profit community-based organisations dramatically expanded their role in the TANF service delivery system. TANF agencies also established new relationships with for-profit organisations, but on a far more limited basis. Box 7.1 highlights the range of service delivery systems put in place by describing systems in three sites.

Of all the study states, Wisconsin took this path the furthest by developing a new administrative structure that integrated welfare programmes (TANF, food stamps, and Medicaid) and workforce development programmes into a single state agency. Although most states did not go so far as to undertake a complete overhaul of the welfare system, some did use welfare reform as an opportunity to completely revamp their service delivery systems and develop new administrative structures for managing and operating TANF.

Box 7.1: Profiles of three TANF service delivery systems

Milwaukee (Wisconsin) Shortly before federal welfare reform, the state welfare and workforce development agencies in Wisconsin were reorganised: administrative responsibilities for cash assistance and related supports (childcare and food stamps) were brought together with employment, training, and workforce development programmes under a newly created department. The state required county welfare agencies to meet specified performance standards to operate the TANF programme (known as W-2). Milwaukee County, as well as several others, did not meet these standards. As a result, the state contracted with four non-profit, and one for-profit, organisations to operate W-2. Staff at these agencies are responsible for all aspects of W-2, including: eligibility determination, assessment, programme assignment and monitoring, referrals for services at other agencies, and job placement. Federal regulations do not allow non-government employees to handle food stamp and Medicaid eligibility, so Milwaukee County staff are responsible for these functions and are physically located in the offices of private W-2 agencies.

Minneapolis (Minnesota) The local welfare agency is responsible for TANF (known as the Minnesota Family Investment Program (MFIP)), eligibility determination and the provision of benefits. Two workforce development agencies (one for Hennepin County and one for the city of Minneapolis) are jointly responsible for MFIP employment services and contract with a variety of providers for these services. As of 2000, there were 32 employment services providers, the majority being non-profit organisations. These provide direct employment services such as job search assistance as well as case management services such as assessment, programme assignment, and monitoring. Policy, programme and fiscal decisions about TANF are made by an interagency workgroup consisting of top administrators from the local welfare and workforce development agencies.

San Diego (California) The local welfare agency administers the TANF programme in six areas in San Diego, with some variation across the region. Eligibility is administered by the welfare department throughout San Diego. However, in four of the six areas, case management (providing monitoring and oversight while individuals participate in employment services) and employment services are provided by three contractors – both for-profit and non-profit agencies. Some of these agencies, in turn, contract out to other organisations to provide job search assistance, while others provide this service in-house. In two areas, the county handles TANF eligibility and welfare-to-work case management, with the two functions carried out by separate types of staff. The county welfare department also contracts with a range of organisations for assessment, mental health, substance abuse, and domestic violence services.

Many welfare agencies contracted with a variety of different organisations for services they were not themselves equipped to provide. The most common reason for contracting with outside providers was to obtain direct employment services, such as job search or education and training classes. Some sites also contracted for case management services – such as monitoring and tracking client participation and determining compliance with programme requirements. Others contracted for specialised services for the hard-to-employ. For example, in Jersey City, New Jersey, an outside health services provider was hired to provide assessments and referrals at the TANF office for recipients with substance abuse problems. Some also developed or enhanced their capacity to establish and monitor contracts with service providers, while others delegated this responsibility to the workforce development agency.

The use of contracting and other inter-organisational partnerships served an important capacity-building function. Rather than significantly expanding in-house capability to meet the new demands of welfare reform, welfare agencies typically responded to the mandate to make welfare more employment focused by transferring some or all of their TANF work programme responsibilities to different agencies and forging new organisational linkages with outside service providers. Without the involvement of other organisations, most welfare agencies would not have been able to 'ramp up' as quickly for initial TANF implementation or develop a more comprehensive service mix over time.

Most localities have also modified their up-front intake and eligibility process to include a stronger emphasis on employment by letting individuals know how the terms and conditions of welfare receipt had changed. In some places, such as Denver, Colorado or Detroit, Michigan, applicants must complete a job search before their eligibility for cash assistance will be approved. However, the more frequent practice is to supplement the eligibility determination process with more specific information about work requirements, time limits, available services and supports, and sanctions for non-compliance. These aspects of welfare reform are typically conveyed during individual or group orientation sessions and by posting information on work requirements, time limits, and sanctions in office waiting rooms.

Some welfare agencies also developed new staffing patterns and responsibilities within local welfare offices. Although welfare agencies generally do not attempt to deliver all relevant supportive and employment services for TANF recipients in-house, some welfare agency staff have been given new or expanded responsibilities for assessing employability, identifying barriers to work, monitoring participation, and coordinating work-related services. Some places have merged these responsibilities with eligibility-related work but, at least in our 17 case study sites, most have separate staff to handle initial and ongoing eligibility matters.

While the importance of promoting work and reducing dependency among welfare recipients has become part of the institutional culture, the welfare agency still maintains its traditional responsibility for all eligibility-related matters – determining initial and ongoing eligibility, issuing benefits, and enforcing sanctions for non-compliance. The increased emphasis on work notwithstanding, eligibility continues to be the primary focus of welfare offices in many places.

Implementation challenges in the new welfare system

Although most localities were successful in developing new services for welfare recipients as well as a new system for providing these services, implementing these institutional and programmatic changes has been a major undertaking. First, the development of the new welfare system was time consuming and labour intensive, requiring significant financial and human resources. Creating the new set of services and administrative and organisational mechanisms to provide them, required substantial staff resources at several levels. In particular, defining the roles and responsibilities of organisations involved in the system took time, and sometimes several variations were tried before inter-organisational arrangements came together and worked smoothly. In addition, establishing working relationships with organisations that often had little or no prior experience with the welfare agency required educating partners on the mission and rules of TANF. Development of the new system was facilitated by significantly more resources than before being available to create different institutional arrangements for service delivery.

Second, sites experienced communication problems among the different organisations involved in providing services on such issues as tracking participation, determining exemptions, and imposing sanctions. Often, one organisation is responsible for tracking an individual's participation in programme activities, while another may be responsible for enacting sanctions or exempting individuals from programme activities. This requires linkages between different staff from different organisations so that information on the status of individual clients can be accessed. However, the lack of good management information systems generally hindered adequate communication. Sites that co-located services offered by different providers found it improved communication and coordination.

Finally, the increased complexity of the TANF service delivery system, greater involvement of workforce development agencies, and general proliferation of providers involved in the system led to the development of new arrangements for paying providers, monitoring performance, and ensuring quality and accountability. Facing this difficult and ongoing implementation issue, sites have tried a variety of management tools, contracting approaches, and performance measures. Many sites increased their use of performance-based contracting under TANF and found this a useful approach for building capacity and providing services. However, several experienced significant implementation challenges associated with developing and collecting the information needed to maintain these contracts.

Overall, the fact that the first five years of welfare reform under PRWORA was fraught with many implementation problems is not surprising given the magnitude of programmatic and institutional change undertaken in such a short period. At the same time, the system itself has become more complex as a result of these changes, making its administration and ongoing implementation all the more challenging.

Effects of welfare reform on families and children

The enactment of PRWORA has clearly resulted in significant changes in federal and state welfare policy – which in turn have substantially altered the welfare service delivery system at the local level. However, the key question is how these changes have impacted on those who the programmes were designed to assist – families and children receiving cash assistance. Since the enactment of PRWORA, there has been extensive research conducted on the effects of the welfare reform law that paints a mixed picture in terms of the law's accomplishments, although outcomes in some areas are still unclear. This section provides a brief review of this research thus far, including its effect on employment, earnings, welfare receipt, and poverty; the incidence and status of families who return to welfare and of those who remain on welfare for long periods; the effect of the law on children; the type of employment services that are most effective in moving individuals into work, and the status of families who reach the time limit on cash assistance.

Since the passage of PRWORA, a significant number of welfare recipients have found jobs. As shown in Figure 7.2, 64 per cent of those who left the welfare rolls between 1997 and 1999 and remained off welfare were working in 1999 (Weil, 2002). In addition, employment rates among those receiving cash assistance has also increased, in part due to the increased earnings disregards, with approximately one third of the TANF caseload working (Loprest, 2002a). At the same time, welfare caseloads fell dramatically – over 50 per cent between 1996 and 2002. In part, this is due to the work-first approach – along with incentives that encouraged work (for example, increased earnings disregards) and stricter sanctions for non-compliance (for example, termination of benefits) – which proved particularly effective in moving significant numbers of recipients into jobs and off assistance. Researchers continue to debate how much of the decline in the caseload should be attributed to welfare reform and how much to low unemployment or to other policies such as increases in the minimum wage (for example, see Council of Economic Advisors, 1999).

As the number of people on welfare dropped after PRWORA was enacted, federal and state funds far exceeded the amount necessary to maintain benefits at previous levels. This gave states and localities substantial resources to build and modify their welfare service delivery systems, and also to serve low-income families who were not receiving cash assistance on a monthly basis but who were still eligible for TANF-funded services.

Although many welfare recipients left welfare for work under the 1996 welfare law, most of these individuals are not faring well in the labour market.

Figure 7.2: Work status of former TANF recipients (1999ª)

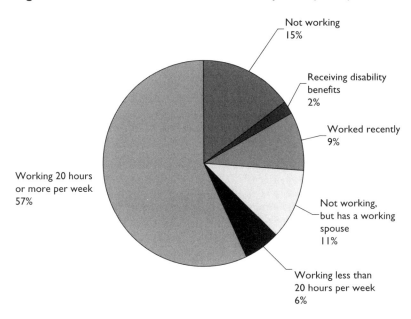

Not working
15%

Receiving disability
benefits
2%

Worked recently
9%

Working 20 hours
or more per week
57%

Not working,
but has a working
spouse
11%

Working less than
20 hours per week
6%

ªThose who left welfare between 1997 and 1999 and remained off welfare in 1999.
Source: Weil (2002), based on data in Zedlewski and Loprest (2001)

One study with a nationally representative sample found that those who left TANF for work in 1999 had a median wage of $7.15 per hour (Loprest, 2002a). Moreover, individuals who leave welfare for work are unlikely to receive employer provided healthcare coverage or paid sick or vacation leave. About 52 per cent of those who left welfare in 1999 had incomes below the poverty level (Loprest, 2001). Many of these individuals are poor, both because their hourly wages are low and because they are not working full time and year round.

Because welfare recipients tend to have less education and fewer skills than workers in general, they are likely to move into jobs that require limited skill and offer low wages. About half of former recipients' jobs are in the service sector, which primarily consists of low-paying occupations. Only 10 per cent are in the manufacturing sector, which tends to have higher paying jobs for workers without a college education (Loprest, 2002a).

In spite of their low wages, the combination of earnings and work supports, such as childcare, child support and refundable tax credits, has made low-income children and single mothers financially better off in the aggregate than they were before welfare reform. Disposable income for all families with children and for single-parent families increased between 1996 and 1998, with improvements in earnings accounting for most of the increase. At the same time, however, a higher proportion of persons in single-parent families are living in extreme poverty under welfare reform – primarily because they do not receive public benefits for which they are eligible, particularly TANF and food stamps (Zedlewski, 2002).

Research on the effects of PRWORA has also found that a substantial portion of cash assistance recipients are not able to keep jobs once they leave welfare and return to the rolls. In a national survey, of those who left welfare between 1997 and 1999, 22 per cent were back on welfare in 1999. Many of these returning recipients had originally left assistance for work. Former recipients with little education, limited work experience, and poor health are particularly at risk of needing welfare again (Loprest, 2002b). This finding, along with the low wages of those who find jobs, underscores the importance of the states' and localities' efforts to improve their employment retention and advancement services.

There are also concerns about the status of long-term recipients who have not found jobs, many of whom face significant barriers to work. As shown on Figure 7.3, one national study found that long-term recipients were more likely than other recipients to have less than a high school education (50 per cent compared with 38 per cent of other recipients), and were more likely to have last worked more than three years ago (34 per cent compared with 20 per cent). Moreover, 40 per cent of long-term recipients have two or more barriers to employment (Loprest, 2002a). Again, the growing efforts of states and localities to modify their work-first approach to accommodate the diverse needs of the hard-to-employ population reflect these findings. Policy and programmatic interventions for long-term recipients are particularly important, given looming time limits on benefits.

Another concern is those who leave welfare but have no visible means of support. As shown on Figure 7.2, one in seven adults in a family with someone employed, are not themselves employed, or are receiving disability or welfare payments (Weil, 2002). Little is known about the status and well-being of these families, although they appear to be very disadvantaged – one third have less than a high school diploma, almost half had not worked in three years, and 50 per cent reported being in poor physical or mental health (Loprest, 2002a).

Research has also addressed the impacts of welfare reform on children, although we are only just beginning to develop an understanding of this issue. While welfare is intended to benefit children, most welfare policies and attempts to reform welfare are focused on the behaviour of parents. Studies have found that programmes that increase parental employment and income by providing a supplement to the earnings of welfare recipients when they go to work improve the school achievement of their elementary school children. However, some programmes have negatively affected adolescents' school achievement and progress, with the data too limited to draw conclusions about infants and toddlers (Morris et al, 2002). At this point, the research suggests that children in welfare families and in families that have left welfare are at similar risk for poor developmental outcomes and that there have been no major shifts in the well-being for either group (Weil and Finegold, 2002).

There has also been a significant level of research conducted on what types

Figure 7.3: Potential barriers to work among current TANF recipients (1999) (%)

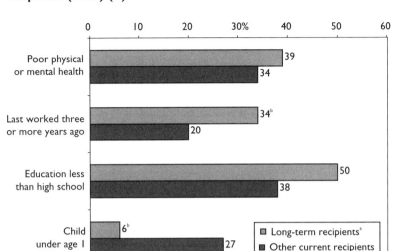

Notes:

[a] Those who have received TANF continuously for two or more years.

[b] The two groups are significantly different at the 90% confidence level.

Source: Loprest (2002a)

of employment services are most effective in moving welfare recipients to work. Evaluations of numerous welfare-to-work programmes have consistently shown that a 'mixed strategy' – one that provides job search, education, and training as part of a programme whose central focus is employment – have been the most effective in increasing employment and earnings and reducing welfare receipt and sustaining that success over time (Gueron and Hamilton, 2002). One site (Portland, Oregon) in a multi-site random assignment study produced impacts that are among the largest ever seen in welfare-to-work programmes – a 21 per cent increase in employment, a 25 per cent increase in earnings (over $5,000 over five years), and a 22 per cent reduction in the time spent on welfare compared to control group members (Hamilton et al, 2001).

The Portland programme substantially increased participation in education and training programmes – particularly post-secondary education and training – and placed a strong emphasis on job quality while maintaining an employment focus. The primary programme activities included education, training, and job search. Other key features included services that were tailored to meet individual needs and an emphasis on job quality. The Portland programme also resulted in the largest improvements in job quality – programme enrollees experienced an increase in hourly wages and in those who had jobs with employer-provided health insurance.

A final issue receiving considerable attention by researchers is determining the effects of time limits on cash assistance on families. It is generally too early to understand the results of this policy because so few families have reached their time limit. Nationally, about 231,000 families have done so – with about 93,000 families having their welfare case closed due to a time limit, and another 38,000 having had their benefits reduced. Most of those who have had their benefits terminated have been concentrated in a few states with time limits shorter than 60 months. As of December 2001, families had begun reaching the federal time limit in fewer than half the states (Bloom et al, 2002).

Given the evidence available thus far, the circumstances of families who left welfare due to time limits appear to be mixed – in some states, many of those who reach a time limit are working, while in others the outcomes are more diverse. The variation across states in terms of the effects of time limits is primarily due to differences in state welfare policies such as sanctions or earnings disregards which affect who reaches the time limit and state time-limit extension policies that determine who will actually be cut off. Most studies find that time-limit leavers have very low household incomes, although they may continue to receive food stamps, Medicaid, and other assistance. However, those who left welfare due to a time limit are not consistently experiencing more or fewer hardships than families who left welfare for other reasons (Bloom et al, 2002).

Overall, welfare reform in the United States has clearly moved more individuals into employment and reduced the cash assistance caseload. However, individuals are primarily working in low-paying jobs with limited benefits, and a significant portion return to welfare. There are also concerns about the prospects for long-term recipients who face significant barriers to work, as well as those who are neither working or on welfare. There is still much to be learned about the long-run effects of welfare reform, particularly on children. In addition, few individuals have been subject to one of the major provisions in the law – the time limit on cash assistance.

Conclusion

States and localities moved forward quickly to implement welfare reform and have made significant progress in transforming the welfare service delivery system to include a strong focus on work and services with more organisational partners. Even at this point, states and localities are continuing to develop new programmes as well as services that they modify to accommodate a greater range of client needs.

While significant progress has been made, welfare reform is a continuing process and future challenges lie ahead. The first five years show what can happen when states and localities are given substantial discretion to design and modify their programmes at a time when the economy is strong and a significant level of resources is available that can be spent on services rather than monthly cash assistance payments. It appears that the next five years may present a different landscape for the continuing implementation of welfare reform.

At the time of writing, the US is experiencing a slowdown in the economy and an increase in unemployment. In addition, the US Congress is about to embark on the reauthorisation of the programme, which could possibly tighten work requirements, reduce funding, or restrict flexibility. Moreover, more families will begin to reach the time limits, which will also bring new programmatic challenges. Within this environment, it is critical to focus attention and resources on several issues.

First, given the barriers facing those who return to welfare and long-term recipients as well as the low-paying jobs most recipients obtain, the state and local efforts to improve services for the hard-to-employ and for low-income workers described in this chapter are a step in the right direction. However, there is considerable variation in this area and further progress is necessary. Overall, career advancement services for TANF recipients are less developed than job retention services; both retention and advancement services lag behind efforts to reduce job barriers for hard-to-employ recipients; and assessment and service strategies for those with multiple barriers are not as developed as work-first employment services for the job-ready.

Second, less attention has been paid to developing a strong education and training component within the framework of an employment-oriented programme. This is an area that should receive further consideration, as studies have found that work-focused programmes that include education and training services are the most effective in increasing welfare recipients' employment and earnings, above all in the long run. Particularly in a weaker economy, education and training may be even more important for both finding and sustaining work, and should be considered an important element of both pre- and post-employment programmes.

Even under the favourable conditions of the past five years, implementation has proved extremely challenging and has taken tremendous effort on the part of agency staff at all levels, service providers, and community stakeholders. As states and localities seek to address a broader and more complex set of client needs through their TANF programmes, continued attention and effort will be required to build the administrative infrastructure to carry out this ambitious agenda, including strong, diverse, and coordinated inter-organisational linkages; the ability to track and share information across agency and programme staff; sufficient staff capacity and capability; and accountability through monitoring and performance-based measures.

Finally, given the number of organisations and the range of services involved in many TANF systems, more attention needs to be paid to ensuring that services are consistently high quality. The performance-based systems that are increasing under TANF provide some accountability, but they can also encourage 'creaming' or a focus on the job-ready. Programme administrators need to develop a range of performance measures and accountability mechanisms that will allow them to accurately assess and improve the quality of services, particularly in areas where the welfare system has less experience, such as services for hard-to-employ and low-income working families.

Notes

[1] The views expressed are those of the authors and do not necessarily reflect those of the Urban Institute, its board or its sponsors.

[2] This cash assistance programme, known as the Aid to Families with Dependent Children, was one of the three original public assistance programmes created by the Social Security Act (SSA) of 1935. SSA set the basic framework for the American 'welfare state' and contains both social insurance and public assistance programmes.

[3] See Holcomb (1995) and Cammisa (1998) for a more complete account of the history of welfare reform in the US.

[4] Although not covered in this chapter, PRWORA also made important changes to the treatment of eligibility to public benefits (including but not limited to TANF) for legal non-citizens, child support policies, and the childcare subsidy system.

[5] The TANF block grant is set at $16.5 billion per year and distributed among the states by a formula established in the law.

[6] In 2002, states were required to place 50 per cent of all families receiving cash assistance in work-related activities for 30 hours per week to meet the participation requirement. Participation rates are adjusted in each state to account for recent caseload declines – whereby the rate is reduced by the same percentage points that the state's TANF caseload declined since 1996.

[7] States may tailor their work requirements to permit or require recipients to engage in other types of activities than those prescribed by the federal law, including allowing greater participation in education and training than called for by PWRORA. However, there is less incentive for states to permit or require activities that cannot be counted towards the federal participation rate, given that failure to meet the prescribed rate can result in a reduction in a state's total TANF block grant. Thus, the extent to which states permit recipients to engage in activities that cannot count towards the participation rate standard depends in part on whether they can allow this range of activities and still meet federal requirements.

[8] Many states now make TANF available on a fairly equal basis to families with single and married parents, which reverses a longstanding rule that may have discouraged marriage. However, the programme still primarily serves single mothers with children – less than 10 per cent of the caseload consists of two-parent families. Twenty states have adopted family caps that deny additional benefits to adults who have children while they are on welfare (Weil and Finegold, 2002).

[9] The case studies included interviews with management and line staff from key agencies and service providers from both the TANF programme and the workforce development

system. State summaries and other reports based on these case studies are available at www.newfederalism.urban.org.

[10] This section of the chapter is drawn from other reports completed for the Assessing the New Federalism project. See Holcomb and Martinson (2002a); Holcomb and Martinson (2002b); and Martinson and Holcomb (2002).

[11] A few sites implemented a 'mixed service' approach where work-first services were blended with education and training or an 'enhanced mixed service' approach where work-focused activities were supplemented with services to reduce employment barriers.

[12] The workforce development system encompasses a broad range of employment, vocational education, and training services and programmes for employers, job seekers, and students. As authorised by the 1998 Workforce Investment Act, the primary focus of the workforce development system is to provide universal access to workforce services – such as information about the labour market, job openings, and education and training programmes – at one-stop career centres.

References

Acs, G. and Loprest, P. (2001) *Synthesis report of the findings from ASPE's 'leavers' grants*, Washington DC: US Department of Health and Human Services.

Bloom, D., Farrell, M. and Fink, B. (2002) *Welfare time limits: State policies, implementation and effects on families*, New York: Manpower Demonstration Research Corporation.

Cammisa, A.M. (1998) *From rhetoric to reform? Welfare policy in American politics*, Boulder, Colorado: Westview Press.

Council of Economic Advisors (1999) *The effects of welfare policy and the economic expansion on welfare caseloads: An update*, Washington DC: Office of the President.

Gueron, J. and Hamilton, G. (2002) *The role of education and training in welfare reform*, Welfare reform and beyond, policy brief 20, Washington DC: The Brookings Institution.

Hamilton, G., Freedman, S., Gennetian, L., Michalopoulos, C., Walter, J., Adams-Ciardullo, D., Gassman-Pines, A., McGroder, S., Zaslow, M., Brooks, J. and Ahluwalia, S. with Small, E. and Ricchetti, B. (2001) *How effective are different welfare-to-work approaches? Five year adult and child impacts for eleven programs*, Washington DC: US Department of Health and Human Services, Administration for Children and Families and Office of the Assistant Secretary for Planning and Evaluation; and US Department of Education, Office of the Under Secretary and Office of Vocational and Adult Education.

Holcomb, P. (1995) 'Family support and welfare reform', in G. Galster (ed) *Reality and research*, Washington, DC: Urban Institute Press, pp 65-84.

Holcomb, P. and Martinson, K. (2002a) 'Putting policy into practice: five years of welfare reform', in A. Weil and K. Finegold (eds) *Welfare reform: The next act*, Washington, DC: Urban Institute Press, pp 1-15.

Holcomb, P. and Martinson, K. (2002b) *Implementing welfare reform across the nation*, Series A, No A-53, Washington, DC: Urban Institute Press.

Loprest, P. (2002a) 'Making the transition from welfare to work: successes but continuing concerns', in A. Weil and K. Finegold (eds) *Welfare reform: The next act*, Washington, DC: Urban Institute Press, pp 17-31.

Loprest, P. (2002b) *Who returns to welfare? Assessing the new federalism*, policy brief B-49, Washington, DC: The Urban Institute.

Loprest, P. (2001) *How are families that leave welfare doing? A comparison of early and recent leavers. Assessing the new federalism*, policy brief B-36, Washington, DC: The Urban Institute.

Martinson, K. and Holcomb, P. (2002) *Welfare reform: Institutional change and challenges. Assessing the new federalism*, occasional paper no 60, Washington, DC: The Urban Institute.

Meyers, M.K., Glaser, B. and Mac Donald, K. (1998) 'On the front lines of welfare delivery: are workers implementing policy reforms?', *Journal of Policy Analysis and Management*, vol 17, no 1, pp 1-22.

Morris, P., Knox, V. and Gennetian, L.A. (2002) *Welfare policies matter for children and youth: Lessons for TANF reauthorisation*, New York: Manpower Demonstration Research Corporation.

Nightingale, D. S. (2002) 'Work opportunities for people leaving welfare', in A. Weil and K. Finegold (eds) *Welfare reform: The next act*, Washington DC: Urban Institute Press, pp 103-20.

Rowe, G. (2000) *Welfare rules databook: State TANF policies as of July 1999. Assessing the new federalism*, Washington DC: The Urban Institute.

Thompson, T., Holcomb, P., Loprest, P. and Brennan, K. (1998) *State welfare-to-work policies for people with disabilities*, Washington DC: Office of the Assistant Secretary for Planning and Evaluation, US Department of Health and Human Services.

Weil, A. (2002) *Ten things everyone should know about welfare reform: Assessing the new federalism*, policy brief A-52, Washington DC: The Urban Institute.

Weil, A. and Finegold, K. (eds) (2002) *Welfare reform: The next act*, Washington DC: Urban Institute Press.

Zedlewski, S.R. (2002) 'Family incomes: rising, falling, or holding steady?', in A. Weil and K. Finegold (eds) *Welfare reform: The next act*, Washington DC: Urban Institute Press, pp 53-77.

Zedlewski, S.R., Merriman, D., Staveteig, D. and Finegold, K. (2002) 'TANF funding and spending across the states?', in A. Weil and K. Finegold (eds) *Welfare reform: The next act*, Washington DC: Urban Institute Press, pp 225-46.

Zedlewski, S. and Loprest, P. (2001) 'Will TANF work for the most disadvantaged families?', in R. Blank and R. Haskins (eds) *The new world of welfare*, Washington DC: Brookings Institution Press, pp 311-44.

EIGHT

Social policy in the East Asian tiger economies: past, present and future[1]

Ian Holliday and Paul Wilding

Introduction

Since the late 1980s, there has been a growth of academic interest in social policy in the East Asian tiger economies – Hong Kong, Singapore, South Korea and Taiwan. Four main factors account for this. First, social policy analysts from western societies looked with envious fascination at the high rates of economic growth sustained by these four societies over many years down to the Asian financial crisis of the late 1990s. Second, once the economic growth records of the East Asian tigers were subjected to detailed scrutiny, it became clear that these societies combined significant degrees of economic freedom and a wealth of economic dynamism with quite a broad range of social policies. Third, it was also increasingly apparent from comparative statistical data that low levels of public expenditure nevertheless generated good social outcomes on a range of key indicators. Finally, a developing interest in comparative study raised concerns as to whether and how these systems might fit into emerging classifications of welfare regimes. In this analysis of the past, present and future of social policy in the East Asian tiger economies, we do four things. We introduce the four societies and present an overview of their social policies. We draw out similarities and differences in their social policy approaches. We evaluate their social provision; and we explore the sustainability of their approaches to social welfare.

Tiger societies and tiger social policy

One important question hanging over tiger social policy is whether it forms a distinct cluster, an East Asian welfare model or regime (Goodman et al, 1998). We will address that question here. However, before doing so we need to provide thumbnail sketches of the social policy systems of our four societies set in the context of their wider economic and political systems.

Hong Kong

The crucial moment in Hong Kong's dramatic economic development was a ban on trade with China, imposed at the start of the Korean War in 1950. The ban forced the colony to turn to export-oriented industrialisation, producing textiles, plastics and consumer electronics. By the end of the 1950s, domestically produced exports were of greater value to Hong Kong than re-exports. The rise of this vigorous domestic manufacturing sector, characterised by small- and medium-sized enterprises, meant that there was little need for direct state promotion of domestic production, as in South Korea or Taiwan, or for state efforts to attract multinational corporations, as in Singapore (Chiu et al, 1997). Between 1970 and 1990, Hong Kong's economy again changed dramatically as it gradually shifted from manufacturing to services because industry moved to southern China to take advantage of lower wages. In those years the contribution of manufacturing to GDP virtually halved.

Politically, Hong Kong down to July 1997 was a British colony ruled by a governor and a small group of key civil servants (Miners, 1998). The governor was assisted and advised by Executive and Legislative Councils, but until the early 1990s they were part of the formal rather than the effective constitution. It was not until the arrival in 1992 of the last governor, Chris Patten, that any serious attempt was made to introduce democracy to the territory (Dimbleby, 1998). Under the colonial system, many elite business figures had excellent connections into the government, and helped to ensure that the needs of business were fully understood by policy-makers. Since the July 1997 handover from Britain to China, the structures of the Hong Kong polity have changed only gradually (Lau, 2002). The most significant reform came in July 2002, with the introduction by Chief Executive Tung Chee-hwa of a ministerial system. This comprised the creation of a small number of political appointees at the apex of a government historically run by civil servants. The new ministers were personally appointed by Tung, who himself was chosen by a small election committee widely held to be fiercely loyal to Beijing.

The colonial government's first and most important welfare initiative came in housing. A massive programme of subsidised public housing launched in the mid-1950s in response to critical conditions in squatter settlements meant that by the 1990s around half the population lived in public housing (Castells et al, 1990). In the early 1960s the government began to acknowledge a responsibility to provide medical care. In the early 1990s this generated a tax-funded hospital system effectively free at the point of use (Grant and Yuen, 1998). In 1971, a system of public assistance was established, and primary education became compulsory. In 1978, compulsory education was extended to nine years. In the 1980s and early 1990s, state-funded higher education expanded dramatically (Wilding et al, 1997). Thus, despite a proclaimed philosophy of 'positive non-interventionism', the Hong Kong government has for many years intervened actively in social sectors. Today, policy is a mix of regulation, funding and actual provision. In education, the state provides most of the funding for primary and secondary schools, although provision tends to be organised by non-state bodies. Tertiary education is heavily subsidised by the state. In health, the state is active as both funder and provider of secondary care, and individual co-payment is minimal. In housing, around half of the population pays subsidised rent in public housing. In social security, a limited social safety net is funded purely by taxation. The state also regulates a mandatory provident fund, setting terms and conditions of membership, but contributions are shared between employers and employees. Castells (1992, p 45) writes of "a decisive role by the state in creating the conditions for economic growth". In particular, government-subsidised housing has made a significant contribution to holding down wages and thereby helping to maintain competitiveness in the global economy (Castells, 1992).

Singapore

When Singapore gained independence from Britain in 1959 and then from Malaysia in 1965, its future looked unpromising. Like Hong Kong, it had long made its living as an entrepôt. In 1960 over 90 per cent of its exports were re-exports. On leading the nation to independence, the People's Action Party (PAP) under Lee Kuan Yew thus launched a vigorous state-directed strategy of export-led industrialisation (Rodan, 1989). Lee and the PAP calculated that to survive Singapore had to prosper. Their strategy was to increase foreign direct investment. To do that it was necessary to show that Singapore was stable, that there was a compliant and educated workforce, and that there was an efficient infrastructure. Lee and the PAP set about providing each of these conditions through a formally democratic regime that was often highly authoritarian in practice. Stunning economic results gave the policy, and the regime, a measure of popular legitimacy. The striking element in Singapore's economic development was the dominant role played by foreign firms – by the 1970s, they were producing over 70 per cent of manufacturing output (Huff, 1999). Today, some 5,000 multinational corporations have their headquarters in Singapore. Forceful and activist government intervention in many spheres of economic and social life makes Singapore a very clear example of the developmental state (Low and Johnston, 2001).

There are four key aspects to the welfare role of the Singaporean state: hostility to welfarism in public discourse and public policy; a massive public housing programme; a multipurpose Central Provident Fund (CPF); and a drive to raise the educational level of the workforce. The ruling PAP has always been deeply hostile to all ideas of social rights and collective responsibility for meeting social needs. "Possibly the second most pejorative term (after liberalism) in the PAP lexicon is 'welfarism'" (Rodan, 1996, p 80). However, this ideology did not prevent the government from launching a substantial public home building programme to stimulate ownership. By controlling the price of land, the government was also able to subsidise flat prices through its building programme. More than 90 per cent of Singaporeans now own, or are currently purchasing, their own apartments. Politically, the state housing programme has helped to legitimate PAP rule and social policy strategy. The CPF, the key engine of social policy in Singapore, is essentially a compulsory savings scheme to which workers and employers contribute. Contributions are high: normally around 20 per cent of wages for both workers and employers. The initial aim of the scheme was to provide an income in retirement, but the scope has now widened to embrace saving for home purchase, medical care and education (Singapore Central Provident Fund Board, 1995). The scheme also provides vast investment funds for the state to deploy. As with home ownership, the CPF gives people a crucial and stabilising stake in the existing economic and political order (Low and Aw, 1997). The most obvious problem with the CPF, as with all work-based systems of social provision, is that it offers nothing for those not in employment or in forms of employment not covered by the scheme. To date, the number of such individuals has been low because employment has been high, but this could change in the future. Finally, from the very start the PAP saw the crucial importance of the quality of the workforce to its strategy of encouraging multinational corporations to locate in Singapore. Education to improve the quality of the labour force became a key plank in government policy.

South Korea

Korea was a Japanese colony from 1910 to 1945. In the mid-1950s, the southern part of a newly divided society emerged from the Korean War 'a war-torn wreck'. Some 40 years later, South Korea had become the world's 11th largest economy (Lee, 1999). Its GDP per capita is now estimated to be almost 20 times that of North Korea, and the contrast between a vibrant and booming capitalist economy and a bankrupt and collapsing communist economy could scarcely be starker. From the 1960s the South Korean economy grew rapidly under the planned direction of the state. As with our other societies, the key strategy was export-led industrialisation. The aim was "legitimation through economic performance" (Kwon, 1999a, p 20). Two sets of factors worked to South Korea's advantage. Falling transport costs and trade barriers and low labour costs compared to the US helped to boost economic performance (Wade, 1992). South Korea also joined Taiwan in sitting on what Wade describes as the fault line of post-Second World War global politics. This ensured US concern for the country's stability and prosperity, and brought US aid and privileged access to US markets.

Until the late 1980s, South Korea was essentially an authoritarian dictatorship with firm, and sometimes brutal, repression of dissent. In the late 1980s, however, a political thaw began to set in (Chu, 1998). A range of social movements emerged and put welfare issues squarely on the political agenda. A sense of civil and political rights also began to develop. At the 1987 election the presidential candidates enthusiastically competed in promising developments in national health insurance and pensions. South Korea is now a fully-fledged and energetic democracy.

Significant social policy measures introduced at a relatively early stage comprised Industrial Accident Insurance in 1964, a programme of public assistance in 1965, and National Health Insurance in 1977. In 1989 a National Pension Scheme was implemented and in 1995 a programme of employment insurance was introduced. The very tightly drawn public assistance programme was modified during the Asian financial crisis to make eligibility for benefits rather wider. A drive to extend educational opportunity resulted in more than 40 per cent of young people entering higher education in the 1990s. In Kwon's view social policy developments have been shaped by the need for legitimation:"democratic deficiency engenders a need for social policy" (Kwon, 1999a, pp 2-3). South Korean social policy has always had a strongly productivist orientation, prioritising economic growth over meeting social needs.

Taiwan

Taiwan was a Japanese colony from 1895 to 1945, geared to serving the economic needs of the imperial power. In 1949, the communist victory in mainland China prompted the Kuomintang (KMT) to flee to the island. Economic development was seen as the route to legitimation of its imposed authority. In this the KMT was triumphantly successful, and Taiwan has enjoyed almost uninterrupted economic growth since the mid-1970s. Taiwan's economic story in the years after 1949 is one of state-guided development through various major transformations: import substitution, export of labour-intensive manufactured products, and the development of heavy industry. In the 1980s came diversification and high-technology production (Lam and Clark, 1998). There were essentially five factors in Taiwan's economic success: a growing world economy and expanding world trade, carefully crafted government policy, high savings ratios, an easily disciplined labour force, and external support from the US. This support had a number of strands, including a massive aid programme, heavy investment, and a market that never took less than 30 per cent of Taiwanese exports between 1970 and 1990 (Ku, 1997).

Until the late 1980s, Taiwan was an authoritarian state with a clear economic development orientation. For Gold, the state's role in economic development was "absolutely crucial across the board" (Gold, 2000, p 92). Democracy came to Taiwan in the late 1980s, and has flourished. This, plus the rise of voluntary associations, created a new politics of welfare. Taiwan's political trajectory has many parallels with that of South Korea. Taiwan is now an open, and in some respects rather chaotic, democracy.

Taiwan introduced its first significant welfare measures in the 1950s with the establishment of social insurance schemes for military servicemen, government employees and some key workers. The overriding aim was to cement the loyalty of important groups to the state. From the 1960s educational development was emphasised, and nine years of free and compulsory education were established in 1968. There was also a drive to extend technical education. This made viable a switch to more skill-intensive production (Wade, 1995). In 1980, a limited national scheme of public assistance was introduced. In the early 1990s, a National Pension Programme became a key focus of debate and in 1995 coverage for healthcare became effectively universal. Ku describes the scheme introduced then as "the most significant welfare effort of the Taiwanese state in the post-war era" (Ku, 1998, p 119).

The East Asian welfare model

Serious analysis of social policy in the East Asian tigers dates from the mid-1980s. In 1986, Midgely wrote of "East Asian welfare regimes", implying a shared approach to welfare. In 1990, Jones described our four societies as "oikonomic welfare states" (p 25). By this she meant that each state's major concern was good household management. In their approach to welfare, these societies, she argued, showed a common core of beliefs, values and priorities. These included an overriding primacy for economic growth, faith in the family as a provider of welfare, belief in order and social stability as the very basis of welfare, low expectations of the state, a lack of interest in social justice, social rights and redistributive policies, and an underlying anxiety about the implications of western-style welfare state policies. Alongside this pattern of similarity she also noted very clear differences, for example in the organisation and funding of healthcare, in the role the state assumed in housing, and in attitudes towards and use of the mechanism of social insurance. Three years later Jones returned to the same four societies. This time she retitled them "Confucian welfare states" (Jones, 1993, p 198), making very clear what she saw as their central shaping characteristic. She also argued explicitly that "they [made] up an 'own brand' of welfare state" that did not fit into Esping-Andersen's typology (p 199).

The next significant contribution to debate about welfare capitalism in the region was Goodman and Peng's analysis of social policy in Japan, South Korea and Taiwan. They held that "there may be a case for discussing what might be called 'East Asian social welfare regimes'" that could be said to "deviate fundamentally from Western experience" (Goodman and Peng, 1996, pp 193-4). The characteristics said to distinguish them from western welfare states were the common language of Confucianism, the putting of the group before the individual, the dominance of economic considerations, the resistance to government provision of welfare, the emphasis on the family, and the hostility to western approaches.

The developing debate came of age in the edited collection *The East Asian welfare model* (Goodman et al, 1998), which analysed Japan and the four tigers. In the introduction, White and Goodman confronted directly the question of "whether ... an EAWM actually exists and, if so, what it is and how it developed" (White and Goodman, 1998, p 4). Their conclusion was that welfare systems in the region "constitute a distinct welfare experience with shared common elements" (p 13). They went on to argue, however, that "it is misleading to think in terms of one homogeneous, over-arching 'East Asian Welfare Model' common to these five societies" (p 14).

In earlier work we sought to contribute in two ways to the debate prompted by *The East Asian welfare model*: by summarising and assessing evidence for the existence of such a model (Wilding, 2000); and by revising and refining the terminology to describe more accurately what actually exists (Holliday, 2000). Wilding's conclusion was that the concept was helpful as long as it was not pushed too far. Holliday sought to get away from two restricting and potentially misleading elements in the concept: the geographical element, and the use of the term 'model'. He saw the concern for production and economic growth as a powerful unifying force transcending lower order policy differences. On this basis he defined the five societies as examples of productivist welfare capitalism (Holliday, 2000, p 710).

Similarities and differences

Clearly there are differences in the social policy approaches taken by our four societies. However, we see them as essentially differences of method, detail and emphasis within a broadly shared common orientation comprised of six core characteristics. Here we analyse those characteristics in turn.

Political purposes have always been primary

In all four tigers, a preoccupation with political concerns rather than with welfare needs has driven social policy development. From the 1950s onwards, the primary concerns were social stability, political legitimation and nation building. Government activity was geared to these linked ends. Kwon (1998, p 54) describes the early welfare initiatives of General Park's military government in South Korea as "a pre-emptive strike to compensate for its lack of political legitimacy". Much the same could be said of social policy reforms introduced by Chiang Kai-shek's KMT in Taiwan. In Hong Kong, Tang (2000, p 129) sees welfare development as "pivotal in ensuring social stability" after 'Cultural Revolution' riots in 1966/67. Tremewan (1994) argues that in Singapore the two key welfare policies, the CPF and public housing, were both primarily concerned with social stability and political legitimacy. In all four societies, governments have used social welfare to incorporate key groups and bind them to the regime. All provide generous benefits, such as pensions, sick pay and healthcare, for their own employees, while deploring the debilitating effects such provision would have on the general population. By the early 1990s, as much as 75 per cent of the Taiwanese central government's welfare expenditure went on civil servants and the military (Ku, 1997). In the East Asian tigers, writes Tang (2000, p 139) "social security is a weapon to target politically important interest groups".

Governments have defined economic growth and full employment as the main engines of welfare

Since economic take-off in the 1960s, all four societies have been driven by growth (Morley, 1999). Growth came to be seen as the only viable way to tackle the huge economic, social and political problems the societies faced, and rapidly became their core commitment. Growth and full employment were also seen as the best engines for promoting welfare. Patten, when Governor of Hong Kong in the mid-1990s, argued that "full employment should be the government's most important social objective" (Patten, 1995, p 6). Jacobs holds that "The importance of full employment in East Asian economies can hardly be overstated in an overview of their social welfare systems" because "East Asian welfare states are built around it" (Jacobs, 1998, p 66). The belief underlying this orientation is the trickledown theory of development, which holds that increasing national wealth will naturally filter through the social layers to the benefit of poorer classes, thereby obviating the need for complex systems of redistribution or social service provision. Tang holds that "the Asian tigers ... are ardent believers in the trickle down theory of development" (Tang, 2000, p 139). Given their belief in the cascading benefits of growth, many aspects of western-style social policy became unnecessary.

Productivist welfare has been the goal

The tigers' essential welfare orientation is captured in the description 'productivist'. Deyo characterised their approach as "developmentally supportive social policy", social policy "driven primarily by the requirements and outcomes of economic development policy" (Deyo, 1992, pp 289-90). Goodman and Peng concluded that "welfare policy has been dominated by economic rather than social considerations" (Goodman and Peng, 1996, p 198). Tang argued that social welfare institutions were "merely adjuncts to the capitalist economy" (Tang, 2000, p 156). Holliday (2000, p 707) identified a world of 'productivist welfare capitalism' in East Asia. The essence of this argument is that social policy is utilised chiefly to assist the core function of the developmental state, which is promotion of economic development. Furthermore, the tigers appear to have been highly successful in making social policy contribute to growth. Deyo's judgement is that "economic development has been energised by social policies" (Deyo, 1992, pp 304-5).

Welfarism has been shunned

The other side of the tigers' productivist orientation has been a denigration of welfarism. All have sought to build what Lee Kuan Yew calls "a fair, not welfare, society" (Lee, 2000, p 95). For all of the tigers, individual responsibility was key to economic advance, and had to be protected from the debilitating effects of excessive state welfare. All are instinctively hostile to universal publicly provided social security and social care. Social security is generally regarded as a burden on the economy, as undermining individual and familial responsibility, and as fostering dependency. There is little or at best only a very weak sense of welfare as a right of citizenship or of a general public responsibility for the needy. All four societies have exhibited clear hostility to the European welfare state. Ramesh (1992, p 1103) points to "ideological opposition to the welfare state" in Singapore, Quah (1998, pp 105-6) identifies "rejection of the welfare state" as one of nine policies making up the Singaporean model of development, Tang (2000, p 131) describes the Taiwanese state as "profoundly anti welfarist" and Hong Kong as "anti welfarist in orientation". His conclusion is that the tigers are "pervaded by mistrust of social welfare" (Tang, 2000, p 135).

The family has been accorded a key welfare function

In all four societies there is great emphasis on the centrality of the family to social welfare and social stability. One key strand in East Asian opposition to European-style welfare states is the belief that state provision weakens family bonds, and erodes social stability. In South Korea and Taiwan, legislation has been passed requiring individuals to support family members, including children, spouses, parents and siblings. In Singapore, older people have been able since 1996 to take their children to court if they fail to support them. Although there is no such law in Hong Kong, survey evidence reveals strong support for it. Extensive family provision has been used to justify and legitimate limited state provision because it is unnecessary when families do their duty. Governments have therefore set out to promote family care. In relation to Singapore, Ramesh writes of "A sense of urgency in the government's determination to ensure that individuals and families remained responsible for their needs in old age" (Ramesh with Asher, 2000, p 163).

States have been strong but limited

Our four societies all have strong but consciously bounded states. Tiger states are strong in the sense that they are active and efficient in the social welfare field. However, their role tends to be restricted to regulating, enabling and organising rather than funding and providing. Our states organise national health insurance schemes and national pension schemes, or they make provident fund membership compulsory. They play a large role in education, but engage to only a limited extent in actual provision. They set deliberate limits to their role, stopping short of funding and actually providing in domains where European states have tended to do both. Standing behind this is a commitment to small government, compromised by simple pragmatism. When it matters, pragmatism nearly always wins out over ideology. Thus, despite their public philosophies, both Hong Kong and Singapore got into public housing provision in a very big way because it was defined as vital on political, economic and social grounds. Pragmatism rather than principle led to the development of health insurance schemes in South Korea and Taiwan. These strong states are bounded states partly because of ideology and partly because they have no vision of the future that is different from the past. Without a social vision, pragmatism rules. Tang speaks of welfare development in Taiwan since the Second World War as "piecemeal, reactive and lacking in grand vision" (Tang, 2000, p 78). He describes the colonial state in Hong Kong as having "no clear social vision, and no comprehensive future plan" (p 126). Goodman and Peng's judgement on development in East Asia is that "the states' approach to welfare has been haphazard, and extremely pragmatic" (Goodman and Peng, 1996, p 211). Such a philosophy tends to make for limited government.

Assessing similarities and differences

In the East Asian tigers, a broad commonality of approach and orientation at the macro-level of social policy sits alongside real differences at the micro-level. Within a generally shared philosophy of welfare, actual policies differ in sometimes significant ways. Funding is very different. In Hong Kong, welfare has always been basically tax-funded. In Singapore, compulsory private saving via employer and employee contributions to the CPF has been key. In South Korea and Taiwan, by contrast, the core funding mechanism is social insurance. Such differences generate distinct institutional frameworks. Different approaches lead, predictably, to different outcomes, for example the nature of access to healthcare. Among our four societies there are also significant overall and specific differences in levels of state expenditure on welfare, although the figures are not easy to handle. Jacobs (1998) calculates that Hong Kong and Singapore spend some 5 per cent of GDP on welfare and South Korea and Taiwan about twice as much. Finally, specific policy variations are visible among our four societies. Housing policy exhibits the most striking variations. Both Hong Kong and Singapore have had major public programmes, although with rather different slants. The South Korea and Taiwanese governments have done no more than dabble in housing.

Evaluating tiger social policy

How successful have our four societies been in attaining the classic central goals of social policy, such as improving access to services according to need, extending opportunity, improving quality of life on key social indicators, reducing poverty and generating society-wide minimum standards of provision? The record is impressive but variable.

In education all four societies have long achieved virtually universal free primary and secondary education. They all have high rates of literacy and score impressively in league tables comparing national performance in, for example, mathematics. In recent years all have greatly expanded their systems of higher education, moving from elite to mass provision. In Hong Kong the percentage of young people proceeding to higher education in the territory increased from 3 per cent in the 1980s to 18 per cent in the late 1990s – and the target is 60 per cent enrolment by 2010. Singapore, South Korea and Taiwan have comparable or even higher rates of entry to higher education. In 30 years all four societies have created high-quality modern educational systems virtually from nothing.

In healthcare, all four tigers register impressive outcomes in terms of mortality rates and life expectancy. Partly, this reflects lifestyle factors, partly it is because all four have had young populations. But all four have also built healthcare systems that effectively offer healthcare according to need. Each has a large private sector, covering most of primary care and most of traditional medicine, which remains significant in all four societies. Access is most straightforward in Hong Kong because of unconditional use of the tax-funded system. In Singapore, the balance in an individual's CPF account plays an important role in regulating access. In South Korea and Taiwan, access depends on insurance records, and there are predictable problems in ensuring equality of access to rural populations. High co-payments also act as a barrier to access. All four societies have some form of safety net for those who fall through the gaps. In all the systems quality is variable but, at best, high.

Although there are still significant housing problems in the four societies, the problem of absolute national shortages has been largely eliminated. The problems that remain are essentially problems of distribution. Access for particular needs groups, such as city dwellers, new immigrants, older people, and the poorest members of society, is a problem. The need to improve the quality of older estates is also an issue. The stress on extending home ownership in Hong Kong and Singapore has inevitably been to some degree at the expense of those unable to afford to buy their own homes. The very residual role assumed by the state in South Korea and Taiwan has meant a shortage of provision for those on low incomes, particularly in the rapidly expanding cities.

Social security raises perhaps the sharpest questions about the achievements and potential of 'productivist' welfare. None of the four societies has a comprehensive social security system covering all basic contingencies. South Korea and Taiwan have the most substantial systems, but there are still significant gaps. Neither has a system of children's allowances. South Korea's pension scheme will not reach maturity for some years and there are doubts about its long-term financial viability (Kwon, 2001). Taiwan has yet to put in place a national pension scheme, and existing pension cover is only very partial. Singapore's CPF only covers those in secure employment, and around half the contributors find on retirement that the balance in their CPF account cannot secure them an adequate income (Asher, 1998; Ramesh with Asher, 2000). Hong Kong only created its mandatory provident fund, a shadow of the Singaporean system, in 2000. Until that matures, comprehensive social security assistance covers basic contingencies, supplemented by an allowance system for older people that yields only tiny benefits. Neither Hong Kong nor Singapore makes specific provision for unemployed people. Crucial to the effectiveness of social security in eliminating poverty is the level and accessibility of benefits.

In our four societies the level of benefits is very variable but the level of bottom line social assistance is generally below what would be seen as necessary to provide a very basic standard of living. In addition, the stigma for claimant and family is a strong deterrent to making claims. There is considerable evidence for the existence of significant poverty in all four societies (Tang, 2000).

The East Asian tigers have considerable welfare sectors. Social security is their least developed social policy area. The strong ethic of individual and family responsibility, dynamic economies, beliefs about the debilitating effects of comprehensive social security provision and youthful populations have all worked to restrict its development. In contrast to education, healthcare and housing, social security makes no obvious contribution to economic growth. This is the major reason why it remains underdeveloped in these productivist social policy systems. In other sectors, the East Asian tigers tend to make significant social policy provisions.

Assessing the sustainability of the East Asian welfare model

How strongly grounded is productivist welfare capitalism? How resilient is it likely to be in the face of future shocks and challenges? The nature of the pressures and changes likely to be registered varies across our four societies, and similar pressures and changes will obviously produce distinct responses in different societies. However, we can make a general assessment by noting that the tiger approach of productivist welfare capitalism has for many years rested on five main pillars: significant economic growth, a young population, strong families, limited social protest and pressure, and successful government criticism of the western welfare state. These five pillars all look less secure than they did in the mid-1990s.

The most important short-term development is the 1997 Asian financial crisis and its aftermath. The crisis had very different impacts on our four societies. Nevertheless, more than five years after its onset, the tiger economies are still seeking to recover their earlier dynamism. The apparent end of rapid and sustained economic growth, and of the economic confidence engendered by it, is a major challenge to the tiger approach to social policy, which has always been largely based on faith in economic growth as the main engine of welfare and as the main solvent of social and political problems. Crucially, the check to economic growth weakened the belief that growth is the best road to welfare. It also ended the easy financing of social programmes through the fiscal dividend. It created unemployment and pressures for an extension of social security benefits. The most obvious and immediate effect was increased unemployment, which was devastating for systems "built around full employment" (Jacobs, 1998, p 12). As Jacobs puts it, 'tough' welfare states can work in a booming economy but "Once a Korean like crisis appears it seems that there is no alternative to the old fashioned unemployment insurance" (p 19).

In the longer term, ageing populations provide a sharp challenge to current patterns of social provision in the East Asian tigers. Because of declining fertility and longer life expectancy, the future will see larger numbers of older people dependent on a smaller working population. Older people will also be dependent for longer, either on social security systems of one kind or another, or on personal savings or family support. Current social security provision for old age in the tigers is very limited and faces increasing strain. Pressures to create new schemes and/or improve existing schemes are likely to become significant.

In providing income and care for the needy, the family has been the linchpin of tiger welfare systems. The strong ethic of family responsibility has made the low level of public service provision much less problematic than it would otherwise have been. For roughly half of older people in South Korea and Taiwan, children are the main source of income (Kwon, 1999b). In the late 1980s and the 1990s, 65 per cent of older people in South Korea and 74 per cent in Taiwan lived with their children (Kwon, 1999b). What is very plain, however, is that children have been providing a declining proportion of income for older parents in both societies (Kwon, 1999b). Co-residence is also declining. The supportive role of the extended family has weakened, not because of moral decay but because of nuclearisation, increased geographical mobility, and the greater integration of women into the formal labour market. Smaller families mean that there are fewer family members to care. The result is a growing income and care gap that politicians have been reluctant to acknowledge because of the expenditure implications. Nevertheless, as Jacobs concludes, "it is very likely that states will have to fill the gap" (Jacobs, 2000, p 11). Pressure to do so will certainly be strong.

Emerging ideas of rights, albeit so far only rather tentative, are likely to provide a further challenge. In South Korea and Taiwan, the development of democracy since the late 1980s has been paralleled by a growth of social movements pressing for extensions of the rights of particular needs groups (Ku, 1998). A similar trend is visible in Hong Kong (Chow, 1998). Notions of rights of access to services, of services as a right of citizenship, of equality of opportunity, are potentially powerful forces for the development of social welfare. In 1997, Goodman et al (p 377) described the East Asian welfare model as being "under threat from democratic political pressures". Democratisation operates in various ways to bring pressure to bear on the state. Most importantly, perhaps, it inaugurates an era of competitive politics. In both South Korea and Taiwan, oppositional parties successfully forced social policy discussion onto and up the political agenda, and on this basis won power. Rising expectations also help to drive social policy change. Increasing affluence, better education and broadening awareness of provision in other states are key factors. Three obvious areas exposed to these pressures of rising aspirations and emulation in the tigers are social security provision, policies to promote equal opportunities for women, and policies to safeguard and improve the environment.

Once all these factors come into play, it may be difficult for East Asian states to hold in place the fifth and final pillar of their social policy systems – denigration of western-style welfare capitalism. As economic, social and political pressures mount, the kind of social provision made in many European states may be difficult to resist even in polities with a tradition of fierce hostility to it.

Conclusion

The future of social policy in the East Asian tigers is of course hard to predict. The impact of the Asian financial crisis and the varied responses to it brought out just how different our four societies actually are despite all their similarities. Hong Kong sought to cut expenditure. Singapore temporarily reduced employer contributions to the CPF, in effect cutting wages at a stroke. South Korea expanded its network of welfare provision through enhanced unemployment insurance and public assistance. It seems probable that diversity of response will be the key future pattern. For various reasons, Hong Kong and Singapore are likely to retain limited systems of social provision, whereas South Korea and Taiwan are likely to move in the direction of expansion. The factors that explain this probable parting of the ways are to be found in the institutions of the East Asian social policy systems themselves, and of the wider political systems to which they belong.

The more interesting cases are South Korea and Taiwan. Ramesh argues that South Korea has "an embryonic welfare state" (p 88) and that "Taiwan is in the early stages of transforming into a welfare state" (p 89). Both, he argues, are "on their way to transforming into conservative welfare states" (Ramesh, 2003: p 98). One reason for this is that in both societies a strong insurance-based welfare infrastructure has been put in place that is likely to generate its own growth dynamic. A second reason is that both are now vibrant and contested democracies that generate social and political pressures for welfare extension. A third reason relates to globalisation. Ramesh (2003) argues that the internationalisation of the South Korean economy has probably contributed to rather than hindered the expansion of social security because once South Korea joined the Organisation for Economic Co-operation and Development (OECD) it was exposed as a welfare laggard. Equally, the Taiwanese government saw democratisation and social policy development as crucial to improving Taiwan's international standing and securing the much-desired legitimating membership of international organisations. There are counter-arguments. Tang (2000) finds no sign that the still powerful KMT in Taiwan is changing its anti-welfare stance. But the forces pushing for social policy growth appear to have the upper hand in both South Korea and Taiwan.

In Hong Kong and Singapore, by contrast, factors driving in the direction of welfare extension are likely to be less forceful. Jacobs argues that "Hong Kong and Singapore's existing institutional frameworks are mature in the sense that further growth would require major institutional shifts which they have failed to initiate so far" (Jacobs, 1998, p 85). In Hong Kong, the limits of a tax-funded system in a society committed to low rates of taxation are very plain. In Singapore, the CPF is probably already overstretched in terms of what can be provided simply by employer and employee contributions. Tang concurs, describing the Hong Kong Government as "relentless in bringing back the residual state" (Tang, 2000, p 166), and finding little sign in Singapore of any significant changes to the CPF. Each society is also less democratic, in practice, than either South Korea or Taiwan. Each has less reason to seek international legitimation. Hong Kong is not a state, and cannot seek membership of many international organisations. Singapore is a much less contested state than either South Korea or Taiwan.

In all four East Asian tigers, many pressures point in the direction of a larger role for the state and increased expenditure. Equally, in all four societies there are also counter-pressures, the most obvious being lower rates of economic growth, a smaller fiscal dividend, and strong business pressure against enhanced social provision. Looking beyond pressures to institutions and their likely responses, it is possible that the coming years will witness increasingly divergent social welfare responses among the four East Asian tigers (Ramesh, 2003). For now, however, there remain strong elements of productivism in all four social policy systems.

Note

¹ This chapter draws on Ian Holliday and Paul Wilding (eds) (2003) *Welfare capitalism in East Asia: Social policy in the tiger economies*, Basingstoke: Palgrave. Much of the material reported here is taken from the chapters in that book written by Yeun-wen Ku, James Lee, and Ka-ho Mok. We thank our colleagues for insights into tiger social policy, and Lo Yat-wai for research assistance. The usual disclaimer applies.

References

Asher, M. (1998) 'The future of retirement protection in Southeast Asia', *International Social Security Review*, vol 51, no 1, pp 3-30.

Castells, M. (1992) 'Four Asian tigers with a dragon head', in R.P. Appelbaum and J. Henderson (eds) *States and development in the Asian Pacific Rim*, Newbury Park: Sage Publications, pp 33-70.

Castells, M., Goh, L. and Kwok, R.Y.W. (1990) *The Shek Kip Mei syndrome: Economic development and public housing in Hong Kong and Singapore*, London: Pion.

Chiu, S.W.K., Ho, K.C. and Lui, T.L. (1997) *City-states in the global economy: Industrial restructuring in Hong Kong and Singapore*, Boulder CO: Westview Press.

Chow, N. (1998) 'The making of social policy in Hong Kong: social welfare developments in the 1980s and 1990s', in R. Goodman, G. White and H.J. Kwon (eds) *The East Asian welfare model: Welfare orientalism and the state*, London: Routledge, pp 159-74.

Chu, Y.W. (1998) 'Labor and democratization in South Korea and Taiwan', *Journal of Contemporary Asia*, vol 28, no 2, pp 185-202.

Deyo, F.C. (1992) 'The political economy of social policy formation: East Asia's newly industrialized countries', in R.P. Appelbaum and J. Henderson (eds) *States and development in the Asian Pacific Rim*, Newbury Park, CA: Sage Publications, pp 289-306.

Dimbleby, J. (1998) *The last governor: Chris Patten and the handover of Hong Kong*, London: Warner Books.

Gold, T. (2000) 'The waning of the Kuomintang state in Taiwan', in K.E. Brodsgaard and S. Young (eds) *State capacity in East Asia: Japan, Taiwan, China, and Vietnam*, Oxford: Oxford University Press, pp 84-113.

Goodman, R. and Peng, I. (1996) 'The East Asian welfare states: peripatetic learning, adaptive change and nation building', in G. Esping-Andersen (ed) *Welfare states in transition: National adaptations in global economies*, London: Sage Publications, pp 192-224.

Goodman, R., White, G. and Kwon, H.J. (1997) 'East Asian social policy: a model to emulate?', in M. May, E. Brunsdon and G. Craig (eds) *Social Policy Review 9*, Canterbury: Social Policy Association.

Goodman, R., White, G. and Kwon, H.J. (eds) (1998) *The East Asian welfare model: Welfare orientalism and the state*, London: Routledge.

Grant, C. and Yuen, P. (1998) *The Hong Kong health care system*, Kensington: School of Health Services Management, University of New South Wales.

Holliday, I. (2000) 'Productivist welfare capitalism: social policy in East Asia', *Political Studies*, vol 48, no 4, pp 706-23.

Huff, W.G. (1999) 'Turning the corner in Singapore's developmental state', *Asian Survey*, vol 39, no 2, pp 214-42.

Jacobs, D. (1998) *Social welfare systems in East Asia: A comparative analysis including private welfare*, London: Centre for Analysis of Social Exclusion, London School of Economics and Political Science.

Jacobs, D. (2000) 'Low public expenditure on social welfare: do East Asian countries have a secret?', *International Journal of Social Welfare*, vol 9, no 1, pp 2-16.

Jones, C. (1990) 'Hong Kong, Singapore, South Korea and Taiwan: oikonomic welfare states', *Government and Opposition*, vol 25, no 4, pp 446-62.

Jones, C. (1993) 'The Pacific challenge', in C. Jones (ed) *New perspectives on the welfare state in Europe*, London: Routledge, pp 198-200.

Ku, Y.W. (1997) *Welfare capitalism in Taiwan: State, economy and social policy*, Basingstoke: Macmillan.

Ku, Y.W. (1998) 'Can we afford it? The development of national health insurance in Taiwan', in R. Goodman, G. White and H.J. Kwon (eds) *The East Asian welfare model: Welfare orientalism and the state*, London: Routledge, pp 119-38.

Kwon, H.J. (1998) 'Democracy and the politics of social welfare: a comparative analysis of welfare systems in East Asia', in R. Goodman, G. White and H.J. Kwon (eds) *The East Asian welfare model: Welfare orientalism and the state*, London: Routledge, pp 27-74.

Kwon, H.J. (1999a) *The welfare state in Korea*, Basingstoke: Macmillan.

Kwon, H.J. (1999b) *Income transfers to the elderly in East Asia: Testing Asian values*, London: Centre for Analysis of Social Exclusion, London School of Economics and Political Science.

Kwon, S. (2001) 'Economic crisis and social policy reform in Korea', *International Journal of Social Welfare*, vol 10, no 2, pp 97-106.

Lam, D. and Clark, C. (1998) 'The cultural roots of guerilla capitalism', in S. Chan, C. Clark and D. Lam (eds) *Beyond the developmental state: East Asia's political economies reconsidered*, Basingstoke: Macmillan, pp 120-30.

Lau, S.K. (ed) (2002) *The First Tung Chee-hwa administration: The first five years of the Hong Kong special administration region*, Hong Kong: Chinese University Press.

Lee, H.K. (1999) 'Globalization and the emerging welfare state – the experience of South Korea', *International Journal of Social Welfare*, vol 8, no 1, pp 32-7.

Lee, K.Y. (2000) *From Third World to first – the Singapore story: 1965-2000*, New York: Harper Collins.

Low, L. and Aw, T.C. (1997) *Housing a healthy, educated and wealthy nation through the CPF*, Singapore: Times Academic Press.

Low, L. and Johnston, D.M. (eds) (2001) *Singapore Inc: Public policy options in the third millennium*, Singapore: Asia Pacific Press.

Midgely, J. (1986) 'Industrialization and welfare: the case of the four little tigers', *Social Policy and Administration*, vol 20, no 3, pp 225-37.

Miners, N. (1998) *The government and politics of Hong Kong*, Hong Kong: Oxford University Press.

Morley, J.W. (ed) (1999) *Driven by growth: Political change in the Asia-Pacific region*, New York: M.E. Sharpe.

Patten, C. (1995) 'Hong Kong: our work together', address by the governor, the Right Honourable Chris Patten, at the opening of the 1995/96 session of the Legislative Council, Hong Kong: Government printer.

Quah, J.S.T. (1998) 'Singapore's model of development: is it transferable?', in H.S. Rowen (ed) *Behind East Asian growth: The political and social foundations of prosperity*, London: Routledge, pp 105-25.

Ramesh, M. (1992) 'Social security in Singapore: redrawing the public–private boundary', *Asian Survey*, vol 32, no 12, pp 1093-108.

Ramesh, M. with Asher, M.G. (2000) *Welfare capitalism in Southeast Asia: Social security, health and education policies*, London: Palgrave.

Ramesh, M. (2003) 'Globalisation and social security expansion in East Asia', in L. Weiss (ed) *States in the global economy: Bringing domestic institutions back in*, Cambridge: Cambridge University Press, pp 83-100.

Rodan, G. (1989) *The political economy of Singapore's industrialization: National state and international capital*, Basingstoke: Macmillan.

Rodan, G. (1996) 'State–society relations and political opposition in Singapore', in G. Rodan (ed) *Political oppositions in industrialising Asia*, London: Routledge, pp 95-127.

Singapore Central Provident Fund Board (1995) *The CPF story: 40 years serving Singapore*, Singapore: CPF Board.

Tang, K.L. (2000) *Social welfare development in East Asia*, Basingstoke: Palgrave.

Tremewan, C. (1994) *The political economy of social control in Singapore*, Basingstoke: Macmillan.

Wade, R. (1992) 'East Asia's economic success: conflicting perspectives, partial insights, shaky evidence', *World Politics*, vol 44, no 2, pp 270-320.

Wade, R. (1995) 'Resolving the state–market dilemma in East Asia', in H.J. Chang and R. Rowthorn (eds) *The role of the state in economic change*, Oxford: Clarendon, pp 114-36.

White, G. and Goodman, R. (1998) 'Welfare orientalism and the search for an East Asian welfare model', in R. Goodman, G. White and H.J. Kwon. (eds) *The East Asian welfare model*, London: Routledge, pp 3-24.

Wilding, P. (2000) 'Exploring the East Asian welfare model', *Public Administration and Policy*, vol 9, no 2, pp 71-82.

Wilding, P., Huque, A.S. and Tao, J.L.P.W. (eds) (1997) *Social policy in Hong Kong*, Cheltenham: Edward Elgar.

Part Three:
In focus: Pensions and old age

With falling stock markets, lower interest rates, frequent media coverage of the pensions 'crisis' and the value of pensions declining, the 'pensions issue' is very much on the agenda. The chapters in this section consider pensions and ageing from a range of different perspectives including labour market and comparative dimensions, New Labour's pensions settlement, questions of agency and social structure, and pension sharing from a gendered perspective.

Giuliano Bonoli and Benoît Gay-des-Combes begin the section with a review of the pension reforms adopted in 8 Western European countries which have been instituted by governments to take account of labour market changes and participation patterns. They argue that the measures adopted depend on the inherited institutional structure of the pension system in these particular countries and that the crucial difference lies in the initial choice between a social insurance and a multi-pillar system.

The following chapter, by Jane Falkingham and Katherine Rake considers New Labour's pension settlement and the challenges arising from the demographic, economic and policy legacy of the 20th century. They consider a range of criteria they believe necessary to underpin a sustainable pension system and use these to evaluate the extent to which the reforms will deliver adequate incomes for pensioners of today and those of tomorrow. They conclude by saying that now might be the time for Labour to start 'thinking the unthinkable' by going 'back to basics' in relation to the basic state pension, an option that is gaining currency in policy and academic circles.

Kirk Mann brings together structures, risk and reflexivity in the context of retirement and pensions policy. His chapter contrasts the structural features of capitalist societies, including pension funds and their investment strategies, risk management, and the importance of these funds in the money markets with sociological accounts such as risk and reflexivity. He explores the tensions between these sociological approaches that are 'new' to social policy with 'older' traditions and ideas. In doing this he suggests that we can bring fresh insights which may help inform social policy.

Finally, Debora Price adds a gender dimension to these concerns, with a consideration of pension sharing on divorce. Two perspectives are used for a consideration of the financial position of divorced women. The first, based upon a view of the UK as a paradigm male-breadwinner nation state considers pension provision for women, particularly those who live alone. The second, considers the policy solution adopted by the government to the 'problem' of divorced women's retirement income. Price concludes that UK pension legislation has been deeply gendered in its effects on those of working age in the accumulation of pensions. Furthermore in its treatment of pension rights on divorce the law is not neutral or independent, but itself helps institutionalise gender inequality and attempts to reduce the complexity of the social world to a 'pensions sharing' law is unlikely to improve the prospects for divorced women in old age.

NINE

Adapting pension systems to labour market changes in western Europe

Giuliano Bonoli and Benoît Gay-des-Combes

Introduction

During the post-war years, all western European countries have seen the construction and the consolidation of comprehensive pension systems. The pre-war rudimentary schemes that offered modest coverage to some sections of the population only were expanded, combined with minimum guarantees, and with supplementary pensions. The result was that by the late 1970s, virtually every country in western Europe could provide reasonably good pension coverage to the whole resident population.

These pension systems were clearly designed to serve the typical male career profile of that period. In other words, the sort of coverage they offer is optimal for someone who has worked without interruptions, full time and from an early age. Today's labour markets, however, contain a much wider variety of career profiles. To a large extent, this has been the result of the gradual but massive entry of women into labour markets since the 1960s. Very often, women's career profiles are characterised by relatively long interruptions and by part-time employment. In addition, the end of full employment means that today's workers are more exposed to the risk of both cyclical and long-term unemployment than was the case for previous generations. Finally, the knowledge-based economies that are emerging across OECD countries require constant skill updating from workers who do not want to be left behind: an activity that may result in career interruptions.

In most countries the career profiles induced by the events described above will generate pension entitlements below the optimum level. Over the last few years, however, pension systems have been adapting to these new patterns of labour market participation. Even though coverage for the so-called 'atypical' workers remains suboptimal, many countries have over the last few years, adopted improvements in the provision for non-standard workers.

In this chapter, we review the reforms adopted in eight western European countries in order to deal with this issue. Our argument is that the measures adopted depend on the institutional structure of the pension system that countries have inherited from the post-war years, and before. In particular, what seems to be crucial is the initial choice between a social insurance and a multi-pillar system. The chapter starts with an overview of labour market changes that have taken place since the end of the period the French call the *trente glorieuses*, the 30 years between 1945 and 1975 characterised by fast economic growth, full (male) employment, rising wages, family stability and so forth. It then moves on to look at how different pension systems deal with the new forms of employment that have become so common over the last decades. Finally, it discusses the key measures that our eight countries have adopted to deal with these issues.

Labour market changes and atypical[1] workers

Since the end of the period of the *trentes glorieuses*, some profound labour market changes have happened in all the countries considered in this chapter. Indeed, the predominance of career profiles characterised by full-time employment and without interruption that were the norm during those years has decreased and new atypical career profiles (for instance part-time and temporary work and career interruptions due to unemployment, parenthood, or retraining) have gained in importance in the labour market. In addition, the same period has also seen changes in family structures and in their stability, such as the development of single-parent households, and the increase in the divorce rate. As a result, the clear predominance of the typical male career profile of the *trente glorieuses*, which provided the basis for post-war pension systems, is a thing of the past (see Price, this volume).

The most visible development is certainly the gradual but massive entry of women into the labour market (see Table 9.1). The importance and predominance of the male breadwinner family model, in which women used to stay at home without professional activity and to do all domestic work, has begun to decrease since this period. This substantial increase in the participation rate of women in the labour force has happened in all the countries taken into account regardless of the initial level (1970 in our case).

Even though women have entered the labour market in large numbers, they continue to play the key role in performing unpaid caring and household work, often at the expense of full or continuous labour market participation. The increase in female employment thus means that a large proportion of current workers are likely to have working careers characterised by interruptions and part-time employment: two features that are associated with lower pension entitlements.

A second change concerns the end of full employment that characterised the post-war years. The persistence of a high level of unemployment, in addition to the substantial proportion of long-term unemployment compared to total unemployment, involves career interruptions and job insecurity for a significant section of the workforce. This high level of unemployment has been relatively widespread among the countries studied in this chapter for about 25 years.

Table 9.1: Female employment ratios (female employment/female population, aged 15-64)

	France	Germany	Italy	Sweden	UK	Switzerland	Denmark	Netherlands
1970	47.9[a]	47.8	30.3	58.4	50.2	52.3	61.2[a]	28.6[a]
1980	49.2	50.6	34.5	72.4	55.8	54.0	65.0[b]	34.7[b]
1990	50.3	52.2	36.2	81.0[d]	62.8[d]	66.4[c]	70.6	46.7
2001	55.2	58.6	41.1	73.5[d]	64.7[d]	70.4	71.4	65.3

[a] Data of the year 1973.

[b] Data of the year 1983.

[c] Data of the year 1991.

[d] For women between 16 and 64.

Source: OECD, various issues

In addition, long-term unemployment has also remained at a high level in these countries. Indeed, the proportion of unemployed people for whom the entitlement period exceeds 12 months has remained important, even though there are substantial differences among the countries covered.

Tables 9.2 and 9.3 show that unemployment is a key feature of post-*trente glorieuses* Europe. Despite the employment policies adopted in most countries and the occasional limited reductions in the rate, unemployment continues to remain high throughout the continent. In addition, the proportion of long-term unemployment in total unemployment has tended to increase during the last ten years in most of these countries. The increased incidence of long-term unemployment will almost certainly result in higher proportions of pensioners with insufficient acquired rights, as the time they spend out of the labour market does not generally generate pension entitlements to the same extent as paid employment.

The third set of labour market changes that can have an impact on the constitution of pension entitlements concerns the increased diversification of forms of employment. The last two decades have seen an increase in the size of part-time and temporary employment, as well as, especially in the 1990s, a

Table 9.2: Standardised unemployment rates as a percentage of the total labour force

	France	Germany	Italy	Sweden	UK	Switzerland	Denmark	Netherlands
1983	8.1	7.7	7.7	3.9	11.1	n/a	n/a	9.7
1990	8.6	4.8	8.9	1.7	6.9	n/a	7.2	5.9
1995	11.4	10.5	11.5	8.8	8.5	3.5	6.8	6.6
2000	9.3	8.1	10.4	5.9	5.4	2.6	4.4	2.8

Source: OECD, various issues

Table 9.3: Incidence of long-term unemployment as a percentage of total unemployment

	1990		2000	
	6 months and over	12 months and over	6 months and over	12 months and over
France	55.5	38.0	62.0	42.6
Germany	64.7	46.8	67.6	51.5
UK	50.3	34.4	43.2	28.0
Switzerland	27.5	17.0	45.7	29.0
Italy	85.2	69.8	77.6	61.3
Sweden	22.2	12.1	41.5	26.4
Netherlands	63.6	49.3	n/a	n/a
Denmark	53.2	29.9	38.1	20.0

Source: OECD (2002)

significant rise of self-employment as a proportion of total employment. As seen above, family changes and the increased number of women in the labour market may partly explain the increased proportion of these new forms of employment. Increased demand for flexibility by firms can also account for these developments. We have less clear explanations for the "partial renaissance of self-employment" (OECD, 2000, Chapter 5). The causes that are most often mentioned in the literature include attempts by firms to sidestep what they regard as an overly rigid labour market and high levels of social contributions, changes in the organisation of industrial production, and governments' efforts in a number of countries to favour the expansion of self-employment.

One can easily note that the proportion of part-time work in total employment has increased in most of the countries covered. Even though part-time employment has remained the prerogative of women, the proportion of male part-time work in total employment has also increased in these countries (Table 9.4). In addition to part-time work, the incidence of temporary work has also increased, sometimes substantially, in almost all the countries under scrutiny (Table 9.5). Both forms of employment tend to generate lower pension entitlement than 'standard employment': part-time work because it means lower wages; temporary work because it is often accompanied by career interruptions between one job contract and the next. In addition, in general, both forms of employment tend to be less secure and more associated with marginalisation than permanent full-time standard employment.

These two forms of atypical employment can also be combined and hence increase job insecurity. In most of the countries covered, the proportion of temporary work (in 1997) in total employment is more important in part-time work than in full-time work (OECD, 1997, Table 1.9).

Self-employment is also considered an atypical form of employment. In most countries, it does not benefit from the same level of pension coverage as

Table 9.4: Importance and variation of part-time work since 1990

	% of part-time work in total employment		% of part-time work in total employment (men)		% of part-time work in total employment (women)		Women in part-time work	
	1990	2000	1990	2000	1990	2000	1990	2000
France	12.2	13.8	4.4	5.3	21.7	24.3	79.8	80.4
Germany	13.4	n/a	2.3	4.8	29.8	33.9	89.7	n/a
Italy	8.8	12.2	3.9	5.7	18.2	23.4	70.8	72.6
Sweden	14.5	17.8	5.3	7.3	24.5	21.4	81.1	79.2
UK	20.1	n/a	5.3	8.4	39.5	40.8	85.1	n/a
Switzerland	22.1	24.8	6.8	8.4	42.6	44.7	82.4	80.1
Denmark	19.2	14.5	10.2	8.9	29.6	23.5	71.5	66.5
Netherlands	28.2	33.0	13.4	13.4	52.5	57.2	70.4	76.3

Source: OECD (2002)

does standard waged employment. With the exception of France and Denmark, the size of self-employment has increased over the last two or so decades in the countries covered in this study (Table 9.6).

Beside these different labour market trends, another change concerns the overall economy and one can present it as the "development towards a post-industrial economy characterised by the employment of the vast majority of the population in the services sector" (Sarfati and Bonoli, 2002, p 2). Indeed, we have witnessed for three decades a 'tertiarisation' of employment. For instance, in our eight countries, the average proportion of service employment of total employment was about 63.4 per cent in 1990 and 68.0 per cent in 1998.

Table 9.5: Importance and variation of temporary work since 1983

	1983	1994	Average (1983/94)
Denmark	12.5	12.0	11.4
France	3.3	11.0	7.8
Germany[a]	10.0	10.3	10.6
Italy	6.6	7.3	5.8
Netherlands	5.8	10.9	8.6
Sweden[b]	12.0	13.5	11.2
UK	5.5	6.5	6.0

[a] Data for 1984 and 1994. Data refer to western Germany prior to 1992.

[b] Data for 1987 and 1994.

Source: OECD (1996)

Table 9.6: Non-agricultural self-employment as a share of non-agricultural civilian employment (1973-98)[2]

	1973	1983	1994	1998
Denmark	9.3	8.5	6.8	6.9
France	11.4	10.5	8.8	8.2
Germany	9.1	7.4	8.5	9.4
Italy	23.1	20.7	22.3	22.7
Netherlands	n/a	8.6	9.4	9.7
Sweden	4.8	4.8	9.0	9.0
UK	7.3	8.6	12.0	11.4

Source: OECD (2000)

Obviously the notion of 'service employment' is a complex one, which encompasses very different types of occupations and career profiles. In addition, this services sector is very heterogeneous and all its components have not evolved in the same way. But one key feature of service employment is that it bifurcates between high-skill, high-wage professions (for example, producer's services) and low-skill, low-wage jobs (distributive and personal services). The constitution of pension entitlements can be problematic at the most disadvantaged end of the distribution: low wages that tend to lag behind those of the rest of the population may result in minimal pension coverage, even when employment is continuous and full time. Of course, the pension coverage that low-skill service workers will receive depends on a large number of factors, including the rules of the pension system and labour market regulations. Nevertheless, what seems clear is that it was much easier to guarantee a decent retirement to an industrial worker whose salary increased year after year than it is to a low-skill service worker stuck in a dead-end job.

Table 9.7 shows the main trends in service employment. Generally, over the last two decades, we can see an increase in the share of producer services and social services in total employment in most of the considered countries. On the other hand, the level of distributive and personal services as a proportion of total employment has been rather constant during this period or even decreased; nevertheless, this level of distributive and personal services has remained relatively high in these countries and these two sectors have a significant number of low-skill, low-wage workers.[3]

These trends in service employment do not only mean that a pension system needs to take into account the existence of a large proportion of low-skill, low-wage workers, but also, as the OECD (2000, p 113) puts it, that: "the analysis of educational qualifications and occupational mix indicates that the shift of employment toward services increases the premium on formal schooling". As a result, workers in a predominantly service-based economy are under pressure to constantly update their skills, by following retraining, further education and

Table 9.7: Evolution of the share of service employment[a]. Levels in 1998 (%) and percentage-point changes between 1984, 1989, 1994 and 1998

	Producer services				Distributive services				Personal services				Social services			
	Changes			Level	Changes			Level	Changes			Level	Changes			Level
	1984-89	1989-94	1994-98	1998	1984-89	1989-94	1994-98	1998	1984-89	1989-94	1994-98	1998	1984-89	1989-94	1994-98	1998
DK	2.2	1.3	0.1	11.4	-0.4	-0.4	0.6	21.1	-0.4	0.4	0.0	5.8	-1.4	0.3	0.8	31.2
F	1.1	2.4	0.1	11.9	-0.4	0.0	-0.2	19.9	0.4	1.0	0.5	8.3	2.2	2.6	0.8	29.2
D	1.4			10.9	-0.9			19.9	-0.1			7.1	1.4			24.8
I			1.7	9.3			0.0	21.6			0.3	8.0			0.3	22.0
NL	1.6	1.8	1.3	14.3	0.1	0.6	-0.7	22.0	0.7	0.5	-0.4	6.2	0.0	0.0	-1.0	27.6
S			0.8	12.2			0.4	19.4			0.1	5.9			-1.4	33.4
CH		0.3	1.8	15.3		0.6	-0.1	19.6		-0.5	-1.4	10.0		2.1	2.8	24.3
UK	2.2	2.4	1.2	14.7	0.6	-0.5	-0.2	21.8	-0.1	-0.1	0.5	9.2	0.3	3.2	0.2	25.7

[a] For a more detailed typology of the services sector, see OECD (2000).

Source: OECD (2000)

language courses. In most cases this means more time spent out of the labour market and, all other things being equal, lower pension entitlements.

These different labour market and economy changes have profoundly modified the former employment landscape characterised by the prevalence of the male breadwinner family model, full employment and economic growth. New atypical career profiles have emerged over the last three decades and welfare states are under pressure to take into account their new needs and aspirations. Generally speaking, the career profiles induced by the events described above will generate pension entitlements below the standard level, regardless of the institutional structure of a pension system. Indeed, the labour market changes presented before often cause career interruptions and hence contribution gaps. The size of the gap, however, may vary substantially depending on the type of pension coverage available.

Pension systems and the new career profiles

The labour market changes outlined above represent a major challenge for current pension systems. Unlike the demographic challenge, however, what is at stake here is not their financial sustainability but their very effectiveness. Failure to adapt could mean the return of widespread old age poverty, a social problem that most western European countries had left behind after the post-war years. Different pension systems, however, are affected differently by these developments. Depending on their institutional structure, they may be more or less able to integrate given non-standard career profiles.

Social insurance versus multi-pillar countries

A convenient way to classify pension systems is with reference to the number and type of schemes that perform the bulk of the intergenerational transfer. In fact, if by the late 1970s virtually every country in western Europe was able to provide reasonably good pension coverage to the whole resident population, the roads taken by individual countries to set up comprehensive pension systems differed sharply, and followed on from decisions taken at earlier stages of pension policy-making. As a result, today one can identify two types of pension systems: social insurance and multi-pillar pension systems. This divergence has generally been recognised in the literature on comparative pension policy, which however, has not yet adopted a consistent terminology to label these two 'worlds' of pension provision. The social insurance/multi-pillar distinction presented here roughly corresponds to the Bismarck versus Beveridge distinction (Bonoli, 1997; Myles and Quadagno, 1997), the mature systems versus latecomers (Myles and Pierson, 2001); and the social insurance versus latecomers (Hinrichs, 2001; Schludi, 2001). The main difference is that it focuses not only on the sort of benefits that are distributed but also on the way in which pension schemes are financed. This distinction reflects only in part the more influential classification of welfare states that distinguishes between social-democratic, conservative and liberal regime types (Esping-Andersen, 1990).

Social insurance pension systems are based, predominantly, on one or more pension schemes of Bismarckian inspiration, granting earnings-related benefits to former workers on a contributory basis. Typically, benefits depend on the contributions made while in work. In addition, social insurance pension systems generally include a means-tested minimum pension, provided to those who reach the age of retirement without having paid contributions, or with a contribution record that is not sufficient to grant them a decent pension. These schemes are financed on a pay-as-you-go basis, which means that current pensions are financed by current contributions. Because of the earnings-related nature of public pension coverage in social insurance countries, private pension provision did not develop to any significant extent, at least until very recently. The generosity and encompassing character of social insurance pension systems have crowded out private provision. To this 'world' of pension provision belong most continental European countries, including Germany, France, Italy and Sweden.

Multi-pillar pension systems are found in countries where state pensions provide only a flat-rate minimum benefit, sufficient to cover basic needs only. Typically, the objective of this sort of provision is not income maintenance during retirement, but the prevention of poverty among the older population. This limited role of the state in pension provision has left ample room for the development of private and/or occupational pensions, which have gradually been integrated into the pension systems of the relevant countries, often on a compulsory or quasi-compulsory basis. Multi-pillar pension systems combine two different financing methods: their basic pensions are of the pay-as-you-go type, like public pensions in social insurance systems, whereas their private and occupational pensions are generally fully funded, with current contributions used to finance future benefits. These systems exist in the UK, the Netherlands, Denmark and Switzerland, where the basic pension is only moderately earnings-related.

The distinction between social insurance and multi-pillar pension systems is visible in relation to the relative importance of the first and second pillars in a pensions system. Social insurance countries spend a considerable amount of their GDP on public pensions and have a small private pension sector; multi-pillar countries spend a lower proportion of their national income on public pensions but have larger private pension systems. Table 9.8 provides an overview of pension systems in selected OECD countries according to these two dimensions.

The pension coverage of atypical workers

At the end of the *trente glorieuses* (late 1970s), regardless of the model adopted, European pension systems were able to fulfil the two essential functions of pension provision: poverty prevention in old age and income replacement during

Table 9.8: Public pension expenditure as a % of GDP (1996) and financial assets of pension funds (1998 or most recent), selected OECD countries

	Expenditure on public pensions % GDP	Financial assets of pension funds % GDP
Social insurance countries		
France	10.36	na
Germany	10.29	3.3
Italy	10.99	3.2
Sweden	8.27	2.7
Average	9.97	3.1
Multi-pillar countries		
Denmark	7.73	21.5
Netherlands	6.75	85.6
Switzerland	6.71	74.9
United Kingdom	6.46	83.7
Average	6.91	66.4

Source: OECD SOCX (CD-ROM); OECD, Institutional Investors Statistical Yearbook 2000, Table S.8)

retirement. Whether they did this with a large social insurance scheme and a means-tested minimum, or through a modest basic pension supplemented by private or occupational provision, did not have a substantial impact on the living standards of older people. From the 1990s onwards, however, it has become clear that the institutional structure of a pension system matters considerably in terms of its vulnerability to given social, economic and demographic developments (Bonoli, 2003: forthcoming; Haverland, 2001). Among these the most important as far as pension policy is concerned is probably population ageing. This distinction, however, seems relevant also in relation with the challenge that is dealt with in this chapter.

Social insurance systems may be in theory better able to adapt to labour market changes because the state determines a higher proportion of the replacement income than is the case in multi-pillar systems. Even though social insurance schemes usually respect the so-called 'equivalence principle', they have in recent years been modified by the introduction of contribution credits that are attributed to insured people during periods of inactivity (or unpaid activity).

Multi-pillar pension systems deal with atypical employment in a differentiated manner. Usually, their first pillars do not penalise part-time workers or people whose career is punctuated by interruptions. Whether entitlement is residence based (Denmark, the Netherlands) or contributory, (UK, Switzerland), a drop in income resulting, for example, from working reduced hours, does not affect the level of the benefit, which is flat-rate in these countries (nearly flat-rate in

Switzerland). Similarly, career interruptions due to child rearing, education, unemployment or sickness do not generally have an impact on the amount of the basic pension.

Things are rather different insofar as the second pillar is concerned. Here the limited extent of risk pooling (an economic sector or a company) means that the sort of corrections adopted in social insurance pensions and in first pillar schemes are unlikely. Contribution credits granted for career interruption would have to be financed by other scheme members.[4] This would be particularly difficult to implement in precisely those sectors of industry in which they would be most needed, essentially those with a high proportion of female staff, those exposed to cyclical unemployment, and to disability/sickness risks. As a matter of fact, pension funds do not generally grant contribution credits for career interruptions. In general, as a result of the absence of contribution credits, pension fund members will have to face the full cost of career interruptions (unless future earnings allow them to catch up through additional savings).

As a result, the quality of coverage provided to atypical workers in multi-pillar pension systems depends very much on the level of provision guaranteed by the first pillar or basic pension. This varies across the four countries covered. In the Netherlands and in Switzerland the basic pension replaces 40 and 35 per cent of the average wage respectively; in Britain the same figure is below 20 per cent while in Denmark it reaches 31 per cent (including a full ATP supplement). None of these countries offers generous basic provision, but the extent of variation between them is substantial.

A crucial issue in relation to the ability of multi-pillar systems to provide decent pension coverage to atypical workers in the future will be the indexation method of their basic pension. In Denmark and the Netherlands the basic pension follows developments in average earnings.[5] In Britain and in Switzerland the basic pension does not follow wage increases, which means that over time the proportion of the wage that will be replaced will decline. This process is already under way. In Britain, where indexation is based on consumer price inflation, the value of the basic pension has declined from 21.0 per cent of average earnings in 1986 to 17.3 per cent in 1995 (recalculation of data from DSS, 1997, Table 3.13, p 56 and Table 6.14, p 143). In Switzerland, where the basic pension is increased according to a 'mixed index' equal to the arithmetic average of changes in consumer prices and wages, the replacement rate has declined from 37 per cent of the average wage in 1979 to 35 per cent in 1999 (Bonoli, 2001a).

These developments may have an important impact in the years to come on the ability of pension systems to provide coverage to atypical workers. The fact that they are not well covered by second pillar pensions combined with the decline in relative value of the basic pension may result in insufficient income in retirement and reliance on means-tested benefits. Because pension rights are accumulated over a four-decade period, it is difficult to make projections of the potential size of the population which is likely to reach retirement age with insufficient coverage. A simulation carried out for the Swiss case has shown that if current rules are kept in place for the next three decades, individuals with atypical career profiles, but who have spent most of their working life in paid employment and who have made a substantial contribution to a second pillar pension, may still end up with income packages lower than the means-tested pension (Bonoli and Gay-des-Combes, 2002). In Britain, the existence of cohorts of atypical or low-paid workers who are slowly approaching the age of retirement without adequate pension coverage has long been recognised by the government as a policy problem. The initiatives taken in the late 1990s (see below) can be seen as attempts to pre-empt a possible major pension coverage crisis in the future.

The effectiveness of pension systems, understood as their ability to provide a reasonable replacement income to retirees on a universal basis, has been undermined by changes in the labour market. The institutional structures in place seem to be more or less vulnerable to this socioeconomic development in a way that mirrors the pattern of robustness/vulnerability seen in relation to demographic ageing. If multi-pillar pension systems are probably better equipped to withstand the demographic challenge, they seem to be less able to integrate new and expanding forms of work. That is why some authors believe that the image of a 'demographic time-bomb' ticking in social insurance pension systems is matched by one of a 'social time-bomb' in multi-pillar systems (Lourdelle, 2002).

Integrating the new career profiles in the existing pension systems

The 1990s and early 2000s have seen in virtually all western European countries an unprecedented level of policy-making activity in the field of pensions. The main objective of reform was, in general, to contain expenditure and to prepare for the expected worsening of demographic conditions. However, on several occasions, reforms have included measures that deal with the problem of providing improved coverage to non-standard career profiles. The type of measures taken depends very much on the pre-reform structure of pension systems.

Reforms in social insurance countries

All four social insurance countries[6] covered in this study have legislated pension reforms during the 1990s. The main objective, in all cases, was to guarantee the sustainability of public pension schemes in the face of demographic ageing, but often cost-containment measures have been accompanied by improvements in the coverage of non-standard career workers. Where this has not been the case (for example, in France) it is because these measures had been introduced earlier.

Italy has seen an overhaul of its very generous pension system, which has become more uniform – for example by eliminating advantages for privileged civil servants – and less costly, especially by phasing out the generous provision for early retirement (*pensioni di anzianità*). The 1995 Italian reform has also changed the pension formula from defined benefits to notional defined contributions. This means that contributions paid during the whole working life will be relevant to the calculation of the benefit (Artoni and Zanardi, 1997; Ferrera, 1997). The reform has also introduced measures that improve the coverage of non-standard workers. For instance pension contributions are credited for periods of inactivity due to maternity (5 months) or parental leave (10 months), sickness or accident (12 months), unemployment and military service. Parents can also claim contribution credits for short periods of time spent caring for a sick child (five days per year). The amounts credited are based on the average salary of the recipient. Contributions are not credited for years spent as a student, nor for longer periods of non-employment spent caring for children. These career interruptions can be compensated, but the missing contribution years must be 'bought' (*riscatto*) by the insured person. Non-working partners of employed persons, essentially housewives (*casalinghe*), can obtain pension coverage, but need to pay for it (Leonardi and Peruzzi, 1995; INPS, 2001).

A shift to defined contributions was part also of the Swedish reform (Palme and Wennemo, 1997; Ståhlberg, 1997; Anderson, 1998). In addition, the new pension formula contains parameters related to demography and the overall performance of the economy. These should produce automatic downwards adjustments of benefits if demographic or economic conditions are worse than expected. Third, the reform has also introduced new legislation on private pensions. A small portion of the contribution to old age insurance (2.5 per cent of earnings) must now be paid into a pension fund chosen by the insured person (Anderson and Weaver, 2001). Like Italy, Sweden has also introduced improvements for non-standard workers. The new system, for example, grants contribution credits for having children, periods of unemployment and sickness. With regard to children, if a parent reduces working hours in the four years following the birth of a child, contributions are credited to his/her pension account on the basis of previous earnings. If he or she stops working completely, then the contribution credit will be based on 75 per cent of the average wage. Finally, if parents continue working as before having a child, their credited contributions will be based on their earnings plus one base amount. Parents can claim only one child credit at any one time, but they remain entitled to it as long as they have children younger than four. Individuals who are not working because of unemployment or sickness receive contribution credits based on their insured earnings (Riksförsäkringsverket, 2001).

Germany first shifted pension indexation from gross to net wages (Schmähl, 1993) and has more recently modified the pension formula so as to gradually reduce the replacement rate from the current 70 per cent for a full contribution record to around 64 per cent in 2030.[7] Together with these cost containment measures Germany has also introduced provision for a fully funded private pension, to which private sector employees can contribute tax free up to 4 per cent of their earnings (Nöcker, 2001; Hering, 2003: forthcoming). At the same time, however, parents in Germany are entitled to contribution credits equal to those payable on an average wage for each child under the age of three living in the same household. The contributions are credited to the mother, unless the parents request a different arrangement. Contributions are credited also to individuals who spend at least 14 hours per week performing caring tasks, if not working more than 30 hours per week. Students are entitled to contribution credits for a period of three years after the age of 17. Recipients of unemployment benefit maintain pension coverage (BMA, 2001).

In France the period over which the reference salary is calculated and the number of contribution years required for a full pension have both been extended, with the result of either reducing benefits for a given contribution record, or encouraging workers to delay retirement to maintain pre-reform pension rights intact (Ruellan, 1993; Bonoli, 2000, Chapter 5). More recently the Jospin government has introduced legislation that encourages the setting up of 'wage earners funds' (*fonds d'épargne salariale*), which benefit from tax concessions but have a time horizon limited to ten years. Wage earners funds may turn out to be the functional equivalent of occupational pensions, depending on the use that employees make of them. Like other social insurance countries, France too has introduced mechanisms to compensate for career interruptions or reductions in working hours due to family care. These are linked to the receipt of a specific family benefit that is paid to parents who reduce working hours or stop working completely in order to provide care. Beneficiaries of this benefit are credited with pension contributions equal to those due on a salary of €1,127 per month (in 2002). These measures, however, have been in force since the 1970s (CNAV, personal communication).

Reforms in multi-pillar countries

In multi-pillar countries, because of their more extensive reliance on funding for the provision of retirement income, the demographic challenge is not perceived to be a serious threat to the long-term sustainability of the pension systems. As a result, reforms in these countries have not been so much concerned with cost containment. Instead, the overall direction of reform here has been towards improving occupational pension coverage for workers like part-time or low-income employees who have a somewhat marginal position in the labour market. This can also be seen as a response to the changes in the composition of the labour force outlined at the beginning of this chapter.

In Denmark the 1990s have seen the expansion of occupational pension coverage, which as a result of a series of collectively negotiated agreements has increased to 80 per cent of private sector employment in 1996 (CEC, 1997). Denmark has long been an exception in western Europe for not providing compulsory or generalised earnings-related pension coverage. In fact, the Danish second pillar (ATP) delivers modest flat-rate benefits, and occupational pension coverage was rather limited throughout most of the post-war years. During the 1980s, however, it became clear that the Danish pension system was producing substantial inequalities in retirement provision between those who had access to occupational pensions and those who did not. As a result, the trade unions campaigned for an extension of supplementary pension coverage by requesting the introduction of a central pension fund, available to all employees and managed by the unions. The proposal was met with little enthusiasm by other political actors, and it was only in 1991 that a breakthrough in expanding pension coverage came about. This, however, was not the result of new legislation, but of a collective agreement signed by the Industrial Workers' Union, which included generalised supplementary pension coverage. The fund was to be managed jointly by representatives of employers and employees. Other trade unions followed suit and introduced similar schemes, with the result of dramatically expanding pension coverage (Kvist, 1997; Ploug, 2000).

In the Netherlands, the 1990s have not seen major reforms of the pension system. An important issue has been to increase the coverage rate for occupational pensions, which has gone from around 80 per cent in the 1980s to 91 per cent of employees in the late 1990s (van Oorschot and Boos, 1999). In 1997 an agreement between the social partners and the government was reached, which included the objective of further increasing the coverage rate. Those who are not covered by a second pillar pension are either employees of employers who do not offer a pension fund (2 per cent of cases), or are excluded from coverage by the funds' rules. These can provide coverage only to employees older than 25, hired on a permanent contract, or whose earnings are above a given threshold. The effects of the 1997 agreement were evaluated in 2001 (SZW, 2001). Other reforms have concerned aspects such as freedom of choice for scheme members and how to improve pension funds' investment performance.

Switzerland adopted a pension reform in 1995, which has affected the basic pension only, and is currently debating a further reform of both the basic pension and the second pillar system. The 1995 reform increased the age of retirement for women and introduced contribution credits for carers and contribution sharing between spouses. It was essentially a cost-neutral operation designed to modernise the scheme. In contrast, the current reform aims at adapting the pension system to population ageing. Among the measures that are being considered is an increase in VAT to help finance the basic pension over the next few decades, and the abolition of widows' pensions. With regard to second pillar pensions, the minimum contribution rates, set by legislation, are going to be increased in order to compensate for the longer life expectancy at age 65. The issue of expanding coverage, currently at about 90 per cent of employees, is also high on the agenda. Affiliation to a pension fund is compulsory only for employees earning above 35 per cent of average earnings, a threshold generally exceeded by full-time workers but not by part-time employees, who are often women. The trade unions and the Social-Democrats asked for the removal of the threshold, but employers and right-of-centre parties opposed the move. At the time of writing (January 2003) it is not clear if this proposal will eventually be adopted.

Finally, in the UK, the 1990s have seen the adoption of policies aimed at improving pension coverage for low-income workers. The issue had become particularly pressing after the 1986 pension reform that reduced the level of the state second pillar pension (SERPS) that provided a supplementary pension to those who did not have access to occupational coverage. Many of them bought private pensions and found afterwards that this sort of pension coverage was not suitable for their low earnings. The high administrative charges of a private pension can swallow a good proportion of the contributions paid by a low-income individual. In order to improve coverage for the low paid, the Blair government has turned the state earnings-related scheme into a flat-rate pension designed to cover workers with very low average earnings and interrupted careers (state second pension). For those on low earnings, the new flat-rate benefit will be higher than the equivalent earnings-related pension. For workers with moderate earnings who do not have access to an occupational pension, the government has introduced a new quality label (stakeholder pensions) that is attributed to personal pensions that meet certain criteria. Administrative charges for any individual account cannot amount to more than 1 per cent of assets, there can be no penalties for contribution interruptions and schemes must be governed by a trust (DWP, 2001).

Conclusion

Faced with similar labour market challenges, the countries covered in this study are developing distinctive pension policy solutions that are related to the institutional structure of their pension systems. Social insurance countries have focused their efforts on carers, by introducing contribution credits for time spent out of the labour market or working reduced hours because of caring. This is a suitable strategy for the provision of decent pension coverage to parents or people providing long-term care. However, as seen in the first section of this chapter, the redefinition of the boundaries between labour market and domestic work is not the only labour market change that can impact on pension coverage. Other disadvantaged workers who do not happen to be involved in the provision of care are unlikely to benefit from the reforms discussed in this chapter. On the contrary, they will be left only with the retrenchment measures adopted in order to contain future pension expenditure.

If social insurance systems are in theory better suited to provide inclusive pension coverage to atypical employees, this does not automatically translate into practice. In fact, improved coverage for marginal workers requires the same level of political will, which has made possible the introduction of contribution credits for carers, to be directed towards other forms of disadvantaged employment. This implies, for example, that contribution credits be attributed to all part-time workers, regardless of whether the decision to work reduced hours is motivated by care needs or by other factors, or to temporary workers who are between jobs. In general, low-income workers in a social insurance pension system may find it difficult to obtain higher than minimal pension entitlements. From their perspective, it would be appropriate to adopt pension formulas that include advantages for their career profiles, hence an element of vertical redistribution.

All these measures are politically difficult to legitimate. The provision of credits to carers can be seen as a way to compensate the contribution to society that is made by raising children or taking care of a frail elderly relative. There is a fairly visible element of reciprocity in these measures that makes them politically attractive. In contrast, the vertical redistribution needed to provide decent pension coverage to marginal workers who are not providers of care will be more difficult to justify in political debates.

In multi-pillar systems it may be technically more difficult to provide pension coverage above the basic pension to atypical workers, because this implies that they be included in second pillar occupational pension schemes. This is often costly, and the sort of redistribution that is possible in social insurance schemes is impractical. With a few exceptions, the limited extent of risk pooling that goes on in these schemes (a company, a sector), does not allow the cross-subsidisation of pension entitlements. This problem is compounded by the fact that atypical, marginal workers tend to be concentrated in specific industries, and possibly companies, and as a result covered by the same pension scheme(s).

However, when efforts are made to improve coverage, they tend not to be selective as is the case in social insurance pension systems. The extension of coverage of occupational pensions seen in Britain, Denmark, the Netherlands or in Switzerland does not concern only carers but all those marginal workers whose annual income or working hours are below a certain threshold. Of course, the bulk of part-time workers are women who are at the same time performing caring work, and the political decisions to extend coverage were largely motivated by the needs of this particular group. However, the benefits will be shared more widely than is the case in social insurance pension systems.

Changes in labour markets are putting pressure on pension systems. If these are to continue to deliver income security to older people, beyond the level needed to meet basic needs, then some adaptation is needed. Social insurance systems are in principle better suited to achieve this goal, because a larger proportion of pensioners' income is the result of political decisions. If there is a political will to provide good coverage to atypical workers, there are few technical obstacles in these systems. However, the recent reforms seem to have focused more on cost containment in view of population ageing, and there is little evidence that the political will exists to provide improved pension coverage to marginal workers independently of their family situation. In multi-pillar systems, the quality of coverage available to atypical workers depends both on the level of the basic pension and on the degree of inclusiveness of private/ occupational pensions. To integrate atypical workers in second pillar pensions seems essential here, especially in those countries where the value of the basic pension is not indexed to wages (for example, Switzerland and the United Kingdom), but this is technically difficult.

Notes

[1] In this chapter we use (interchangeably) the terms of atypical and non-standard employment to denote all forms of employment that do not conform to the (ideal) typical male career profile of the post-war years (full-time, uninterrupted employment, for 40-45 years).

[2] Data for Switzerland are not available in this case, but we can surmise that tendencies in the field of self-employment are practically the same in this country (see Flückiger et al, 2001).

[3] For producers and social services, low-skill jobs represent on average about 20 per cent of high-skill professions. The same figure for distributive and personal services is respectively 60 per cent and 80 per cent (OECD, 2000, Table 3.6).

[4] The recently introduced German second pillar pensions (known as 'Riester's pensions', from the name of the Minister for Social Affairs), include an ingenious mechanism that is equivalent to a contribution credit, in the shape of a subsidy.

[5] In the Netherlands for several years during the 1980s the amount of the basic pension was frozen in order to deal with budget problems. As a result, the value of the pension relative to average wages dropped by 1.7 percentage points (van Oorschot and Boos, 1999).

[6] More in-depth comparative accounts of pension reform in social insurance countries can be found in Bonoli (2000); Hinrichs (2001); Schludi (2001).

[7] The government has claimed that the replacement rate will decline to 67 per cent only, but this figure is based on earnings net of the non-compulsory contribution paid to a private pension. The figure of 64 per cent is based on net earnings according to the pre-reform definition, and hence comparable with the current replacement rate of 70 per cent (Nöcker, 2001).

References

Anderson, K. (1998) 'The welfare state in the global economy: the politics of social insurance reform in Sweden 1990-1998', PhD dissertation, Seattle: University of Washington.

Anderson, K. and Weaver, K. (2001) 'Pension policy in Sweden: fundamental reforms in a policy cartel', paper presented at the Swiss Political Science Association annual conference, Fribourg, Switzerland, 9 November.

Artoni, R. and Zanardi, A. (1997) 'The evolution of the Italian pension system', in MIRE (ed) *Comparing welfare states in Southern Europe*, Paris: Ministry of Social Affairs, pp 243-66.

BMA (Bundesministerium für Arbeit) (2001) Rentenversicherung, www.bma.de/frame.asp?u=/de/sicherung/rente/rente.htm (visited 23 July).

Bonoli, G. (1997) 'Classifying welfare states: a two-dimension approach', *Journal of Social Policy*, vol 26, no 3, pp 315-72.

Bonoli, G. and Palier, B. (2000) 'Pension reforms and the expansion of private pensions in western Europe', *Yearbook of European administrative history*, vol 12, pp 153-74.

Bonoli, G. (2000) *The Politics of pension reform: Institutions and policy change in western Europe*, Cambridge: Cambridge University Press.

Bonoli, G. (2001a) *Quelle couverture retraite pour les travailleurs atypiques? Une simulation de quelques cas à risque*, mimeo, Department of Social Work and Social Policy, University of Fribourg, Switzerland.

Bonoli, G. (2001b) 'Mandating pensions: the Swiss experience', paper presented at the conference, 'The political economy of pension reform', Institute for Advanced Studies, Delmenhorst-Bremen, 3-5 May.

Bonoli, G. and Gay-des-Combes, B. (2002) *L'évolution des prestations vieillesse dans le long terme : Une simulation prospective à l'horizon 2040*, research report, Bern: Federal Office of Social Insurance.

Bonoli, G. (2003: forthcoming) 'Two worlds of pension reform in western Europe', *Comparative Politics*.

European Commission (1997) *Supplementary pensions in the single market: A green paper*, Brussels: CEC, COM (97) 283.

Cesari, R. (2000) *I fondi pensione*, Bologna: Il Mulino.

Department of Social Security (1997) *Social security statistics*, London: The Stationery Office.

Department for Work and Pensions (2001) *Stakeholder pensions*, www.dss.gov.uk/lifeevent/benefits/stakeholder_pensions.htm, (visited 25 August).

Esping-Andersen, G. (1990) *The three worlds of welfare capitalism*, Cambridge: Polity Press.

Ferrera, M. (1997) 'The uncertain future of the Italian welfare state', in M. Bull and M. Rhodes (eds) *Crisis and transition in Italian politics*, London: Frank Cass, pp 231-49.

Flückiger, Y., Ferro-Luzzi, G. and Falter, J.M. (2001) *Le travail indépendant en Suisse*, Rapport scientifique, FNRS; PP Demain la Suisse.

Haverland, M. (2001) 'Another Dutch miracle? Explaining Dutch and German pension trajectories', *Journal of European Social Policy*, vol 11, no 4, pp 309-23.

Hering, M. (2003: forthcoming) 'Turning ideas into policies: implementing modern social-democratic thinking in Germany's pension policy', in G. Bonoli and M. Powell (eds) *Social democratic party policies in contemporary Europe*, London: Routledge.

Hinrichs, K. (2001) 'Elephants on the move. Patterns of public pension reform in OECD countries', in S. Leibfried (ed) *Welfare state futures*, Cambridge: Cambridge University Press, pp 77-102.

INPS (Istituto Nazionale di Previdenza Sociale) (2001) TuttoINPS, www.inps.it/Doc/TuttoINPS/TuttoINPS.htm (visited 23 July).

Kvist, J. (1997) 'Retrenchment or restructuring? The emergence of a multi-tiered welfare state in Denmark', in J. Clasen (ed) *Social insurance in Europe*, Bristol: The Policy Press, pp 14-39.

Leonradi, G. and Peruzzi, M. (1995) 'Pensioni', *Italia Oggi*, vol 5, no 197 (special issue).

Lourdelle, H. (2002) 'Is there a future for the trade unions in social protection?', in H. Sarfati and G. Bonoli (eds) *Labour market and social protection reforms in international perspective: Parallel or converging tracks?*, Abingdon: Ashgate.

Myles, J. and Pierson, P. (2001) 'The political economy of pension reform', in P. Pierson (ed) *The new politics of the welfare state*, Oxford: Oxford University Press, pp 305-33.

Myles, J. and Quadagno, J. (1997) 'Recent trends in public pension reform: a comparative view', in K. Banting and R. Boadway (eds) *Reform of retirement income policy: International and Canadian perspectives*, Kingston, Ontario: School of Policy Studies, Queen's University, pp 247-72.

Nöcker, R. (2001) *The recent pension reforms in Germany: Individual pension accounts as a replacement for state pensions*, mimeo, London: Centre for Pensions and Social Insurance, Birkbeck College, University of London/City University.

OECD (Organisation for Economic Co-operation and Development) (1996) *Employment outlook 1996*, Paris: OECD.

OECD (1997) *Employment outlook 1997*, Paris: OECD.

OECD (2000) *Employment outlook 2000*, Paris: OECD.

OECD (2001) *Employment outlook 2001*, Paris: OECD.

OECD (2002) *Employment outlook 2002*, Paris: OECD.

Palme, J. and Wennemo, I. (1997) *Swedish social security in the 1990s: Reform and retrenchment*, mimeo, Stockholm: Swedish Institute for Social Research.

Ploug, N. (2000) 'The recalibration of the Danish old-age pension system', paper prepared for the International Sociological Association RC 19 Annual Conference, 24-27 August, Tilburg, the Netherlands.

Riksförsäkringsverket (National Social Insurance Board) (2001) *Den nya allmänna pensionen*, www.pensions.nu (visited 23 July).

Ruellan, R. (1993) 'Retraites: l'impossible réforme est-elle achevée?', *Droit social*, vol 12, pp 911-29.

Sarfati, H. and Bonoli, G. (2002) 'Tight constraints, new demands and enduring needs: addressing the labour market versus social protection challenge', in H. Sarfati and G. Bonoli (eds) *Labour market and social protection reforms in international perspective: Parallel or converging tracks?*, Aldershot: Ashgate.

Schludi, M. (2001) 'Pension reform in European social insurance countries', paper presented at the Biennial Meeting of the European Community Studies Association, Madison, Wisconsin, 31 May-2 June.

Schmähl, W. (1993) 'The 1992 reform of public pensions in Germany: main elements and some effects', *Journal of European Social Policy*, vol 3, no 1, pp 39-52.

Ståhlberg, A-C. (1997) 'Sweden: on the way from standard to basic security?', in J. Clasen (ed) *Social insurance in Europe*, Bristol: The Policy Press, pp 40-59.

SZW (Ministerie van Sociale Zaken en Werkgelegenheid) (2001) *The old age pension system in the Netherlands*, The Hague: SZW.

van Oorschot, W. and Boos, C. (1999) 'Dutch pension policy and the ageing of the population', *European Journal of Social Security*, vol 1, no 3, pp 295-311.

Walker, A. (1993) 'Living standards and way of life', in European Commission, *Older people in Europe: social and economic policies*, Brussels: European Commission, pp 8-33.

Whiteford, P. and Kennedy, S. (1995) *Incomes and living standards of older people*, DSS, research report 34, London: HMSO.

TEN

Pensions choices for the 21st century: meeting the challenges of an ageing society

Jane Falkingham[1] and Katherine Rake[2]

Introduction

Pension reform is rarely off the political agenda, despite the fact that by their very nature pensions require planning and stability over a longer period than the normal life of a government. The publication by New Labour in December 1998 of the Green Paper *A new contract for welfare: Partnership in pensions* (DSS, 1998) marked an attempt to forge a new and enduring settlement for the provision of income in retirement to carry Britain through the 21st century. However, we argue in this chapter that the reforms proposed have fallen short of those required, and any consensus that had been created has been quick to disperse. The government itself implicitly acknowledged this failure by introducing a new layer of reforms before the Green Paper itself had been fully legislated. These include revised levels of the minimum income guarantee, the pension credit and the new savings gateways. The delayed legislation for the state second pension, the relatively slow take-up of the new stakeholder pensions at the company level, and the collapse of Equitable Life and subsequent public concerns over private pension schemes all mean that pension reform continues to be firmly on the agenda. In December 2002, a new pensions Green Paper *Simplicity, security and choice: Working and saving for retirement* (DWP, 2002a) was published – just four years on from *Partnership in pensions*.

By way of background, this chapter first examines the challenges facing policy-makers at the start of the 21st century; challenges arising from the demographic, economic and policy legacy of the last century. The chapter then puts forward a number of criteria that we believe are necessary for a sustainable and effective pension system. New Labour's 1998 pension settlement is then evaluated against these criteria and the extent to which the settlement will indeed deliver an adequate income in later life for both today's and tomorrow's pensioners is assessed. Finally, an alternative option for pension provision is considered.

Pension challenges: the demographic, economic and policy legacy of the 20th century

Policy makers within the pensions field face a number of challenges that are the result of changes during the 20th century: changes in the demographic structure of the UK; changes in the pattern of working life; and the legacy of changes in the balance of pension provision due to policy shifts in the last 30 years. Each of these is briefly discussed below, before turning to the last, but by no means least, challenge of enduring pensioner poverty.

Changes in the demographic structure

The changing demographic structure of the population, with an increasing number of older people dependent on a shrinking working-age population, has often been presented as one of the challenges, if not the main challenge, facing contemporary welfare states. The implications for the sustainability and equity of public pensions was dramatically highlighted by the World Bank in 1994 in its report on *Averting the old age crisis*, and discussion of the impact of demographic change is prominent in the opening sections of both the 1998 and 2002 Green Papers (DSS, 1998; DWP, 2002a).

It is the case that past trends in fertility and mortality have resulted in a dramatic increase in the proportion of the population aged over 60 (Figure 10.1). In 1901 those aged 60 and over constituted just 7.5 per cent of the population. In 2001, they made up over 20 per cent and by 2031 it is expected

Figure 10.1: Percentage of UK population aged 60 and over (1901-2031)

%

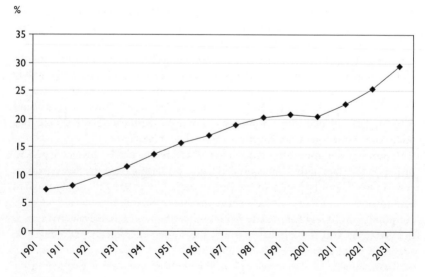

Source: GAD surveys

that they will comprise nearly 30 per cent, as the baby-boom generations start to retire (Evandrou, 1997; ONS, 2002a). Such figures have given rise to the notion of a 'demographic time bomb'. However, while the idea of a time bomb ticking away beneath our feet remains popular within the media, most academic commentators would now agree that this is a myth (see among others, Johnson and Falkingham, 1992; Warnes, 1996; Mullan, 2000; Catalyst, 2002). Substantial changes in the age structure of the British population have already taken place, without any catastrophic affect. The last century saw a tripling of the share of the pensioner population at the same time as the expansion, rather than contraction, of the welfare state. Increases in the population aged 60 and over will be less dramatic in future than many mature welfare states have coped with in the past (Glennerster, 1999). Futhermore, it is increasingly recognised that the welfare support ratio is determined by many other factors in addition to demographic change, not least the proportion of people in different ages who are in work and the design of welfare policy itself (Falkingham, 1989; Hills, 1997). That is not to say that demographic change is unimportant. Recent changes in mortality at older ages have had a significant impact on longevity, with the result that more older people will spend longer in retirement than ever before. Research from the Personal Social Services Research Unit shows how there has been an average increase in life expectancies for men at 65 of 1.7 months for every year from 1980 to 1998; for women the figure is 1.2 months (Bebbington and Comas-Herrera, 2000). This means that a woman retiring at age 60 in the UK today can expect to live, on average, for a further 22.8 years, while a man retiring five years later at age 65 could live for an additional 14.7 years (ONS, 2002b). It is the combination of relatively more older people living longer that presents a challenge for policy-makers, both for the provision of income in later life and for the funding of health and social care services.

Most pension systems were designed for a world where retirement was the exception rather than the norm and where, to quote from Leon Trotsky's diary in exile, "...old age is the most unexpected of all things to happen to a man" (Trotsky, 1935, 1958, p 56). Trotsky's comments, written in 1935, reflected the fact that among those cohorts born in the mid-19th century, only a third survived to 65. Even among the cohort born in 1901 only half survived to 65. However, among those born in 1971, over 80 per cent can expect to survive into old age. Thus, old age is no longer an unexpected or unpredictable risk that needs to be 'insured' against. Given this, it is important to rethink the meaning of later life, our expectations of retirement and how it should be provided for – the notion of retirement as a distinct phase of life, where one is not expected, or 'allowed', to be in employment, is actually a very modern one. So far, politicians have resisted any increase in the age at which statutory pensions are payable. However, a recent report by the new Pensions Policy Institute (O'Connell, 2002) forcefully argues that the time has come to raise the state pension age.

Changes in working life

Just as people are surviving longer, the last 50 years have also seen a number of important changes in the labour market and working life. Since the mid-1970s there has been a dramatic fall in the number of years of life that men spend in employment and a corresponding increase in the number of years spent in other activities such as school, unemployment and especially retirement. In a typical OECD country at the start of the 21st century it is estimated that a man might spend only half his life in employment (OECD, 2000). Analysis of economic activity rates among different birth cohorts within Britain shows that successive generations of men are both entering the labour market later and leaving earlier, and having lower overall participation rates at any given age (Figure 10.2) (Evandrou and Falkingham, 2000). The shorter working lives of men will reduce the period during which they are able to accumulate pension entitlements, and increase the period that they are dependent on such entitlements. At the same time, as is discussed below, changes in the pension system mean that prospects in retirement are now more closely linked to experiences during working life than previously.

It is important to note, however, that changes in the labour market have affected men and women differently. Women from more recent birth cohorts experience *higher* rates of participation in full-time employment at any given age than earlier cohorts, although their participation rates are still lower than those of men (Figures 10.3a and 10.3b). For example, among women born in 1961-65, 54 per cent were working full time at age 26 compared to just 35 per cent of women at the same age born in 1946-50. Furthermore, the extension of women's retirement age to 65 may well shift the employment trajectory

Figure 10.2: Percentage of men in employment by birth cohort

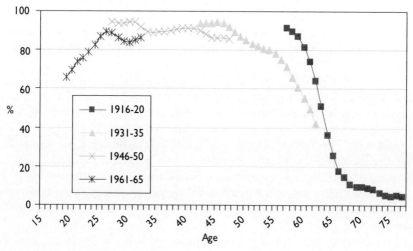

Source: Evandrou and Falkingham (2000)

Figure 10.3(a): Percentage of women in full-time employment by birth cohort

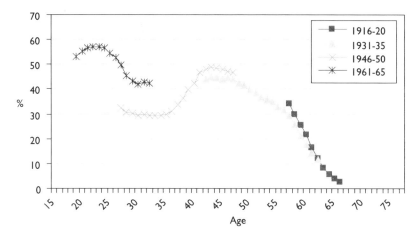

Source: Evandrou and Falkingham (2000)

Figure 10.3(b): Percentage of women in part-time employment by birth cohort

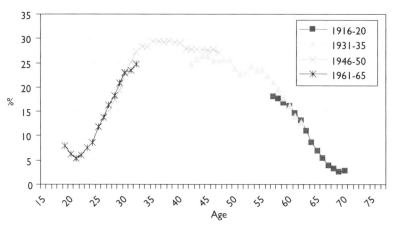

Source: Evandrou and Falkingham (2000)

further out, which will mean that today's younger women will have longer to build up their pension entitlement than previous generations. Today, one in five women reaching state pension age have no entitlement to the basic state pension (BSP), and only a quarter of newly retired women with a BSP based solely on their own contributions receive a full BSP (PPI, 2003). However, it is estimated that by 2025 almost all women reaching state pension age will have some entitlement to BSP, with average entitlements being equivalent to nearly 90 per cent of the full pension (GAD, 1999).

Although changes in working life may be good news for women in terms of entitlement to BSP, the key change in the pension system over the last 20 years has been the shift in the balance of the welfare mix, with a reduction in the value of the BSP and an increasing emphasis on second tier pensions.

Changes in the pension mix

Since 1980, the BSP has been uprated in line with price inflation. The effect of this has taken time to show through. In 1981 the BSP was worth 20 per cent of average male earnings: today it is worth around 14 per cent and if current indexation rules continue, it is estimated that by 2050 its relative value will have fallen to just 7.5 per cent. One important outcome of a devalued basic pension is that second tier pensions are increasingly important in maintaining the living standards of pensioners relative to those of the working population.

Since the 1950s there has been considerable growth in occupational provision, with an increase in members from 6.2 million in 1953 to around 11 million in the 1980s (Figure 10.4) (GAD, 2001). Prior to the mid-1980s, an employee could only opt out of the state earnings-related pension into a final salary occupational pension. Since then, however, employees have been permitted to use money purchase pensions to contract out of the state second tier pensions. An important distinction is that in contrast to a final salary scheme where the employer bears the risk concerning the value of the pension that will eventually be paid, in personal pensions it is the individual that bears the risk. In 1996-2000, a quarter of men in full-time employment were members of a personal pension scheme.

Figure 10.4: Percentage of employees who were members of UK occupational pension schemes (1956-95)

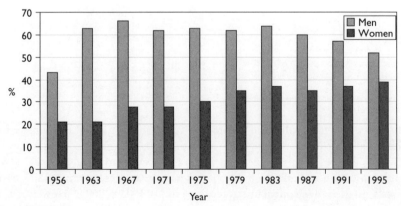

Source: GAD surveys

The growth in private second tier pension coverage has been very uneven. Table 10.1 shows the proportion of employees who are currently members of an occupational or personal pension scheme by gender and socioeconomic group. There is a clear gender imbalance, with significantly higher proportions of men being scheme members, the gender differences being even greater if we distinguish between those women working part time and full time. In particular, there are marked differences across socioeconomic groups, with rates of occupational scheme membership varying from 76 per cent of men working full time in professional occupations to just 15 per cent of women working part time in an unskilled occupation. Similarly, the highest proportions with a personal pension are found among full-time employed men who are employers and managers (32 per cent) or professionals (27 per cent). Only 3 per cent of women working part time in unskilled manual jobs have such pensions.

The emphasis towards a greater role for private pension provision was reaffirmed in the 1998 Green Paper on *Partnership in pensions*. For the first time in a policy document a shift in the balance of pension provision was included

Table 10.1: Percentage of employees who are currently members of private pension schemes, by sex and socioeconomic group

	Professional	Employers and managers	Intermediate non-manual	Junior non-manual	Skilled manual and own account non-professional	Semi-skilled manual and personal service	Unskilled manual	Total
Men full time								
Occupational pension	76	66	70	59	44	43	34	56
Personal pension	27	32	19	20	27	19	15	25
Any private pension	89	83	79	70	64	56	44	71
Women full time								
Occupational pension	71	64	70	52	38	31	27	55
Personal pension	19	20	16	15	16	11	10	16
Any private pension	80	74	78	61	50	40	31	65
Women part time								
Occupational pension	51	40	52	28	23	23	15	28
Personal pension	23	20	12	11	10	7	3	9
Any private pension	63	54	59	36	31	28	17	34

Source: ONS (2001, Table 6.5)

as an explicit goal; with the target being a change from 60 per cent state provision and 40 per cent private provision to 40 per cent state and 60 per cent private. Before moving on to examine the impact of the recent pension reforms in more detail, it is important to mention a final and related challenge facing policy makers – that of persistent pensioner poverty.

Persistent pensioner poverty

The good news is that at the start of the 21st century pensioners enjoy, on average, a much higher level of income than 20 years previously. Figure 10.5 shows that between 1979 and 1996/97 the average incomes of all pensioner households increased by 62 per cent from £137 a week to £223. Over the same period average earnings grew by just 38 per cent in real terms. Thus the position of pensioners has improved relative to others. However, the bad news is that this tells only part of the story. Not all pensioners have benefited equally from this growth in real income. Figure 10.6 shows the income position of pensioner couples within the different quintiles of the pensioner income distribution. Although the incomes of all groups of pensioners have risen, the incomes of those in the richest fifth have increased three times as fast as those in the poorest fifth, which in fact grew by 31 per cent over the period, less than the growth in real earnings – with the result that the poorest pensioners have actually fallen behind relative to others (DWP, 2002b).

The extent to which pensioners are living in poverty is unclear as there is no consensus around a single definition of poverty in the UK. The closest to an officially accepted definition are the relative measures of low income published in the *Households below average income* series. In 2000/01, a quarter of pensioner households had an income below 60 per cent of contemporary median income, that is, a quarter of pensioners were living in poverty (DWP, 2002c). Alternative definitions of poverty compare incomes to an absolute amount estimated as being required to attain a particular standard of living. Two such measures have been calculated by the Family Budget Unit – the 'Low Cost but Acceptable' (LCA) living standard, below which health and social integration are thought to be at risk, and the 'Modest But Adequate' (MBA) living standard that is slightly higher and takes into account the resources necessary to participate in society (Parker, 2002). It was estimated that in 1999 52 per cent of single pensioners and 24 per cent of couples had net incomes after housing costs of less than the LCA threshold (SCSS, 2000).

Pensioner poverty remains particularly concentrated among female pensioners, who tend to have low personal incomes. In 2000/01, 38 per cent of single female pensioners and 81 per cent of married female pensioners have individual gross incomes of less than £100 a week. According to analysis of the dynamics of poverty using the British Household Panel Survey, persistent poverty is also concentrated among older women, with the proportion experiencing such poverty being three times that of the whole population. This reflects both the

Figure 10.5: Rising pensioner incomes: average gross income (1979 and 1996/97)

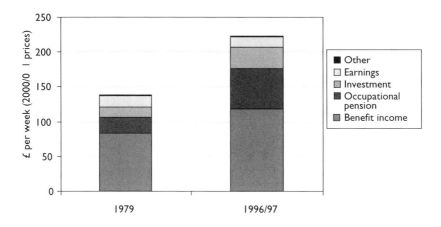

Source: DWP (2002b, Table A1)

Figure 10.6: Rising inequality: median net income of pensioner couples (1979 and 1996/97)

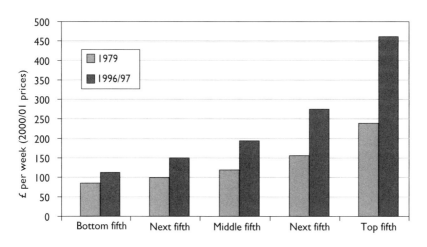

Source: DWP (2002b, Table A13)

lower wages of women while in work – the wage gap – and the fact that they are much more likely to have experienced interruptions to their earnings histories – the pay gap. Changes in the pension mix, particularly the move to greater personal pensions, which are based on contributions made during working life and which may result in the purchase of a single life annuity (and hence no survivors' benefits for women married to men with such an annuity), do not bode well for future trends in women's pension income.

In summary, policy-makers at the beginning of the 21st century are facing a number of challenges. First, there are and will be more older people who are living longer. At the same time as the period spent in retirement is lengthening, people – particularly men – are both entering the labour market later and leaving earlier and having shorter working lives. Thus the period during which men are able to accumulate pension entitlements is shortening, while the period of time that they are dependent on such entitlements is lengthening. Moreover, there is greater diversity within the population, and the last 20 years has seen increasing income inequality both among the pensioner population and the working-age population. Finally, there has been a significant change in the pension mix, with increasing reliance on second tier pensions and a shift from instruments that pooled risk to ones where risk is individualised. Furthermore, the increasing emphasis on earnings-related private pensions means that inequalities in working life are much more likely to be perpetuated into retirement. Thus, at the start of the 21st century, pension reform remains firmly on the political agenda. How should we assess any new pension system proposed to us?

Desirable criteria for pension systems

We believe that at least seven criteria are desirable in any pension system. These are, in alphabetical order:

* adequacy
* administrative efficiency
* affordability
* equity
* political sustainability
* protection of incentives and
* transparency.

The weight given to these different criteria will depend upon the goals of the pension system and the elements within it. For example, for a system targeted at the lifetime poor, issues of adequacy will predominate, whereas a system designed to encourage savings and redistribution across an individual's own lifetime should be assessed according to its effects on incentives. The criteria also operate at different levels, some being more relevant to particular elements of the system and others being pertinent at the overall system level. Thus, the overall pension system needs to be assessed in terms of transparency, affordability, administrative efficiency and political sustainability. Bearing these in mind, let us assess how well the pension settlement outlined in the 1998 Green Paper will deliver.

Evaluating New Labour's pension settlement

Prior to 1998, the British pension system was built around three key tiers. The first tier of state provision was designed to provide everyone with a basic income in retirement. As discussed above, the real value of the basic state pension (BSP) has declined over time and in 1998 anyone with entitlement to only the contributory non-means-tested BSP was also eligible for the means-tested income support. The second tier consisted of three compulsory options: the state earnings-related pension (SERPs), occupational pensions and personal pensions. The third voluntary tier enabled people to make additional savings into their pensions through AVCs (and free-standing AVCs). Thus, even before the 1998 reforms, the British pension system had six main elements.

The reforms in the Green Paper reflected several interrelated goals including: ensuring an adequate income in later life for all; providing a reward for savings; and altering the balance between individual and state provision. A central tenet of the reforms was that where individuals were in a position to save for their own old age they should be encouraged to do so, but for those who were unable to save sufficient amounts either because of low income or interrupted working lives then the state should provide an adequate safety net. The Green Paper highlighted occupational pensions as "one of the great welfare success stories of the century" (DSS, 1998, para 19, p 18,), and an explicit aspiration of the reforms was to share this success story more broadly across the population. The vehicle chosen to do this was the new stakeholder pension (SHP), which became available in April 2001.

In fact, SHPs differ from occupational pensions in a number of important ways. Occupational pensions have worked, in part, by limiting the individuals across whom they pool risk, for example by excluding part-time employees or workers in particular parts of a company or by adopting long vesting periods. Furthermore the level of contributions is generally decided not by the employee but by the company and is set at a reasonably high level. By contrast, membership of SHPs is open. This can be seen as a positive attribute, but there is the risk that some individuals may mispurchase SHPs inappropriate to their circumstances. Furthermore, as there are no set levels of contribution to SHPs, some individuals may under-invest in their pension. Finally, SHPs are defined contribution schemes (mirroring shift within the occupational sector itself) and have no mechanism for pooling risk.

In recognition that private provision through earnings-related second tier pensions are not necessarily suitable for individuals with low lifetime earnings or high levels of absence from the labour market, the reforms also proposed a new state second pension (S2P) to replace SERPS. The government intends that S2P will become a flat-rate benefit at the level of the lower earnings threshold (£11,200 from April 2003). The 1998 Green Paper suggested that the change could come into effect five years after the introduction of stakeholder pensions, that is, April 2006 (DSS, 1998).

The reforms also renamed income support as minimum income guarantee (MIG) (which has enabled the government to introduce differential rates of income support for working- and pension-age populations). Finally, in 2000, the government announced a further element, the pension credit. The guarantee element of the pension credit will subsume MIG and the credit element will act as a complement to MIG. The pension credit, legislated in 2002, will come into effect in autumn 2003. The reformed system will therefore consist of at least seven elements (Table 10.2).

How well will the post-1998 pension system deliver in terms of some of the criteria identified above? Most people would agree that the provision of an income in retirement that is 'adequate' to lift people over the poverty line must be the primary objective of pensions policy. Indeed, the 1998 Green Paper explicitly aimed to reduce pensioner poverty and to deliver a 'secure' retirement for all.

New Labour's pension settlement: delivering adequate pensions?

In assessing the success of the 1998 reforms in delivering adequate pensions, it is important to distinguish between today's and tomorrow's pensioners. First, looking at today's pensioners, the government has chosen to target increases in state provision via the means-tested MIG rather than through an enhanced level of the BSP. Implicit in this choice is the extension of means testing of state provision in later life. The weekly rate of MIG in April 2003 was £100 for a single person. It is striking that this is equivalent to around 20 per cent of average earnings – that is, the level at which the BSP would have been if the link with earnings had not been broken in 1981.

The Chancellor has stated that the MIG will rise in line with earnings for the duration of the current parliament. Thus, from 2003, MIG will be just above the official relative poverty line (half mean household income after housing costs) – with the outcome that pensioner poverty (as defined by the government) will be effectively abolished. This move is to be welcomed, but it is important to note that this assumes that there will be 100 per cent take-up of entitlement – take-up of benefits is known to be lower among pensioners than among the population as a whole. Depending on how it is calculated, figures for 1999/2000 suggest that between 22 and 36 per cent of entitled pensioners failed to claim the means-tested payments they were entitled to, compared with between 13 and 23 per cent of the population as a whole (DWP, 2001). While some of these people would have been missing out on relatively small amounts and so may have thought it not worthwhile claiming, the average weekly amounts of £22 unclaimed were not trivial. In total between £420 million and £940 million went unclaimed. Using data from the Family Resources Survey, about

Table 10.2: The reformed pension system to come into effect in autumn 2003

Pre-1998	Post-1998
First tier state provision • Basic state pension • Income support	• Basic state pension • 1999-2003 Minimum income guarantee • 2003 onwards pension credit (incorporating a guarantee and saving element)
Second tier compulsory options • SERPS • Occupational pensions • Personal pensions	 • (accumulated entitlements under SERPS) • State second pension • Occupational pensions • Stakeholder pensions • Personal pensions
Third tier voluntary options • AVCs	 • AVCs

60 per cent of the non-claimants were over the age of 75 and just over half were living in households in the bottom fifth of the income distribution. An additional £22 a week would make a big difference to the living standards of these people.

As well as the issue of take-up, there are also concerns that a more generous MIG might undermine incentives to save. People who have worked all their lives but who have accumulated only relatively small pension entitlements may end up with an income in retirement that is only a little higher than the MIG. And their income may end up being lower than their neighbour who claims MIG after the value of other passported benefits are taken into account – the so-called 'occupational pension poverty trap'. As the MIG now looks set to rise in line with earnings and BSP with prices, the gap between them will widen over time, increasing the width of the pensions poverty trap. As a response to this, the government has introduced the pension credit (PC), which effectively introduces a taper to MIG but also adds another layer of complexity to the system. Whether new initiatives within the Department for Work and Pensions (National Audit Office, 2002) combined with the introduction of the PC will overcome the problems of take-up and incentives has yet to be determined, but it is likely that significant numbers of older people will remain on low incomes into the foreseeable future.

What about tomorrow's pensioners? The vehicle 'chosen' to deliver adequate incomes in later life to those currently on low pay (those earning less than £10,000 per annum), is the state second pension (S2P). The S2P target group primarily consists of women and manual workers; in 2000, 5 per cent of all male employees and 16 per cent of all women earned less than £10,000. However, 42 per cent of female manual workers and 7 per cent of male manual workers fell into this group (ONS, 2002c).

It remains questionable whether the S2P will indeed deliver an adequate income to these groups when they enter retirement. Previous work investigating the effectiveness of the government's proposals in protecting individuals from a means-tested old age (Rake et al, 1999) estimated that S2P in combination with the basic state pension would provide an income equivalent to just £1 above the basic MIG. Since the time that article was written, the value of MIG has benefited by increases above the rate of real earnings growth. These increases in MIG are to be welcomed in terms of helping to alleviate poverty among today's pensioners. However, increases in the real value of MIG, combined with the government's aspirations to index the PC to earnings growth while leaving BSP and S2P indexed to prices, mean that by 2050 anyone with income from BSP and S2P alone will automatically fall into means testing. Projections by the government Actuary's Department suggest that BSP will be worth 7.5 per cent of average male earnings in 2050 and that the flat-rate S2P will be worth around 10.4 per cent. This implies that together, BSP and S2P will be worth just 17.9 per cent of average male earnings, that is, below the current value of MIG (20 per cent of average male earnings). This raises real questions about the purpose of the state second pension and its relationship with other tiers of the pension system.

Furthermore, S2P will do nothing to solve the issue of providing better coverage to the self-employed (who are not compelled to contribute) or of providing coverage to those not covered by national insurance because of very low/seasonal earnings. In 1998, some 2 million women were below the lower earnings limit, although hopefully this will be fewer today as a result of the minimum wage (McKnight et al, 1998).

New Labour's pension settlement: protecting incentives and providing a reward for saving?

The new pension credit, to be introduced in October 2003, will modify the structure of mean testing for older people by tapering the withdrawal of benefits as pension income rises. Although this will increase income and reward savings for some pensioners, it may actually result in perverse incentives *not* to save for others. By setting the PC threshold at the rate of the full BSP, the credit element will not enhance the incomes of anyone with less than full entitlement and a modest amount of additional savings or pension. This will affect women in particular, as they are most likely to be unable to accrue a full basic pension. Currently 51 per cent of women do not have a direct claim for a full BSP, and research using the Family and Working Lives Survey indicates that significant numbers of women, particularly those that have cared for children and dependent adults, will continue to lack full entitlements in the future (McKay et al, 2000). Forty per cent of women still earn an individual income of £100 or less per week (ONS, 2002c). For these women, who have other immediate demands upon their money, it will make little economic sense to make additional pension savings, as any such savings will be 'wasted'.

This situation may be further exacerbated by the limits placed on credits into S2P, which unlike the current system of home responsibility protection for the BSP, only allow for credits for childcare up to the child's sixth birthday. Furthermore, there are no credits into S2P for unemployment and so increasing numbers of men may also be affected. It is likely that many of those with only partial entitlement to S2P will find that their contributions will not yield any additional income over and above the level of the guarantee element of PC.

The introduction of the PC, with mean-tested thresholds linked to earnings while other retirement income (BSP, most occupational pensions and annuity income from personal pensions) remain linked to prices, will extend means testing in retirement further up the income distribution than previously. Simulations by the Pensions Policy Institute suggest that someone retiring at 65 in 2003 with an income of £100 in *addition* to their full BSP[3] would be entitled to PC after just ten years – despite starting retirement with an income significantly above the PC level (PPI, 2003). And as the gap between PC and BSP widens in the future, more and more people will experience a means-tested old age. Research by PricewaterhouseCoopers suggests that, if current uprating conventions continue, by 2037 someone who enjoyed average earnings throughout their working life would be entitled to PC as soon as they retired at 65 (PwC, 2001).

New Labour's pension settlement: improving transparency?

The new Partnership in Pensions has involved grafting on new mechanisms to a system that was already complex. We would argue that has reduced rather than increased transparency. With the bewildering array of choices to be made, there is now a very real fear among pensions analysts that many young people will make the 'wrong' decision or indeed decide not to save in a pension at all.

In a highly complex pension market there are now at least seven distinct vehicles for providing income in later life. This bewildering choice means that many people may end up with a pension that is inappropriate for their circumstances. At first sight, the 1 per cent cap on charges in stakeholder pensions works in favour of the consumer, ensuring a low-cost pension product and transparent charging structure. However, financial advice will be the casualty of this capping, as the 1 per cent leaves no scope for pension providers to make advice available. Thus financial advice has been squeezed out at a time when people are in need of more information than ever. The large pension providers have already begun to lay off their direct sales teams, contributing further to the advice vacuum.

What is more, for people to make the best choice possible they require information on both their current circumstances and their future earnings and employment patterns. Without a crystal ball, it is likely that the increase in pension choice will lead to more pension mistakes. For those on low pay, and especially those who take time out of the labour market to care or who experience unemployment, it is questionable whether 'stakeholders' will provide the best vehicle. Such people may be better off remaining in the state system or indeed putting their money into an Individual Savings Account, which offers flexibility for a rainy day.

The problem of people 'under-saving' for retirement was highlighted in the 2002 Green Paper *Simplicity, security and choice* (DWP, 2002a). However, the proposals put forward in the new Green Paper concentrate almost exclusively on simplifying the taxation systems and financial products rather than the system as a whole. While the proposals to simplify the taxation of pensions in order to "promote greater transparency, flexibility and consistency of treatment" (DWP, 2002a, p 39) is to be welcomed, we would argue that the primary beneficiaries of these changes will be financial advisers and pension scheme administrators and that any changes are unlikely to provide a substantial stimulus to individual saving.

New Labour's pension settlement: promoting long-term sustainability?

Given all the issues outlined above, we believe that there are real issues regarding the long-term sustainability of the post-1998 system. In particular, there are political risks in that the system now has many separate vehicles, making it very easy for a government in search of budgetary savings to 'pick off' small parts of the pension system. This is a particular problem for the state second pension, which is targeted on the lifetime poor, who have a weak political voice and may not be able to defend it.

There is also a real issue with regard to the overall coherence of the reforms. Since these have been introduced on a piecemeal basis, it has been difficult to evaluate the impact of the whole package; for example, legislation for stakeholder pensions was introduced before the consultation on the 1998 Green Paper had even closed, and the consultation on the pension credit was initiated before details of S2P were published. But now it is clear how all the pieces fit together, it is also clear that there are a number of inconsistencies between the different parts of the system. Finally, we would argue that the system has been designed without due regard to the future and how the package will work across people's lifetimes. Looking into the future, it is evident that most people on S2P or SHP will fall into means testing at some point during their retirement (Falkingham et al, 2002). Surprisingly, like SERPS in 1974, there have been no detailed government forecasts of the future costs of the pension credit. However, it is estimated that by 2025 a staggering 75 per cent of pensioners will be entitled to some means-tested PC and that this will rise to 82 per cent by 2050 (Clark and Emerson, 2002). Work by John Hawksworth of PricewaterhouseCoopers estimates that the additional cost of the savings credit element in PC, over and above the cost of MIG, will amount to 1.2 per cent of GDP in 2050 (Hawksworth, 2002). Reform was swift as soon as Norman Fowler and colleagues realised the real cost of SERPS. It may not be long before Andrew Smith and Gordon Brown follow their example.

Back to the future

So what should any future reform do? First, it is worth reiterating that by their very nature pensions require planning and stability over a longer period than the normal life of a government. Pensions policy is the oil tanker of social policy and needs careful navigating. Second, any reform must bear in mind that we need a system that will deliver both for today's older population and tomorrow's. Given that the majority of today's poorest pensioners are women, it must also deliver equally for them as for men.

One 'radical' option that is gaining currency in the academic and policy world outside Westminster is to 'go back to basics' and to raise the basic state pension to the level of MIG and index its value to earnings. It has been estimated that this would raise direct spending on pensions to 8.5 per cent of GDP in 2050 (Hawksworth, 2002). Although higher than the government's plan of 6 per cent, this is still lower than in all other EU countries. Such a move would score highly on the objectives of securing an adequate pension for all and maintaining incentives for savings. It would also be transparent, administratively efficient and would be popular with the electorate. If this move were combined with reform of eligibility criteria for the BSP, including the abolition of the 25 per cent rule[4] and the lower earnings limit, the relaxation of the definition of a contribution year to allow the aggregation of part years or part-time work, and the redesign of pension credits for caring to positively reward caring, it would result in a BSP that recognised the different working lives of women and men. Such a reform would truly deliver, in the words of Mr Blair, "dramatically better pension provision for … those unable to work because they are caring for children or a relative who is ill or disabled", and ensure that "everyone can look forward to a secure retirement" (DSS, 1998, p iii). Perhaps now is the time for New Labour to start 'thinking the unthinkable'.

Acknowledgements

The research is part of the ESRC SAGE (Simulating Policy for an Ageing Society) Research Group (sage@lse.ac.uk) funded under grant number M565-21-1001.

Notes

[1] Co-Director ESRC Research Group *Simulating Social Policy for an Ageing Society*. Professor of Demography & International Social Policy, University of Southampton.

[2] Co-Director ESRC Research Group *Simulating Social Policy for an Ageing Society*. Director of the Fawcett Society. This chapter was written while at the London School of Economics and Political Science and the views expressed in it do not necessarily reflect those of the Fawcett Society.

[3] An amount that is broadly equivalent to average net income before housing costs of a single recently retired pensioner.

[4] The 25 per cent rule means that anyone with entitlement to less than 25 per cent of the full BSP gets nothing – and hence any NI contributions they have made are effectively wasted.

References

Bebbington, A. and Comas-Herrera, A. (2000) *Healthy life expectancy: Trends to 1998 and the implications for long term care costs*, Personal Social Services Research Unit Discussion Paper 1695, London: London School of Economics and Political Science.

Catalyst (2002) *The challenge of longer life: Economic burden or social opportunity?*, The report of the Working Group on the Implications of Demographic Change, December, London: Catalyst.

Clark, T. and Emmerson, C. (2002) *The tax and benefit system and the decision to invest in a stakeholder pension*, Institute for Fiscal Studies, briefing note no 28, London: Institute for Fiscal Studies.

DSS (Department of Social Security) (1998) *A new contract for welfare: Partnership in pensions*, Cm 4179, London: The Stationery Office.

DWP (Department for Work and Pensions) (2001) *Income related benefits: Estimates of take up in 1999-2000*, London: Analytical Services Division, DWP.

DWP (2002a) *Simplicity, security and choice: Working and saving for retirement*, Cm 5677, London: The Stationery Office.

DWP (2002b) *Pensioners' income series 2000/01*, London: DWP.

DWP (2002c) *Household below average income 1994/5-2000/01*, London: DWP.

Evandrou, M. (1997) *Baby boomers: Ageing in the 21st century*, London: Age Concern Books.

Evandrou, M. and Falkingham, J. (2000) 'Looking back to look forward: lessons from four birth cohorts for ageing in the 21st century', *Population Trends*, vol 99, spring, pp 21-30, London: The Stationery Office.

Falkingham, J. (1989) 'Dependency and ageing in Britain: a re-examination of the evidence', *Journal of Social Policy*, vol 18, no 2, pp 211-33.

Falkingham, J., Rake, K. and Paxton, W. (2002) 'Modelling pension choices for the 21st century', in R. Brooks, S. Regan and P. Robinson (eds) *A new contract for retirement: Modelling policy options to 2050*, London: IPPR, pp 35-64.

Glennerster, H. (1999) 'Which welfare states are likely to survive?', *International Journal of Social Welfare*, vol 8, pp 2-13.

GAD (Government Actuary's Department) (1999) *National insurance fund long-term financial estimates*, Cm 4406, London: The Stationery Office.

GAD (2001) *Occupational pension schemes 1995 – tenth survey by the Government Actuary*, London: The Stationery Office.

Hawksworth, J. (2002) 'UK state pensions policy at the crossroads', in R. Brooks, S. Regan and P. Robinson (eds) *A new contract for retirement: Modelling policy options to 2050*, London: IPPR, pp 9-34.

Hills, J. (1997) *The future of welfare: A guide to the debate*, York: Joseph Rowntree Foundation.

Johnson P. and Falkingham, J. (1992) *Ageing and economic welfare*, London: Sage Publications.

McKay, S., Heaver, C. and Walker, R. (2000) *Building up pension rights*, DSS Research Report no 14, London: DSS.

McKnight, A., Elias, P. and Wilson, R. (1998) *Low pay and the national insurance system: A statistical picture*, Manchester: Equal Opportunities Commission.

Mullan, P. (2000) *The imaginary time bomb: Why an ageing population is not a social problem*, London: I.B. Tauruis.

National Audit office (2002) *Tackling pensioner poverty: Encouraging take-up of entitlements*, report by the Comptroller and Auditor General, HC31 Session 2002–2003, London: The Stationery Office.

O'Connell, A. (2002) *Raising state pension age: Are we ready?*, London: Pensions Policy Institute.

OECD (Organisation for Economic Co-operation and Development) (2000) *Reforms for an ageing society*, Paris: OECD.

ONS (Office for National Statistics) (2001) *Living in Britain: Results from the 2000 General Household Survey*, London: The Stationery Office.

ONS (2002a) *National population projections 2000-based*, Series PP2, no 23, London: The Stationery Office.

ONS (2002b) *Population trends*, no 110, winter, London: The Stationery Office.

ONS (2002c) *New earnings survey 2002*, London: The Stationery Office.

Parker, H. (ed) (2000) *Low Cost but Acceptable incomes for older people: A minimum income standard for households aged 65-74 years in the UK*, Bristol: The Policy Press.

Parker, H. (ed) (2002) *Modest but adequate: A reasonable living standard for households aged 66-74*, York: Joseph Rowntree Foundation/Age Concern.

PPI (Pensions Policy Institute) (2003) *The pension landscape*, London: PPI.

PwC (Pricewaterhouse Coopers) (2001) *Live long, die poor? Pensions projections for the millennial generation*, press release (www.pwcglobal.com/extweb/ncpressrelease.nsf/DocID/3F28EFAC6A6845B780256C4D004F90EA).

Rake, K., Falkingham, J. and Evans, M. (1999) '*Tightropes and tripwires: New Labour's proposals and means-testing in old age*', Centre for Analysis of Social Exclusion discussion paper no 23, London School of Economics and Political Science.

SCSS (Select Committee on Social Security) (2000) *Select Committee on Social Security 7th report – pensioner poverty*, London: House of Commons.

Trotsky, L. (1935, 1958) *Trotsky's diary in exile – 1935*, Translation published in 1958, Cambridge MA: Harvard University Press.

Warnes, A. (1996) 'The demography of old age: panic versus reality', in R. Bland (ed) *Developing services for older people and their families*, London: Jessica Kingsley, pp 26-42.

World Bank (1994) *Averting the old age crisis*, New York: Oxford University Press.

The schlock[1] and the new: risk, reflexivity and retirement[2]

Kirk Mann

Introduction

This chapter explores questions of agency and social structure in relation to retirement and pensions policy. Some sociological accounts of risk, reflexivity, identity, 'lifestyle' and consumption are contrasted with structural features of contemporary capitalist societies; pension funds and their investment strategies, risk management, and the significance of these funds in the money markets.[3] It will be claimed that there are tensions between these 'new' – or at least new to social policy – sociological approaches and the 'older' ideas and traditions within social policy. However, by considering retirement in the context of risk, identity and reflexivity we can try to evaluate the usefulness of both the 'old' (the schlock) social policy approaches and the new as we rethink social policy (Lewis et al, 2000). Viewing social policy through these 'new' lenses can provide some fresh insights and important challenges. Simultaneously, they may obscure some older sociological landmarks that structure opportunities and restrain reflexivity (Giddens, 1991, 1994, 1998; Beck, 1992, 2000; Adam et al, 2000; Mann, 2001; Taylor-Gooby, 2001).

Changes and chances in a risk society

Over a quarter of a century ago (so hardly very new) Baudrillard (1975, p 144) suggested people are "mobilised as consumers, their needs become as essential as their labour power". And in the context of retirement Mike Featherstone observed 16 years ago that "Pre-retirement planning today is presented as the management of life-style and consumption opportunities to enable retirement to be a progressive set of options and choices" (1987, p 134). However, for most of the 20th century pensioners were assumed (erroneously perhaps) to have rather modest expectations and despite the evidence of relative poverty there was an oft-stated commitment to a universal pension funded by revenue collected by the state (Abel-Smith and Townsend, 1965; Townsend, 1979). Retirees were generally portrayed as deserving and their welfare dependency rarely evoked criticism. Yet by the last quarter of the 20th century some retirees appeared to be quite comfortably off, while some (paid) workers were noticeably struggling on low incomes. Retirees appeared to have higher expectations of what their retirement lifestyle would be like and many seemed reluctant to wait until they reached the state pension age before enjoying their retirement (PIU, 2000). This shift in expectations and lifestyles provides a major challenge to the traditional 'universal' models of welfare (the schlock?) and requires social policy to consider some of the new(ish) ideas that offer a response.

There are a number of indicators that could be used to show how expectations have changed but two basic trends should suffice – first, the trend towards early retirement and, second, the rising incomes of retirees particularly those that have occupational (defined benefit or DB) pensions.

By the start of the 21st century the average age of retirement for men in most OECD countries was closer to 60 than 65 and for women closer to 58. Between 1975 and 1995 male labour force participation rates fell dramatically with alarming predictions about the labour force to dependency ratio (OECD, 1998; Visco, 2001). Undoubtedly, a significant proportion of that fall was due to enforced retirement that often concealed unemployment, but for some it marked a welcome end to their paid working life (Castles, 1997; Tanner, 1997).

Nevertheless, it is plain that for recent retirees the provision of occupationally related pensions (mainly defined benefit schemes) and fiscal welfare (tax privileges for AVCs, FSAVCs[4]) has had a significant and positive impact. Indeed, "The average income of pensioners is known to have increased by 70% between 1979 and 1997, which is considerably faster than average wages" (Walker with Howard, 2000, p 263). The increase has not been uniform across the pensioner population and for those that have to rely exclusively on public welfare the picture is far from rosy. Nevertheless, 64 per cent of recent retirees (that is, since 1996) will be receiving an occupational pension, although again the amounts will vary considerably. With the decline in final salary schemes since the 1980s, and many employers recently closing such schemes altogether, the upward trend in pensioner incomes may soon come to an abrupt end. The evidence is inconclusive but it seems fairly clear that only a small minority feel they can trust the state to meet their retirement needs and expectations in the future.[5] This may be a response to alarmist fears that successive governments have raised but, in part, it may also reflect the success of the private pensions industry in promoting its products.

Positive images and reflexive identities

The private pensions market, including the annuities, life assurance and company-based defined contribution schemes, have also played a part in changing popular perceptions of retirees (Sawchuk, 1995; Aldridge, 1997). For example, adverts by the Prudential had a pensioner riding a Harley Davidson; Egg used a picture of young clubbers; Standard Life's baby, 'James', showed it is never too early to start saving; Scottish Widows' attractive woman made pensions simple; and in

Australia BT Fund Management's double-page spreads banner headlined: "SUPERANNUATION SCARES MOST PEOPLE. AS ALWAYS, FORTUNE FAVOURS THE BRAVE". Unsurprisingly, sellers of pension and savings products promote the benefits of being retired and use positive images of retirement that will be yours if you save with them, although they often exclude images of older old people.

However complicated pensions may seem, the message is clear: a private pension ensures the consumer is planning and making choices. Pension products like other commodities have to engage with the lifestyle and identity of those they are aimed at. These images appear to endorse Giddens' claim that; "... lifestyle choice is increasingly important in the constitution of self-identity and daily activity. Reflexively organised life-planning, which normally presumes consideration of risks as filtered through contact with expert knowledge, becomes a central feature of structuring self-identity" (1991, p 5). Thus people with private pensions want to be in control of their own lives, not dependent on others. Self-reliance is good, dependency bad. Pensions have been repackaged, made 'sexy', ironic and accessible. They are part of our life-planning project, sold by engaging both with our current lifestyle and those we hope to enjoy when retired.

There is an ambiguity in the way that pensioners are being portrayed that needs to be highlighted. On the one hand the images are more positive, less likely to portray frail, childlike characters (Hockey and James, 1993; Featherstone and Hepworth, 1995). There are also more diverse lifestyles and images being presented. In many respects such images might be applauded. On the other hand it presumes that everyone is capable of making rational choices about complex goods and services (Aldridge, 1997). These images make the private pensions carrot appear irresistible and the prospect of living on the state pension a sharp stick prodding us towards the 'obvious' choice. The adverts also reinforce the idea of the 'heroic consumer' but, as Warde (1994) makes plain, the assumption that consumers construct their own lifestyles, that they embark on a lifetime project that involves the presentation of themselves to the world, cannot be taken at face value.

Against this picture of a restructuring of the balance between paid work, consumption and leisure – all fuelled by reflexively informed individuals – it is necessary to reconsider, to reflect, on some traditional questions. Thus the social context within which consumers operate, the constraints on reflexivity and the hierarchy of risks that different social groups confront, all need to be borne in mind.

No more heroes?

For Giddens, whose influence should not be underestimated, the concept of a 'pensioner' and of a fixed age of retirement typify the rigidity of 'universalism' serving to identify and exclude older people:

Old age at sixty-five is a creation, pure and simple, of the welfare state. It is a form of welfare dependency much more widespread than any of the dependencies noted by the rightist interpreters of the underclass (1994, p 170). [And]: A society that separates older people from the majority in a retirement ghetto cannot be called inclusive. (1998, p 120)

Giddens sees the state excluding older workers and discusses the marginalisation of older people, while recognising their desire to be fully active citizens and their potential to contribute to society. He also feels that once they break out of their 'dependency ghetto' they may achieve greater political influence (1994, p 188). Unlocking the chains of welfare dependency is therefore a key feature of his (1994) account. Unfortunately blocking the road to the 'Third Way' (1998) are some traditional obstacles, not least of which are the expectations of retirees and prospective retirees:

> Once established, benefits have their own autonomy ... expectations become 'locked in' and interest groups entrenched. Countries that have tried to reform their pensions systems, for example, have met with concerted resistance. We should have our pensions because we are 'old' (at age 60 or 65), we have paid our dues (even if they don't cover the costs), other people before have had them, everyone looks forward to retirement and so forth. Yet such institutional stasis is in and of itself a reflection of the need for reform..... (Giddens, 1998, pp 115-16)

Quite why pensioners and people looking forward to retirement should be so obstructive, given that they would be liberated from welfare dependency, is unclear. Moreover, if marginalisation and exclusion typify the situation of older people as he claims, it seems unlikely that they are simultaneously so politically powerful they can prevent reform – which he believes would be in the interests of pensioners themselves. By claiming that he understands what is in the interests of pensioners, but that they are unable to appreciate this fact, Giddens reproduces one of the oldest and most negative political traditions. He does not say pensioners are suffering from 'false consciousness' but he certainly implies it. Worse still, the fact that they dare to object to reforms is further evidence that reforms are necessary. Such authoritarianism sits uneasily alongside his suggestion that welfare reforms be underpinned by individuals with a more reflexive, thoughtful and positive sense of their own welfare needs, and of their 'selves' (1991, 1994, 1998). However, Giddens highlights two other features of a post-traditional society that merit further attention; risk and identity.

Risk

Risk and how it is addressed is significant for post-traditional approaches and social policy for four main reasons:

It is claimed that traditional responses to risk are no longer appropriate.

- A key factor highlighting the point above, developed societies are themselves less predictable. Change and flux typify society today. Faith in the ability of the state or scientific experts to manage risk on our behalf has therefore diminished.
- As a consequence of the above, people must anticipate and address risk. Whether this is best achieved by collectively sharing the responsibilities and costs of a risk society, or instead by individuation, becomes a crucial issue.
- Traditional definitions of risk, premised on technical measures, neglect the social construction of these and of the risks themselves. This in turn poses fundamental questions about the way we define welfare and well-being.

These four features of a post-traditional society are difficult to disentangle and they combine to pose advocates of universal public welfare provisions a major challenge (Culpitt, 1999; Kemshall, 2002).

Public welfare provisions provide clear examples of how traditional perceptions of risk are inadequate and how difficult it now seems to find solutions. Responsibility for protecting populations against the risks of modernity was assumed by the state in most countries during the 20th century. Public welfare was aimed, primarily, at protecting men as wage earners and women as mothers until they retired. However, these narrow welfare categories were premised on a view of family and social life that appear to be misplaced. Life expectancy has increased dramatically, fertility rates have declined, industrial restructuring means very few manual workers can expect a job for life, divorce rates have soared, many households and 'families' no longer conform to the heterosexual 'nuclear' norm and many women's relationship to paid labour has changed (Lewis et al, 2000).

Moreover, contemporary developed societies have as a by-product of their successes generated many new and different risks. For example, extending civil and social rights has enabled some women to escape from traditional authoritarian family forms. However, state-run welfare schemes have inadequately covered the new risks associated with, for example, divorce or lone parenthood. The reconfiguration of 'families' that is often seen as a key feature of a post-traditional society is not addressed by traditional welfare solutions predicated on the (insured) male 'breadwinner'.

In their responses to change governments have often added to the uncertainty that many people feel as they approach retirement. Changes to benefit rules, new types of benefits for specific groups, changing and even scrapping the retirement age, trimming entitlements that were 'earned' through insurance contributions and tinkering with the tax liabilities of pensioners have generated further uncertainty, fears and insecurities. Trying to plan for retirement has become increasingly complex and not surprisingly only a minority in the UK feel able to do so with confidence (Boaz et al, 1999). Often it seems that the rules change to suit whatever the economic situation demands, particularly the demand for labour and the level of unemployment. Even planning when to retire is fraught with uncertainty and the constant moving of the goalposts is not peculiar to the UK (Guillemard and Gunsteren, 1991). Individuals must try to anticipate pensions policy, rule changes, and stock market behaviour over the next 10-30 years if they are to make meaningful choices. Good luck, rather than prudent planning, is what the individual needs. This, in turn, creates situations where people of similar ages, work histories and expectations can find they have very different income levels because one person may have realised an opportunity and another 'missed' it. Unsurprisingly post-traditional societies have witnessed a loss of faith in the 'universal' welfare state.

Occupational pensions also began life with a male 'breadwinner' in mind and assumed transfers were from working husbands to dependent wives. For most of the 20th century the actuarial calculations they relied on assumed that the membership were male and on the death of the member any derived benefits would go to widows. Whereas a widow is usually entitled to a proportion of her husband's occupational pension, typically in the region of 60 per cent in a defined benefit scheme, if the 'dependent' spouse of the occupational (DB) pensioner dies, the pension is not reduced, since it 'belongs' to the person who 'earned' it. This apparently benign method of calculating benefits is one reason why women currently have lower incomes in retirement than men, even when they are not relying solely on the state pension (Arber, 1995). These assumptions have had to be revised in the light of women's increased labour force participation in the last quarter of the 20th century. Many more women have accessed occupational pensions, particularly in the public sector, and they will be claiming their full pension for longer than their male colleagues. Consequently the Pickering Report (2002) suggests that derived benefits should be scrapped. This too would reinforce the trend towards individual welfare 'rights', although in this case undermining income transfer arrangements within households (informal welfare) that a great many women have relied upon in order to access occupational welfare.

For many employers in the private sector the prospect of not being able to meet their future pension commitments, in part because they were premised on misplaced assumptions, has encouraged a move to defined contribution (DC) schemes. This change means employers carry little or no risk because the fund will usually be operated by an insurance company. Risk is, therefore, a central concern of the personal and occupational pension providers. By grouping scheme members in terms of age, sex, occupation, and lifestyle behaviours it is possible to calculate the risk of them surviving or, if in a life insurance scheme, of dying. Thus the Association of British Insurers (ABI, 1995) discusses risk largely in terms of the problem that the pensioner poses – will they live to or beyond the projected life expectancy? Whereas anyone contributing to a pension scheme hopes to live to a ripe old age, collecting their pension for longer than the provider had anticipated, the pensions industry relies on their customers dying. However, providers must also consider 'inflation risk': the risk of the funds being incapable of matching inflation and not delivering the anticipated pension; a great deal, too, hinges on how the funds perform in the finance and stock markets. If there is a lengthy period of slow growth it is plain that occupational and personal pension providers run the risk of overcommitting themselves. While the long-term nature of the investment portfolios of the pension funds hedges their bets they are, nevertheless, engaged in some very risky activities (Deaton, 1989; Minns, 2001). They are also central to the operation of finance capital and inherently exclusive.

Exclusion

A measure of exclusion is built into private and occupational schemes due to the way the labour market and pension funds operate. Among these inherent limitations are actuarial assumptions based on length of employment, contribution records and age of retirement, access to the sort of paid work that provides a pension, discrimination within, and the imperfections of, the labour market, employer demands for a more flexible workforce, more part-timers and fewer people on permanent contracts. Most significantly, of course, occupationally related pensions and provisions predicated on labour market access offers nothing to those whose work is unpaid, again affecting mainly women. The inability of the poorest to make large and reliable savings contributions means the private pensions market has historically been reluctant to cater for the poorest 20 per cent of the prospective pensioner population. Simultaneously, private providers are actively opposed to the state competing in the market (Glennerster, 1991; Hamill, 2002).

Pension funds now play a central part in the corporate and finance markets. In Britain in 1963 pension fund assets were 7 per cent of all UK equities, but by 2001 the Myners review, undertaken on behalf of the British government, stated that "UK institutional investors own more than £1,500 billion of assets – over half the quoted equity markets" (Myners, 2001, p 4), a figure that is more than double the size of the US's GDP for 1998. Despite their supposedly conservative investment strategies the growth of the pension funds has been incredible: between 1990 and 1995 the annual rate of growth was 8.9-11.3 per cent (Minns, 2001, p 26). The effect of reforms to the pension system is illustrated by events in Australia. In the early 1980s Australia had one of the lowest per capita savings of any OECD country, but the development of occupationally based superannuation schemes, culminating in the introduction by the Labor government of the 1992 Superannuation Guarantee Charge Bill quickly changed that. Australia's former Federal Treasury Minister, Ralph Willis, stated that "Importantly for the future of Australia, retirement savings are providing an increasing pool of patient capital to support the productive investment that is crucial to sustaining Australia's economic growth and prosperity" (cited in Olsberg, 1997, p 161).

Pensions funds are clearly of considerable structural significance for the finance markets. Consequently any discussion of agency, consumption, lifestyle 'choice' and identity must bear in mind these phenomenal resources. It is, therefore, also vital to consider briefly how financial institutions, fund and investment managers, and pension experts address questions of risk. The sheer size of the funds, persistent queries and contests over their ownership and control, the contrasting functions they must perform and the impact of institutional investment strategies on the finance markets, impose very real limits on what governments feel they can do (Minns, 2001). Simultaneously contests over fund control are likely to intensify because the activities of the funds pose ethical and political questions that some members and trustees will raise. The process may be exacerbated by pressure groups campaigning on ethical investment issues such as the environment, animal welfare, arms trading and so on.

The growth of institutional investment funds as a proportion of all investment funding is also significant because it changes the balance of power within finance capital as a consequence of the concentration and centralisation of pension fund assets. Although concentration and centralisation are different processes, both have the effect of reducing the options for those who seek capital for investment purposes and as such 'distort' the money markets. They are likely to steer investment into areas that are perceived as 'sound' and are unlikely to commit much of their portfolio to entrepreneurial projects (Deaton, 1989). Competition in the finance market is reduced and the impact of investment decisions can then affect other features of the economy. One consequence is that key decisions over savings and investment become institutionalised.

As the pension funds' control of the industrial sector is increased so their fortunes (literally) are tied to the performance of that sector globally. The temptation and tendency for these institutional investors to intervene directly in the strategic decisions of the industrial sector is, therefore, also likely to increase, with the concomitant reduction in any 'real' market forces influencing events. Indeed, the Myners review recommended legislation similar to that in place in the US, which places a duty on "... managers to intervene in companies – by voting or otherwise – where there is a reasonable expectation that doing so might raise the value of the investment" (2001, p 14). In these circumstances investment decisions increasingly look like political decisions, reflecting the ability of powerful elites to mobilise support or agreement for their preferred policy, but once again they raise the possibility for challenges and conflict (Deaton, 1989).

Furthermore, insurance principles, whether the state, insurance companies or occupational pension funds apply them, necessarily involve various techniques of surveillance and specific forms of knowledge. Ewald (1991) illustrates the way that expert knowledge, discourse and power can combine to discipline insured populations. He identifies three economic and financial techniques that developed to enable 'risks' to be insured. First, the techniques had to be rational and demonstrable, thereby disciplining the providers, regulating the insurance market and ensuring a 'level playing field'.

"Second, insurance is a moral technology. To calculate risk is to master time, to discipline the future" (Ewald, 1991, p 207). Prudence, providence and planning impose a severe discipline on many people who feel they must defer pleasure today for security tomorrow. Governments may pronounce their belief in 'choice' (DWP, 2002) but they have been quick to compel compliance among sections of the population deemed to have made the wrong choices. State compulsory 'saving' is complemented by insurers who penalise behaviour they have identified as 'risky'. The appearance of control over fate is possible for those that plan and save and the prudent (cautious and non-risk taking) are therefore defined as deserving.

Those who save for their retirement through insurance schemes also rely on Ewald's third 'technique' of reparation and indemnification. Insurance operates as a system of justice that purports to share risks and redistribute resources according to equitable rules. He states that "The combination of these different dimensions makes insurance a *political technology*.... Insurance makes it possible to dream of contractual justice.... Insurance makes it possible to envisage a solution to the problem of poverty and working class insecurity" (Ewald, 1991, p 207).

The net effect is profoundly misleading; creating a sense of security, whether real or not, defining some forms of behaviour as undeserving and therefore potentially subject to being disciplined, promoting retirement dreams that can not be realised, and creating an illusion of equity and justice when this only applies within the insured population. Although writing of insurance schemes, Ewald's points apply well to the different forms of retirement pension. The various constituent populations of the social divisions of welfare (SDW) are rarely aware of their respective subject identities and how these are framed by the technologies applied to them. They are, however, made aware that their behaviour – their ability to conform to a prudent lifestyle – will enable some to enjoy richer dreams and a better retirement deal than others.

Genetic testing offers the prospect of even more reliable data that could see providers offering benefits tailored to the individual's propensity for illness, disability or death. The fund managers' journal *Pensions World* (December, 2000) speculated that if testing became standard practice, occupational pension funds might wish to exclude certain 'impaired lives' and on this basis employers might also refuse them the job. In contrast life annuity policies might be more generous for those who can be identified as at 'more risk'.

There are powerful pressures to allow testing in the UK and reports of some insurance companies breaking the current restrictions amid government "fears they may create a genetic underclass" (*The Observer*, 8 April 2001). The implications of genetic testing, bearing in mind the overlapping histories of eugenics and social science, are particularly worrying for disabled people and certain ethnic minorities (Dyson, 1999). However, in a global financial market it is not clear that current restrictions can be sustained. According to David Damant (1992, p 7):[6]

> We are in the presence of [a] very definite revolution in investment analysis and portfolio construction.... [And] The change in the way the subject is viewed will be as different as the way in which the structure of societies was viewed after the French Revolution....

The key factors in this revolution are: the globalisation of finance markets; new information technologies; and the development of new theories regarding portfolio and investment modelling. These changes are intimately connected and they are transforming working practices, concepts and assumptions about retirement savings. We are witnessing a very risky historical period for the institutions that manage retirement pensions. What is less clear is how the reflexive individual on a low income might anticipate and respond positively to changes.

The risky society?

Ulrich Beck (1992, 2000) has also drawn attention to the way that technical, scientific measures of risk tend to neglect social factors. Thus the ABI discuss longevity risk, accumulation risk and inflation risk. These are essentially measures of average and general trends for particular social groups, and types of investment, under certain presumed circumstances. In reality these basic measurements cannot be accurately predicted and are well-informed estimates. The ability to assess risks is further complicated for the layperson because risk occurs at various points in the life of a pension. The prospective retiree must consider both how the fund operates during its accumulation/investment period and how to receive the pension: as an annuity, an income stream or some combination of the two. In this context fiscal/tax liabilities and privileges become very important and the interaction between the tax and benefits systems has been vital for specific retirees (HM Treasury, 2002).

Blake et al (1999, p 1) compared DC schemes currently being promoted by companies and the government via stakeholders, with old-style DB schemes, in respect of the options for the accumulation process, and concluded that; "[W]e find that defined contribution (DC) plans can be extremely risky relative to a defined benefit (DB) benchmark (far more so than most pension plan professionals would be likely to admit)". The following year they went on to consider the choices available to a personal (DC) pension scheme member on retirement for converting their fund into an income stream. They concluded that:

> The best programme is therefore an annuity programme rather than an income drawdown programme that leaves a bequest to the policy holder's survivors. The best programme also depends on the policy holder's attitude to risk: if he (sic) is highly risk averse, the appropriate programme is a conventional annuity; if he is more risk loving, the best programme involves a mixture of bonds and equities, with the optimal mix depending on the policyholder's degree of risk aversion. (Blake et al, 2000, p 1)

Hopefully these crucial and critical comments will ultimately be translated by newspaper 'experts', so that those of us who are risk loving can be assured we are not getting a pension product intended for someone who is risk averse!

The important point is that the more accurate and reliable the calculation of risk the less likely it is that 'low-risk' or low-cost groups will be willing to effectively subsidise others. Individuals need to reflect on their behaviour and the risks they take and find the most suitable pension provider. The net result may be that those that can afford to will "buy themselves out of collective responsibility" (Bauman, 1993, p 244) while others will find it very difficult to gain access to a worthwhile life assurance policy, or a meaningful pension. However, at least one insurance company already offers enhanced pensions to 'impaired lives'. According to Budd and Campbell (1998, p 15), "They intend to offer annuities which pay more to those with medical problems which are more likely to cause an early death". Good news for smokers and couch potatoes perhaps, and it ought to reinforce Giddens' calls for individuals to be more reflexive regarding the risks they confront:

> Schemes of positive welfare, oriented to manufactured rather than external risk, would be directed to fostering the *autotelic self*. The autotelic self is one with an inner confidence which comes from self-respect, and one where a sense of ontological security, originating in basic trust, allows for the positive appreciation of difference. It refers to a person able to translate potential threats into rewarding challenges, someone who is able to turn entropy into a consistent flow of experience. The autotelic self does not seek to neutralise risk or to suppose that 'someone else will take care of the problem'; risk is confronted as the active challenge which generates self-actualization. (Giddens, 1994, p 192, emphasis in original)

But as Adam and van Loon (2000, p 7) point out:

> [I]f reflexivity as self-confrontation is to mean anything in this context it is not a confrontation between two sets of calculations.... Instead, reflexivity requires us to be meditative, that is looking back upon that which allows us to reflect in the first place.

This leads neatly on to a discussion of identity, which has also been central to post-traditional accounts.

Identity and difference

Questions of cultural identity are seen by many scholars as indicative of postmodernity and have a particular significance for pensioners, retirees and older people (Hall and du Gay, 1996; Roseneil and Seymour, 1999). Age can form a powerful barrier, both fixing *our* social identities in relation to specific cohorts and identifying *other* age cohorts, for example, the 'baby boomers' and

'Thatcher's children/generation'. Indeed, the language and categories preferred highlights the significance of subject identities. Thus most older people in the UK prefer to be called 'senior citizens' and the identity label of 'retiree' is often preferred to 'old age pensioner' (Boaz et al, 1999). This too may imply a more difficult time for pensioners relying on public welfare because their form of dependency is stigmatised, even by other retirees. How risk is perceived and whether individuals accept responsibility for risk management may hinge on their sense of 'self', their identity. For Giddens, it is crucially important that retired people develop a strong sense of security, self-respect and self-actualisation and in so doing confront their welfare-dependent status. "The management of identity is the centre-point of how far a person's relation to the world ... is experienced as incapacitating or generates opportunities for self-enhancement or self-renewal" (Giddens, 1994, p 187). Individuals as consumers and 'lifestyle managers' are required to reflect on their needs, their behaviour and their 'selves'.

Simultaneously, the term 'senior citizen' asserts some traditional claims – age-based rights rather than tested needs or consumer redress. While Giddens (1994, p 132) may feel that Marshall's citizenship model "does not stand up to scrutiny", that need not prevent senior citizens mobilising successfully around the concept. Indeed, subject identities may become more significant in the near future through a redefinition of citizenship rights. For example, a definition of a working life that acknowledged the right to retire, alongside protection from age discrimination in paid work, could alleviate fears that exit from paid work will shortly only be possible for people with a private or occupational pension (Field, 2002; Mann, 2002).

While 'rethinking social policy' (Lewis et al, 2000), it needs to be recalled that identity, diversity and difference are hardly 'new' to welfare debates but have been mobilising themes against 'the schlock' since the early 1970s (Mann, 1986). As Williams notes, public welfare groups have "grasped the administrative categories (or subject positions) imposed upon them by policy makers, administrators and practitioners and translated these into political identities and new subjectivities" (1996, p 17). Williams' point is that despite the managerialist and individuating discourses, people are not empty vessels into which ideas can be poured without some spillage. Active human subjects adopt and adapt the categories and labels applied to them. Many of the social movements that are cited as indicators of postmodernity and a post-traditional society (for example, ecological, anti-globalisation, disability politics, women's health and welfare groups) testify to the durability of active human subjects. Pensioners, retirees and older people have similarly asserted their social and political agendas. Gray Panthers in the US, public pensioners picketing political conferences in the UK, lobby groups representing superannuants in Australia and a range of consumer and special interest groups across the developed economies testify to the possibilities (Wilson, 2000). However, to date these "entrenched interests" as Giddens describes them (1998, p 115) look rather weak in comparison to the "vested interests" (Field, 1996, p 38) that control the finance and pensions markets.

The marginalisation and social exclusion of older people therefore remains a vital issue for social researchers. Thus Phillipson (1998) advocates a sociology of 'daily living' that would expose the isolation of some older people but also how they resist and reconstruct their 'selves' in circumstances that initially appear to offer little opportunity for resistance. By focusing on resistance, however, it should not be thought that this simply consists of pensioners storming the barricades or occupying post offices. There are examples of such activities but, like most of us, older people resist in less obvious ways too. For example, 'dumb insolence' among residents of a residential care centre when urged to join in with the 'community singing', or teasing staff by 'playing dead' when they bring in the morning tea (Hockey and James, 1993, p 182; Thorpe, 1999).

Furthermore, as Phillipson (1998, p 49) argues, the rate and pace of change in contemporary societies, including the tremendous successes that have produced an ageing society, "seem to have undercut a language and moral space which can resonate with the rights and needs of older people as a group". We are not as fixed by community, class or family as in the past and that adds both to the pleasures of contemporary social life but also the anxieties. Postmodernity throws into doubt established identities and for younger retired people this may be extremely attractive, no longer ghettoised by age. Active and dynamic retirees provide a powerful challenge to negative stereotypes of frail and incompetent victims. But as Paul Hoggett (2001) reminds us, some people are frail, others are incompetent and any welfare system that neglects this fact is in danger of evading responsibility for the weakest and least articulate groups in society. Turning 'experience' into a positive learning process is all well and good, but physical and mental frailty will ultimately overwhelm even the most reflexive individual. As one of my favourite exam howlers put it, "we all tend to die". There are, of course, very big differences in how we experience both physical ageing and when we die. The trend is not uniform and gender, 'race', class and geography all provide very reliable data of differences that mirror socially structured inequalities, but to date no social group or individual has managed to buck the trend.

Consequently it is important to recall Hoggett's (2001, p 42) observations on Giddens' work "... our capacity to be a reflexive agent is often constrained by the difficulties we have in facing our own fears and anxieties. Some ideas and experiences are just too painful to think about, even with the support and solidarity of others, and they therefore get split off". The subject of death and dying is not something we care to ponder in a romanticised and youthful world. Like chameleons we can apparently change identities at will but "we do have bodies which do cause us suffering (and some more than for others) and which do decay and die" (Hoggett, 2001, p 43). No amount of reflexivity can prevent the inevitable decline of the body. Thus it is reasonable to ask at what point are we free of the need to "turn potential threats into rewarding challenges" (Giddens, 1994, p 192)? And when is it legitimate to be welfare dependent or to acknowledge ones own dependency? What if, having reflected on the likelihood of one's dying within the next ten years one wants to enjoy a period of retirement, spend some 'quality time' with one's grandchildren, travel, feel the sun on ones ageing skin and escape from the 'bullshit' (Castles, 1997) of work? How much reflexivity does it take to know that death awaits us all?

These questions are crucial because Giddens (1998, pp 119-20) proposes the scrapping of the retirement age and implies everyone should save for their retirement:

> The concept of a pension that begins at retirement age, and the label 'pensioner', were inventions of the welfare state. But not only do these not conform to the new realities of ageing, they are as clear a case of welfare dependency as one can find.... We should move towards abolishing the fixed age of retirement, and we should regard older people as a resource rather than a problem.

A 'third way', or no way, out?

These views have been echoed by New Labour with successive ministers, government reports and Green Papers emphasising the need to change popular attitudes to retirement (DSS, 1998a, 1998b; PIU, 2000; DWP, 2002; HM Treasury/ Inland Revenue, 2002). Ironically, the main themes and policy proposals to emerge run counter to the social trends that underpin a 'post-traditional' society. Thus the trend to early retirement needs to be halted and older workers need to be encouraged to remain in paid employment, even beyond 65. In future retirees must lower their lifestyle expectations and the idea of a 'right to retirement' – at a fixed age and with a right to public welfare – needs to be undermined.

Although the mantra of 'choice' runs through the various reports and proposals it is plain that individuals are expected to make the right choices. They need to be saving more, working for longer and expecting less from the state. Alistair Darling, the former Social Security Minister, made it brutally clear to the House of Commons on 15 December 1998: "... once stakeholder pensions are established, it is my intention to ensure that we amend the system further so that, if people stay in the state system, they will lose money" (Hansard, vol 337, col 771). Subsequently the Prime Minister, Tony Blair, asserted:

> I hope that our actions as Government will also promote a wider change in attitudes. This cultural change is a long-term project, with high stakes. In a century in which we can expect life expectancy to continue to increase, we will all suffer if we write people off on the grounds of age. (Foreword to PIU, 2000)

Early retirement is portrayed as an economic drain – at a time of low unemployment – and the labour force to public welfare dependency ratio is often cited as problematic. In December 2002, the Secretary of State for Work and Pensions, Andrew Smith, introduced his department's Green Paper; "Our aim is to help people choose how they plan for retirement, how much they save and how long they keep working" (DWP, 2002, p v).

There were merely four proposals set out in the summary. The first was to "help people make better informed choices"; the second reaffirmed that employers play a part but admitted a need for "greater protection for members of occupational schemes"; the third was to encourage simple savings products and broaden access to financial services; and the fourth was proposed to "introduce measures to extend working lives" (DWP, 2002, p 1).

Public sector employees will see their retirement rights curtailed and early retirement is to be made a poorer choice. "Many older people are leaving work unnecessarily early" (DWP, 2002, p 12). It is also plain that 'the voluntarist approach' hinges on people taking advantage of the opportunities offered. These consist of increasing the incentives to continue in paid employment and restricting early exit. The tax system (fiscal welfare) is central to helping people make the right choices. With an annual tax handout of £13 billion to £19 billion (DWP, 2002), and further tax breaks proposed to encourage longer working lives, there is a large financial carrot being dangled in order to promote Blair's 'cultural change'. Reflexivity – translated as choice by the merchants of spin – in this context requires some careful economic calculations, rather than decisions over identity and lifestyle. Ominously for those who might still make the 'wrong' choices, Andrew Smith also intends to establish an 'independent' pensions commission "to advise whether there is a case for moving beyond the current voluntarist approach" (DWP, 2002, p v). Simultaneously the Treasury Green Paper, 'simplifying the taxation of pensions: increasing choice and flexibility for all', slipped in the following announcement: "The concept of normal retirement age will vanish from tax legislation" (DWP, 2002, p 2).

It is against a backdrop of restraining the right to retire and the rights of the retired, by shifting responsibility for retirement risks onto individuals, that questions of identity need to be located. It seems that: "the language of autonomy, identity, self-realization and the search for fulfilment forms a grid of regulatory ideals…" (Rose, 1996, p 145). As consumers, savers and lifestyle managers, individual retirees are making "themselves 'interested' in their own government" (Rose, 1996, p 146).

In contrast, Giddens' reflexive (masculine?) 'self' operates with a chilling rationality and a high degree of autonomy in a world where opportunities and risks are socially structured (Seidler, 1994; Hoggett, 2001). Those subject identities that struggle in circumstances where there are fewer opportunities and more risks (usually the poorest in society) are portrayed as lesser identities. Thus choosing an AVC to top up an occupational pension is an indication of the (deserving) reflexive self. Passively relying on the public pension is 'welfare dependency' and therefore undeserving. Those in the retirement ghetto must be brought out (in some cases kicking and screaming no doubt) into the more worthwhile world of work, and "old age should not be a time of rights without responsibilities" (Giddens, 1998, p 121).

Nevertheless, managing consumption and consumers also generates tensions

(Harrison, 1990). For example, the subject identities of older people may assume more political significance in the near future as the 'baby boom generation' nears retirement. As Giddens (1991) has noted, people in post-traditional societies reflect on and reconstruct their identities in the light of experience. Identities are not fixed but fluid and any change brings with it new possibilities. Anyone persuaded to take out a private pension by the positive images of what retirement may consist of (travel, choice, and consumption), is unlikely to be reassured that their investment was worth making if they subsequently feel politically marginalised or socially excluded. And managing aggrieved consumers is already generating resentment within the pensions industry. "But now the culture of complaint has reached disproportionate level ... the current consumerist faux outrage in the Equitable affair seems to have reached unreasonable heights, with emotions reaching lynch levels" (*Pensions World*, 2003, p 39). Promoting choices, and using positive images of retirees to sell pension products will need to be carefully managed if consumers are not to mobilise around these when things go wrong. Government may wish to shift responsibility to the pensions industry, but it may simply pass it back. Shunting those who saved and planned – the new deserving – into political limbo is a very risky strategy for both government and the pensions industry. It is also likely to make the experience of ageing and retirement even more traumatic (Vincent, 1999). Shared identities in retirement may promote an awareness of common interests and generate 'new' social and political mobilisations but, then again, they may not.

Conclusion

Giddens' positive model of welfare and society has much to commend it. In relation to retirement it offers the possibility of a more balanced view of work, care, leisure and retirement, one in which important options have to be considered. In viewing welfare as more than simply resource transfers, we are reminded of the various campaigns of the 1960s /1980s in which voices were raised about the way that public welfare could discipline and control subject populations. Likewise Beck's account of risk, the problems he sees with scientific and technical measures, the way it is socially manifest and the global implications of trying to manage it, are all clearly relevant to retirement and the possibilities it presents for the reflexive individual. However, the institutions that operate in the insurance, pensions and finance markets do so with models of risk that reinforce existing patterns of privilege.

The risks associated with planning for retirement also illustrate the more general problems confronting populations in the developed economies. Divorce, industrial change and globalisation, are commonplace and illustrate how post-traditional societies impact on both the personal and macro-level. There is a hierarchy of risk that corresponds with some very traditional forms of social inequality and with the different elements of the social division of welfare (Mann, 2001). From this perspective Giddens' and New Labour's 'third way' appears as blinkered by traditional definitions of welfare and dependency as 'the schlock'. It also returns us along a very traditional road paved with Victorian ideas of self-help and populated by the 'reflexive' professional middle classes. Despite the rhetoric of globalisation, which often looks remarkably like the old deterministic view of industrialisation, there is little consideration of the huge resources held by pension funds or of the privileges they, and private pension funds, enjoy. Thus the dismissal of public pensioners (most of whom will be working-class women) as embedded in a culture of dependency is offensive. It neglects the hierarchy or privileges – and the greater risks – imposed by the different elements of the social division of welfare (Titmuss, 1958; Mann, 1992, 2001). Giddens' exclusive focus on public welfare (and he is not alone in this, of course) simply neglects the fact that everyone is welfare dependent (interdependent) in a post-traditional society. Rather than extending the privileges of the rich and the middle classes to all – something that would break with traditional welfare approaches – he promotes an individualistic agenda that blames the poorest for not being more like the middle classes.

Changing the moral fabric of society and establishing the third way is a project that focuses attention on how individuals behave and distinguishes those who reflexively adapt from those who persist with their errant behaviour (Giddens, 1998; Dwyer, 2000; Hoggett, 2001). The modernising project is, therefore, to get subsequent retirees, current workers, carers and consumers, to make their own provisions, to change their behaviours "by finding new ways of *using* the state to impose the discipline of the market on its population" (Walker, 1999, p 538).[7] Consequently, as Peter Taylor-Gooby (2001, p 10) has suggested, the "third way looks increasing like an ideology serving the interests of the more privileged classes by denying the continuing importance of class divisions in vulnerability".

Notes

[1] Schlock: "cheap inferior or trashy (US slang derived from Yiddish)", *Collins English Dictionary*, 1979.

[2] I would particularly like to thank Pete Dwyer for his comments on previous drafts of this chapter.

[3] Although consumption processes and the management of economic institutions are discussed here as distinct and separate, in reality they occur in tandem and are part of the continual processes promoting social change.

[4] AVCs are accelerated voluntary contributions, FSAVCs are free standing accelerated voluntary contributions.

[5] Pessimism, a hallmark of (the old) social policy, needs to be tempered since, according to Andrew Dilnot, 89 per cent of even the lowest paid (earning £10–20k, which is the

stakeholder target group) have some sort of pension provision (Channel 4, 5 October, 2002). However, over on BBC1, *Panorama* on 17 November, 2002, reported that 9 million people had made no pension provisions and only 3 to 4 per cent of their respondents expected the state to provide for their retirement needs. An example, perhaps, of how the media in a risk society can both generate alarm and appear to offer reassurances?

[6] Among many other responsibilities he has been Managing Director of Paribas Asset Management, a subdivision of the 28th largest bank in the world, a member of the International Stock Exchange, former President of the European Federation of Financial Analysts Society and a representative on the Board of the International Accounting Standards Committee, which establishes accounting standards on the world level (Cooke et al, 1992, p xiii).

[7] In this context it is worth noting that compulsory private saving for all is being advocated by a former minister in the Labour government, Frank Field (Pension Reform Group, 2001; Field, 2002).

References

Abel-Smith, B. and Townsend, P. (1965) *The poor and the poorest*, London: Bell and Sons.

ABI (Association of British Insurers) (1995) *Risk, insurance and welfare: The changing balance between private and public protection*, London: ABI.

Adam, B. and van Loon, J. (2000) 'Introduction: repositioning risk: the challenge for social theory', in B. Adam., U. Beck and J. van Loon (eds) *The risk society and beyond: Critical issues for social theory*, London: Sage Publications, pp 1-46.

Adam, B., Beck, U. and van Loon, J. (eds) (2000) *The risk society and beyond: Critical issues for social theory*, London: Sage Publications.

Aldridge, A. (1997) 'Engaging with promotional culture', *Sociology*, vol 31, no 3, pp 389-408.

Arber, S. (1995) 'Discrimination, retirement and pensions', *Work, Employment and Society*, vol 9, no 2, pp 401-02.

Baudrillard, J. (1975) *The mirror of production*, St Louis MO: Telos Press.

Bauman, Z. (1993) *Postmodern ethics*, Oxford: Blackwell.

Bauman, Z. (1998) *Work, consumerism and the new poor*, Buckingham: Open University Press.

Beck, U. (1992) *Risk society: Towards a new modernity*, London: Sage Publications.

Beck, U. (2000) 'Risk society revisited: theory, politics and research programmes', in B. Adam, U. Beck and J. van Loon (eds) *The risk society and beyond: Critical issues for social theory*, London: Sage Publications, pp 211-29.

Blake, D., Cairns, A.J.G. and Dowd, K. (2000) *Pension Metrics II: Stochastic pension plan design during the distribution phase*, ASI-Gamma Foundation, working paper collection no 20, presented at the 4th annual BSI Gamma Foundation conference on global asset management, Rome, October 2000.

Boaz, A., Hayden, C. and Bernard, M. (1999) *Attitudes and aspirations of older people: A review of the literature*, DSS Research Report, no 101, London: The Stationery Office.

Budd, A. and Campbell, N. (1998) *The roles of the public and private sectors in the UK pension system*, London: HM Treasury (www.hm-treasury.gov.uk/pub).

Castles, F.G. (1997) 'Leaving the Australian labour force: an extended encounter with the state', *Governance*, vol 10, no2, pp 97-121.

Cooke, T.E., Matatko, J. and Stafford, D.C. (eds) (1992) *Risk, portfolio management and capital markets*, Basingstoke: Macmillan.

Culpitt, I. (1999) *Social policy and risk*, London: Sage Publications.

Damant, D. (1992) 'The revolution in investment management', in T.E. Cooke, J. Matatko and D.C. Stafford (eds) *Risk, portfolio management and capital markets*, Basingstoke: Macmillan, pp 7-18.

Deaton, R.L. (1989) *The political economy of pensions politics and social change in Canada, Britain and the United States*, Vancouver: University of British Columbia Press.

DSS (Department of Social Security) (1998a) *New ambitions for our country: A new contract for welfare*, Cm 3805, London: The Stationery Office.

DSS (1998b) *Partnership in 'pensions'*, Cm 4179, London: The Stationery Office.

DWP (Department for Work and Pensions) (2002) *Simplicity, security and choice: Working and saving for retirement*, London: The Stationery Office.

Dwyer, P. (2000) *Welfare rights and responsibilities: Contesting social citizenship*, Bristol: The Policy Press.

Dyson, S. (1999) 'Genetic screening and ethnic minorities', *Critical social policy*, vol 19, no 2, pp 195-215.

Ewald, F. (1991) 'Insurance and risk', in G. Burchell, C. Gordon and P. Miller (eds) *The Foucault effect: Studies in govermentality*, Chicago: Chicago University Press, pp 197-210.

Featherstone, M (1987) 'Leisure, symbolic power and the life course', in D. Jary, S. Home and A. Tomlinson (eds) *Sport leisure and social relations*, London: Routledge, pp 113-38.

Featherstone, M. and Hepworth, M. (1995) 'Images of positive ageing: case study of *Retirement Choice* magazine', in M. Featherstone and A. Wernick, *Images of ageing: Cultural representations of later life*, London: Routledge, pp 29-47.

Field, F. (1996) *Stakeholder welfare*, Choice in Welfare Series, no 32, London: Institute of Economic Affairs.

Field, F. (2002) *Debating pensions: Self interest, citizenship and the common good*, London: Civitas.

Giddens, A. (1991) *Modernity and self identity*, Cambridge: Polity Press.

Giddens, A. (1994) *Beyond left and right*, Cambridge: Polity Press.

Giddens, A. (1998) *The third way: The renewal of social democracy*, Cambridge: Polity Press.

Glennerster, H. (1991) 'The radical right and the welfare state in Britain: pensions and health care', in H. Glennerster and J. Midgeley (eds) *The radical right and the welfare state: An international assessment*, Hemel Hempstead: Harvester Wheatsheaf, pp 45-62.

Guillemard, A-M. and van Gunsteren, H. (1991) 'Pathways and their prospects: a comparative interpretation of the meaning of early exit', in M. Kohli, M. Rein, A.M. Guillemard and H. van Gunsteren (eds) *Time for retirement: Comparative studies of early exit from the labour force*, Cambridge: Cambridge University Press, pp 362-87.

Hall, S. and du Gay, P. (eds) (1996) *Questions of cultural identity*, London: Sage Publications.

Hamill, J. (2002) 'The development of the UK pension structure and the making of pensions policy', unpublished PhD thesis, submitted September, Leeds: Leeds University.

Hansard (1999) *Parliamentary questions*, House of Commons, vol 337, London: The Stationery Office.

HM Treasury/Inland Revenue (2002) *Simplifying the taxation of pensions: Increasing choice and flexibility for all*, London: The Stationery Office.

Hockey, J. and James, A. (1993) *Growing up and growing old: Ageing and dependency in the life course*, London: Sage Publications.

Hoggett, P. (2001) 'Agency, rationality and social policy', *Journal of Social Policy*, vol 30, no 1, pp 37-56.

Kemshall, H. (2002) *Risk, social policy and welfare*, Buckingham: Open University Press.

Lewis, G., Gewirtz, S. and Clarke, J. (eds) (2000) *Rethinking social policy*, London: Sage Publications.

Mann, K. (1986) 'The making of a claiming class – the neglect of agency in analyses of the welfare state', *Critical Social Policy*, vol 15, no 2, pp 62-74.

Mann, K. (1992) *The making of an English 'underclass'*, Buckingham: Open University Press.

Mann, K. (2001) *Approaching retirement: Social divisions, welfare and exclusion*, Bristol: The Policy Press.

Mann, K. (2002) 'Faith in the city: absolving employers and protecting vested interests', in A. Deacon (ed) *Debating pensions: Self interest, citizenship and the common good by Frank Field*, London: Civitas, pp 79-83.

Minns, R. (2001) *The cold war in welfare*, London: Verso.

Myners, P. (2001) *Myners review of institutional investment: Final report*, London: HM Treasury, (www.hm-Treasury.gov.uk/docs/2001_report0602,htm.

OECD (Organisation for Economic Co-operation and Development) (1998) *The retirement decision in OECD countries*, Ageing working papers (AWP1.4Eng), *Maintaining prosperity in an ageing society: The OECD study on the policy implications of ageing*, Paris: OECD.

Olsberg, D. (1997) *Ageing and money*, St Leonards: Allen and Unwin.

Pension Reform Group (2001) *Universal protected pension: Modernising pensions for the millennium*, London: Institute of Community Studies.

PIU Report (2000) *Winning the generation game*, London: Cabinet Office, HMSO.

Phillipson, C. (1998) *Reconstructing old age*, London: Sage Publications.

Pickering Report (2002) *A simpler way to better pensions*, an independent report by Alan Pickering. www.nhspa.gov.uk/library/pickering_report. pdf (11 July).

Rose, N. (1996) 'Identity, genealogy, history', in S. Hall and P. du Gay (eds) *Questions of cultural identity*, London: Sage Publications.

Roseneil, S. and Seymour, J. (eds) (1999) *Practising identities: Power and resistance*, Basingstoke: Macmillan.

Sawchuk, K.A. (1995) 'From gloom to boom: age identity and target marketing', in M. Featherstone and A. Wernick (eds) *Images of aging: Cultural representations of later life*, London: Routledge, pp 173-87.

Seidler, V.J. (1994) *Unreasonable men: Masculinity and social theory*, London: Routledge.

Sevenhuijsen, S. (2000) 'Caring in the third way: the relation between obligation, responsibility and care in *Third Way* discourse', *Critical Social Policy*, vol 20, no 1, pp 5-38.

Standard Life (1998) *Life Times*, issue 11, no 2, Edinburgh: Balfour Publishing.

Tanner, S. (1997) 'The dynamics of retirement behaviour', in R. Disney, E. Grundy and P. Johnson (eds) *The dynamics of retirement: Analyses of the retirement surveys*, London: The Stationery Office.

Taylor-Gooby, P. (2001) 'Risk, contingency and the third way: evidence from the BHPS and qualitative studies', *Social Policy and Administration*, vol 35, no 3, pp 195-211.

Thorpe, M. (1999) 'Marginalisation and resistance through the prism of retirement', in J. Hearn and S. Roseneil (eds) *Consuming cultures: Power and resistance*, Basingstoke: Macmillan.

Titmuss, R. (1958) *Essays on the welfare state*, London: Allen and Unwin.

Townsend, P. (1979) *Poverty in the United Kingdom*, Harmondsworth: Penguin.

Vincent, J. (1999) *Politics, power and old age*, Buckingham: Open University Press.

Visco, I. (2001) *Paying for pensions: how important is economic growth? Managing the global ageing transition*, a policy summit of the Global Ageing Initiative, Zurich: OECD.

Walker, A. (1999) 'The third way for pensions (by way of Thatcherism and avoiding today's pensioners)', *Critical Social Policy*, vol 19, no 4, pp 511-27.

Walker, R. with Howard, M. (2000) *The making of a welfare class: Benefit receipt in Britain*, Bristol: The Policy Press.

Warde, A. (1994) 'Consumers, consumption and post-Fordism', in R. Burrows and B. Loader (eds) *Towards a post-Fordist welfare state?*, London: Routledge.

Williams, F. (1996) 'Postmodernism, feminism and the question of difference', in N. Parton (ed) *Social work, social theory and social change*, London: Routledge, pp 61-76.

Wilson, G. (2000) *Understanding old age: Critical and global perspectives*, London: Sage Publications.

TWELVE

Pension sharing on divorce: the future for women

Debora Price

Introduction

Gender divisions in material provision in later life are profound: most of the world's aged are women, and on average they are much poorer than men. These differentials are clearly exposed by an examination of the financial circumstances of individuals who live alone in old age. They result from diverse social policies formed during the 20th century, in countries with different types of governments, different cultures and different histories. Evidently, such persistent and pervasive gender effects cannot be random; how and why things should be so unequal is a substantive concern of feminist, and to a lesser extent mainstream, scholarship.

In the developed world, the welfare state, whether reinforcing or ameliorating this gendered condition of older women, is perceived to be under threat. As Bonoli and Gay-des-Combes outline elsewhere in this volume, all western European countries have been examining and reforming one of their greatest welfare expenditure items, their pension systems. Many reasons have been identified for the stress to these systems, the ageing of the population being perhaps the most significant for pensions, but also dramatic social and political changes (Pierson, 2001). Later marriage, later childbirth, the burgeoning of childbirth outside marriage, increases in single parent and lone adult family units and increasing rates of relationship breakdown are the salient features of family change. These changes in family structures at the micro-social level have been accompanied at the macro-level by globalisation, the move from manufacturing to service employment in post-industrial economies, and the so-called neo-liberal consensus on the importance of the market economy for social welfare provision. In pension terms, the convergence of these factors raises questions of gender inequality in material provision in later life. How older men and women will fare financially in the light of such myriad changes – particularly as marriage becomes less likely to last into old age because of rising divorce rates – becomes an important question of concern.

In this chapter the prospective financial position of divorced women in retirement in England and Wales[1] is viewed from two convergent perspectives. First, the United Kingdom's location within welfare state theory as a paradigm male breadwinner nation state is reviewed. The meaning of this for the pension provision of women, especially those who will live alone, is considered. Second, the chapter focuses on the particular policy solution to the 'problem' of divorced women's retirement income that has been chosen by the UK government, and recently implemented. The courts have been given discretionary powers to allocate pensions between spouses on divorce. Known as 'pension sharing', this 'solution' to a large extent was the one proposed by women campaigners, although its selection also confirms the characterisation of the UK within welfare state theory.

In resorting to the 'family' legal system, women may find that the law fails to affect their income in retirement. Moreover, it precludes the search for other solutions because it operates in a hidden realm wherein it claims to be an objective final arbiter of 'justice' between spouses. Analysis of the exercise of judicial discretion shows that the male-breadwinner paradigm pervades judicial decision-making to the long-term detriment of women. By problematising divorced women, the structural inequities of the overarching welfare regime are marginalised. If women are left without potential income in retirement, then their most rational economic solution may be (if they have the opportunity) to become financially dependent on a man. In this way, the breadwinner/dependent model is reproduced, with no material improvement for women.

Here, the gendered framework for pension accumulation in the UK, and the legal system as an institution for the disposal of pension rights on divorce, are seen as intersecting components of a single system that determines adverse outcomes for older women.

The UK as a gendered welfare regime

In modern capitalist economies, differential income and wealth of older people can be seen as functions of discriminative social policies formulated by the state over time. Family structures, compulsory retirement from paid labour and increasing longevity all create financial dependencies among older people, and democracy and ideology combine to require political sensitivity towards inequality and poverty in old age. Pensions have thus become a major concern in all developed countries in terms of social security, and fiscal and employment policy.

Titmuss (1963) pointed out that these three policy arenas each make distinct and major contributions to state-aided welfare, but are highly divisive in their effects as they reinforce occupational class and privilege differences between men. He did not, however, grapple in any philosophical sense with the vast gender differences within occupations and classes that resulted from the gendered social divisions of labour and care. In Esping-Andersen's seminal work on understanding the origins, evolution and trajectories of welfare within states,

The three worlds of welfare capitalism (1990), his analysis is similarly embedded in class division and class alliance, in the role of ideology, in the political mobilisation of male labour, in divisions of power in industrialised nations, in the control of the economy by the state, and the role of state institutions. He famously classified countries into liberal, conservative/corporate and social democratic 'welfare regimes', noting that welfare is a complex beast, as much comprised of the market and the family as of state transfers. Again though, and notably, he did not conceptualise welfare outcomes for women in any of his regimes: in their relations with men, with children, with care (especially unpaid care) and in their various interactions with the paid labour market.

Yet if the poverty of older women is to be understood, and meaningful ways of tackling it without simultaneously reinforcing gender inequalities are to be found, the place of women in welfare and in the state must be understood too. Critics of Esping-Andersen's welfare regime theory have presented alternative ways of conceptualising the nexus of gender and the welfare state, by reference to the domestic realm of gender relations, caring work and the social construction of male/female dependencies.[2] While there is active debate about precisely how this analytical framework should be formulated, there is broad consensus that key variables are the extent to which partnered men and women continue to be characterised by breadwinning/homemaking or breadwinning/care-giving; the extent to which the welfare regime is structured to favour a familial model of marriage with gendered labour/care division between husband and wife; the extent to which care work is valued economically; the capacity of the state to provide support for mothers who do not live with partners; and the extent to which dual-earner/dual-carer couples are supported in the welfare regime. These variations correspond to more than one 'gendered' dimension of a welfare regime, dimensions including not only breadwinning/financial dependency between partners, but also a care dimension incorporating the domestic division of unpaid care work, and market and state features of paid care work (Lewis, 1992, 1997; O'Connor, 1993, 1996; Orloff, 1993; Daly, 1994, 2000, 2002; Hobson, 1994; Sainsbury, 1994; O'Connor et al, 1999; Daly and Lewis, 2000). Welfare regimes can therefore be considered in the sense of whether they enable, promote or reinforce certain types of family forms and certain types of paid labour/unpaid care divisions over others.

While these gender relations shape the division of welfare, these welfare considerations simultaneously elucidate the role of the state in affecting gender relations and gender hierarchies (Orloff, 1996; O'Connor et al, 1999; Daly and Lewis, 2000). The welfare system here must be interpreted broadly enough to encompass such systems as support care of children, the sick, the disabled and infirm older people; systems (including fiscal, employment and benefit systems) that support part- and full-time paid labour for women; systems that construct marriage as normative and solo parenthood or working motherhood as deviant; and the operation of the market in domestic work and paid care.

In understanding gender dimensions at the level of the state, therefore, and the ways in which gender differences are apparent in individual citizens' articulation with welfare, gender relations in the private/domestic realm become of prime importance. Many of those who have focused on or included the British welfare regime in their analysis have found it useful to characterise domestic relations in terms of the extent to which male/female partnerships and various social policies adhere to a domestic model of breadwinning/ homemaking. Lewis (1992), for example, argued in an influential analysis that Britain was a 'strong' male breadwinner state, with relationships tending towards a male breadwinner/female carer paradigm, which both explains and is the result of women's low rates of participation in the labour market and their low pay, their tendency to work part time, the lack of childcare provision by state or market, and inequalities in access to social security rights. Sainsbury (1994) constructed two ideal-types as an heuristic device for the analysis of welfare regimes: the breadwinner model, where a breadwinner/homemaker family unit is assumed, and an individual model, where men and women are assumed to be both earners and carers. She too characterised the UK as approximating the breadwinner type, albeit with some state recognition of the care work of mothers as a basis for welfare entitlements; Daly (2000), while criticising the simple breadwinner model as failing to fully conceptualise and specify the attributes of the breadwinner household, recognises among British married women a high level of dependence on their husbands for income.

Following a wide-ranging engendered analysis of four 'liberal' welfare regimes: Australia, Canada, Great Britain and the United States, O'Connor et al comment:

> The shift in liberal ideology from gender difference to gender sameness is variously represented in the policy regimes of the four countries, with Britain holding more determinedly to the breadwinner-carer family model than the other three countries.... The United States and to some extent Canada again show a clear and distinct pattern of encouraging families to have recourse to the market for support services, while Britain shows a clear pattern of encouraging the privatisation of need within the family, including continued dependence on former spouses. (O'Connor et al, 1999, p 233)

Reasons given for the strength of the male breadwinner model in the UK include a historical perspective whereby idealised versions of the male breadwinner/female carer family predominated at the time the welfare state was forming (Lewis, 1992) and the powerful separation of state and family, public and private, within liberal ideology (Lewis, 1992; O'Connor et al, 1999). Liberalism essentially targets those most in need, reinforcing the norm of female caring in the private domain for most families (Sainsbury, 1994). All theorists agree that since the origin of the welfare state, there has been a process of political and institutional feedback. In one variant of this loop, used to differing degrees to explain the persistence of the breadwinner norm in UK gender relations, pre-existing unequal personal relationships between men and women are reinforced or compounded by the social processes of the welfare state, encouraging their reproduction.

Women and pensions in the UK

While some welfare state theorists incorporate pension systems in their analysis (for example, Schiewe, 1994; Leitner, 2001), gender theory is not well developed for an ageing society (Arber and Ginn, 1995). Feminist writers have focused on divisions of domestic and paid labour, motherhood, childcare, care work and workforce participation as key empirical indicators of the gender dimensions of welfare states. Each of these has an obvious and measurable impact on the accumulation of pension provision, and state transfers to individuals of pensionable age are a substantial proportion of any welfare budget.

As might be predicted from the UK's generally accepted classification as a liberal welfare state and the resilience of the male breadwinning norm within partnerships, women in the UK have little or no pension compared with men (Field and Prior, 1996; McKay et al, 2000). If they are married, it is generally assumed for policy purposes that sharing of income with their husbands takes place. Their relative poverty is only illuminated by examining the income of those who live alone, currently almost half of all women over 65, and 60 per cent of women over 75[3] (Walker et al, 2001). The vast majority of these women have previously been married, and are either widowed, separated or divorced. Low income in later life is the legacy of their individual poor financial circumstances during marriage, but would generally have been obscured during this period by most data analysis.

This poverty of women pensioners is the result of the way that pension schemes are structured in the UK. Gendered assumptions about households, families, breadwinning and childcare have been institutionalised by the state in the UK pension system, to the detriment of women as individuals. Women were not 'meant' under the Beveridge model of the welfare state to need their own pensions (Beveridge, 1942). Since its conception, pension outcomes (state and private) have been heavily linked to contributions made through paid work by those not on low pay, thus excluding most women (carers) for much of their working lives. It was assumed that women would either be married and therefore part of a household, or if not married, would be childless and would lead 'male pattern' working lives. Married women would depend on the pension income of their husbands and when widowed would depend on a widow's pension inherited from their husbands. Married women, even if in work, were encouraged by financial incentive to opt out of the pension system altogether (the so-called 'married women's stamp').

In a society where marriage tended to last for life, childbirth outside marriage was rare, and full employment for husbands was assumed, the implications of this gender unequal distribution of pension income would mainly be an issue within the marriage between spouses. But in modern UK society over a third of children are now born outside marriage (Ermisch and Francesconi, 2000), and the risk of divorce or separation is relatively high. Yet the assumptions underlying Beveridge's system have not changed within pension policy. Inside marriage, women remain financially dependent on men. The pension structure does not take into account lifetime working patterns interrupted and/or affected by caring and domestic responsibilities, nor the low earnings of women, which in turn are partly a result of the UK's persistent gender pay gap in its highly gender segregated labour market. These factors continue to lead to most women being unable to accumulate sufficient pensions themselves to live comfortably in retirement without financial dependence on a living or deceased partner. The state pensions have been so eroded in recent years by successive governments that despite their generally redistributive effect, they no longer provide sufficient pensions to women to achieve financial independence (for detailed accounts of these issues and the ways that this has happened see Falkingham and Victor, 1991; Ginn and Arber, 1994, 1999, 2001; Waine, 1995; Rake et al, 2000). Concern about whether women, particularly those who will live alone, can look forward to a secure retirement emerges "starkly from virtually every report on pension income" (Falkingham and Rake, 2001, p 67).

Without individual pensions, the risks for women who live alone of poverty in old age are high. While widows have some limited derived rights from the pensions of their deceased husbands, divorcees do not, even if they could reasonably have anticipated this when married (Ginn, 2003).

Ageing divorcees: a policy imperative

In the mid-1990s 37 per cent of divorced women over 65 were in receipt of income support – about two-and-a-half times the proportion of single women in receipt of this benefit, and more than twice the proportion of divorced men (Ginn and Price, 2002). Ginn (2001) showed that in 1998 divorced and separated women over 65 had a median income of only £89 per week, when the means-tested income support level was £70.45. This compared with £112 per week for never married single women, and £100 per week for widowed women (whose individual income is usually boosted by some inherited pension). In policy terms, the poverty of women living alone in retirement observed over recent years has led to very large direct income transfers from state to individual in the form of means-tested benefits, set to become larger with cohort effects of partnership formation and dissolution and recent increases in means-tested benefits in retirement.

The rise in the divorce rate over the last three decades is a well-known and much-written about phenomenon. It is estimated that four out of every ten marriages entered into in the UK in 1996 will end in divorce (Shaw, 1999), where the current divorce rate is the highest in the European Union (Barlow et al, 2002). Few retirees have yet experienced old age as divorcees, but the proportions are growing, as divorce rates have risen for successive cohorts. Within these growing proportions, the numbers of divorced men and women are not symmetrical by gender. Men have a greater likelihood of repartnering after divorce than women, and while repartnering after divorce becomes progressively less likely with age for both sexes, this is especially so for women (Davidson, 1999). By age 65, it is estimated that there are 125 divorced women for every 100 divorced men and it is thought likely that over the next two decades this gender differential will increase (Haskey, 1999). Gender differences within the estimated rapidly ageing divorced population are shown in Figure 12.1.

In 1996 the highest proportions of divorcees were in the age group 35-44, but in 2021 the highest proportions, which are growing all the time, are projected to be in the age group 55-64. Projections are that by 2021 there will be 840,000 divorced women over 65, and 626,000 divorced men (Shaw, 1999).

The relative poverty of older divorced women reflects two institutionalised processes: the gendered accumulation of pension provision, and the divorce process.

Breadwinners, carers and divorce law

Welfare state analysis has tended to focus on the norms of partnership formation and their interactions with the state and market, with emphasis on the state's institutionalisation of particular types of family form. But gender arrangements within partnerships and as assumed by the institutions of the state can also be directly observed in the field of family law, and in particular in laws relating to marriage and divorce (Smart, 1984b; Smart and Neale, 1999). While law is viewed in this context by government as neutral, and an infallible method for achieving 'justice' between men and women (qua divorcing spouses), Smart (1989) has argued that in constructing itself as powerful within gender relations

Figure 12.1: Proportion of men and women divorced, by age group, 1996 and projected to 2021

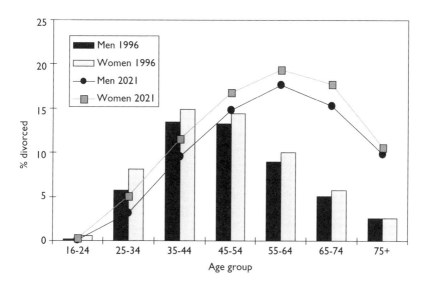

Source: GAD; Shaw (1999, from Table 1)

it has extended its reach into the most intimate spheres of women's lives and served to reinforce their inequalities. A resort to law is constructed as the 'cure' for gender inequalities but instead in practice reveals itself as bad as the original abuse that it was intended to ameliorate (Smart, 1989, p 161). Other feminist work has shown how legal norms are founded in masculine experience and how "gender constructs become embedded in case processing" (Haney, 2000, p 651).

In the context of explaining motherhood Pfau-Effinger (1999) has argued that it is insufficient to examine only the welfare policies of states, however broadly those policies are defined. The position of mothers is the product, rather, of institutions, culture and women's agency, and cannot be explained save in these terms. The male breadwinner/female dependent relationship is only one dimension within a broader concept of the gender–cultural relationship, and itself can be subdivided into female full-time carer, and female part-time carer models. This 'gender culture' derives partly from the construction of the role of women in the family economy and the social construction of childhood, recognising that the social actors negotiating these have different power and resources. These cultural models are not determined by but interact with welfare state institutions, which inter alia determine the extent of state involvement in caring. 'Gender systems' – the macro-level cultural and institutional frameworks that also determine work–care orientations of women – take the gender culture as a dominant frame of reference. The resulting 'gender arrangement' is the frame produced by the gender system and the gender culture.

In considering the financial prospects in old age for divorced women, Pfau-Effinger's approach provides an analytical framework for interpreting and understanding the gendered social process of the pension outcomes of divorce litigation. While sustained by policy-makers, the legal system is a macro-level state institution peopled by individual judges, themselves part of the construction of the gender culture, and this forms part of the gender system. Corresponding to other empirical classifications of the UK's welfare regime outlined earlier, Pfau-Effinger categorises the UK as a male breadwinner/female part-time carer regime.

Connecting these approaches, it is argued here that the dominant gender culture which constructs married men as breadwinners/providers and married women as carers and at best part-time workers, feeds the judiciary who operate a powerful part of the gender system, which in turn serves to reinforce the culture, leading to pension poverty for divorced women.

Financial division on divorce

The resolution of issues about pensions and old age that arise within divorce is but one facet of more complex gendered financial outcomes of divorce generally. Pahl's (1989) work exposed the fallacy of the assumption of equal resource sharing within marriage in part by an examination of the finances of women who divorced or separated. Divorced women suffer higher risks of poverty and greater falls in their standard of living after divorce than men do (Weitzman and Maclean, 1992), and the intervention in the UK of the government by creating the Child Support Agency is not likely to change this, geared as it is towards reducing state transfers rather than improving mothers' income (Lister, 1994). Space does not here permit an analysis of judicial approaches to all financial outcomes of divorce, although some are referred to below. Rather, this chapter focuses on the embeddedness of a particular cultural bias that leads to systematic sidelining of long-term financial outcomes for women.

Women achieved the right to claim substantive financial provision on divorce only in 1970 with the Matrimonial Proceedings and Property Act, which became the 1973 Matrimonial Causes Act (the 1973 Act). These rights reflect mostly the arrangements between the parties during marriage, and not the effect of the marriage on their subsequent lives. The 1973 Act continues to form the basis of the prevailing law for the financial resolution of divorce cases in 2003. If divorced, the financial process of divorce determines the starting point for women of their financial position in later life, but the 'gender arrangement' determines to what extent this is able to change after dissolution.

The 1973 Act gave judges wide discretion to award and adjust many forms of property between divorcing spouses including housing, investments and income. These powers were virtually unfettered, provided that the judges took into account a wide list of relevant factors.[4] The judiciary could interpret this legislation at will, legitimately using their personal cultural frameworks in deciding cases. In empowering the 'law' as the sole arbiter of the financial outcomes of divorce, parliament created an opaque and largely unaccountable system for the resolution of cases.

The 'problem' of pensions and divorce: how judges viewed the issue of pension rights

At the time of the divorce law reforms in 1970, the Law Commission were concerned that once divorced, former wives could no longer become widows and receive widows' pensions in the event of the death of their former husbands (unwittingly reflecting Beveridge), but the wider issues surrounding pension ownership were not seen as causing injustice (Law Commission, 1966). The only property reform relating to pensions that was formally included in the 1973 Act was a requirement to have regard to a loss of widow's pension on divorce. In practice, however, judges generally ignored the loss of widow's pension, which would usually only be received, if at all, decades away from the marriage.

The Court of Appeal soon determined two cases. The reasoning of the judges was binding on all lower courts, by the system of legal precedent, leading to these cases being of considerable influence throughout the 1980s. In the first (*Priest versus Priest*, 1978), the couple had been married for 13 years and had three children, in a traditional breadwinner/homemaker marriage. Mr

Priest could retire from the Royal Marines in 1983, with a gratuity and a pension income, after 22 years' service. The Court of Appeal ruled that Mrs Priest should receive only a third of her husband's gratuity. She received no compensation for loss of a widow's pension, and no share of Mr Priest's pension. The justification in the judgment for this tiny amount being granted to Mrs Priest as security in her retirement was that any more than this would be unfair as the gratuity would increase in value over time, *during which the parties were not married*. By implication she could not appropriately be construed as a dependent outside of marriage, despite her financial position at that time being entirely a function of her dependent status within her marriage. The relative prospects for Mr Priest with his Royal Marines career and pension, and Mrs Priest, divorced, not in paid work, and with their three young children to care for, are quite clear.

Shortly after, the Court of Appeal similarly decided the case of Mr and Mrs Milne (*Milne versus Milne*, 1981), a couple in their mid-50s married for over 30 years with three children. Mr Milne had ten years to retirement when he would be entitled to a lump sum of about £16,000, which was a quarter of the value of his pension fund. Mr Justice Purchas said:

> The wife has mothered and brought up the children and it is a classic case in which the wife is entitled to recognition in a practical way in respect of this great contribution that she has made to the family and the marriage. (*Milne versus Milne*, 1981, p 288B)

In this way, he reflected the idealised version of family, which necessarily includes virtually complete economic dependence by a wife on her husband, but he did not translate this into a share of the money or wealth earned by the man to be utilised by Mrs Milne outside of the relationship. He went on to order that upon receipt of his pension lump sum, Mr Milne should pay his wife half of it (amounting to only one eighth of the value of his pension fund), saying:

> ... there is no magic in the fraction 'one half'. The reason I have reached that particular amount is that there has been a very long marriage. If the husband survives to the date of retirement, the figure with which one is dealing is itself only one quarter of the capitalised effect of his pension. If he dies while in service, the second wife, if there is to be one, is still protected under the provisions of the scheme, because, under those provisions, she receives, of course, not the 2 years' salary by way of a lump sum, but she does receive other compensation as the widow. (*Milne versus Milne*, 1981, p 289E)

Mrs Milne received no compensation herself for loss of the widow's pension. In addition the dominant cultural hegemony of heterosexual marriage including female economic dependence is confirmed in the transference of this idealised version of marriage to a second wife, also economically dependent on her husband, who does not yet exist either in reality or in the contemplation of Mr

Milne. The present Mrs Milne's financial resources following divorce are made subject to the financial rights within this normative construction of marriage, of this hypothetical person.

These cases ensured that if retirement age was more than ten years away, pension capital and income was not considered a relevant factor on divorce. Second, even if a wife passed this hurdle, one half of the maximum commutable lump sum – itself only a small fraction of the pension – became a maximum figure, only awarded to those who were perceived as virtuous and dutiful homemakers and carers during their marriage. Pension income was not considered at all, nor was a wife's long-term financial security or well-being.

The 'clean break': a policy objective

Wives would have taken on domestic and childcare responsibilities in a marriage, which reduced their ability to earn and enhanced that of their husbands, yet those seeking maintenance from their former husbands were quickly labelled 'alimony drones' (Smart, 1984a). Within a few years of the 1970 divorce and property laws coming into force, the courts began introducing the policy of 'clean break'.

This meant, in practice, that wives with their financial disadvantages should not receive ongoing maintenance from their former husbands. Despite an admission at the time that there were 'inadequate factual data' against which to judge the operation of the clean break, the Law Commission recommended that the clean break policy be formalised in a new law. They considered in the process that having inadequate factual data was not a powerful enough reason to hold up reform when there was "widespread grievance at the existing law" (Cretney, 1986, pp 39-40). The widespread grievances were the grievances of men at having to pay maintenance to their first wives, particularly when they had a second. The judiciary, the Law Commission and parliament were combining powerfully to support the ability of men to advance their careers and to remarry without financial burdens, thus creating anew the family structure of a breadwinner and financially dependent wife, at the expense of the first wife and her children. The clean break policy was ultimately embodied in divorce legislation, imposing a duty on courts to consider ordering the cessation of maintenance (1984 Matrimonial and Family Proceedings Act, section 3).

There was at this time a simultaneous shift of policy focus towards child-support,[5] driven by the perceived cost of welfare for mothers bringing up children without the financial assistance of fathers. This contributed to a judicial framework for consideration of former-spouse support only as an adjunct to child support. By implication, spousal support once children were adults was seen as undesirable, and contrary to the principle of the 'clean break' between divorcing adults. Now, wives seeking maintenance became known colloquially in the courts as seeking 'a meal ticket for life', but with no examination of how they should provide for themselves, their children and their retirement, often as single mothers in an environment of low pay for women, having sacrificed work and opportunity to their marriages.

The process of reform: pension sharing on divorce

In 1993, Dawn Barnett was in her mid-50s, with a depleted teacher's pension, having taken career breaks to raise three children. Her husband, with a good pension from an unbroken career, was divorcing her. Despondent at the law, she and a similarly positioned woman, Sally Quin, founded Fairshares – a lobbying group on the single issue of pensions and divorce. The loosely formed, non-hierarchical organisation grew quickly through word of mouth and newspaper articles, at one time having a membership of 1,500 and handling 15,000 enquiries in five years (Select Committee on Social Security, 1998: evidence given by Sally Quin at questions 490-9). Many well-educated middle-class divorced women saw their retirement looming in parlous circumstances – particularly when compared with their former husbands. The group began to insist on the right to acquire a share of their husbands' pensions on divorce, gaining considerable political influence.

Two factors are important. First, this is not the advocating of a new cultural model of marriage, lone motherhood, old age, law or welfare, but a plea to view accrued pension rights as having a financial value. This view, because of the high profile of population ageing, was becoming irresistible in any event, with government urging the population to accrue pension funds from a young age. Thus it did not threaten existing dominant hegemony within the law or welfare policy; indeed it supported one interest of the state in potentially reducing the financial dependence of single women on state welfare and returning it to the private familial sphere.

Second, the focus was very much on men and women of the middle classes. Although divorce law has always been technically concerned (and remains) with both state and private pensions, there are substantive class divisions in pension accumulation that interact with gender in different ways, making it less likely to be an issue that could be raised in a divorce case for working-class women. Their lack of pension accumulation would probably project them on to means-tested benefits in any event, and they are more likely to be married to working-class men, who are less likely than other groups to have substantial enough pensions accumulated to transfer in a divorce settlement (Joshi and Davies, 1991, 1992; Price and Ginn, 2003: forthcoming).

While the Conservative government of the day opposed any reform, Fairshares garnered support from opposition MPs in the Labour Party. Critical support for the reform was also found in the unelected House of Lords, where a powerful cross-party coalition of female peers introduced a change in the law just short of pension sharing. These provisions were to become known as the 'earmarking' provisions.

Earmarking: the law, the judges and the lawyers

The 'earmarking' laws of 1995[6] demanded that pension assets be formally considered on divorce, whatever the ages of the parties. Pension trustees could now be ordered to pay life insurance, part of the lump sum and/or part of the annuity of a pension to a divorced spouse. 'Considering' pensions though does not necessarily mean much, other than a requirement to recognise that they exist. There was no simultaneous requirement to consider the ability of the parties to provide for their retirement. The judges quickly rendered these new provisions virtually ineffective in a series of judgments.

In the case of Mr and Mrs T (*T versus T*, 1998), Mrs T, aged 47, had paid work when younger, but for the latter half of her 14-year marriage, she had been a homemaker. Mr T was an executive director of a bank. Mrs T had a tiny amount of deferred pension from her earlier employment, whereas Mr T could anticipate pension income of £88,000 per annum. Mr Justice Singer stated that the new 'earmarking' provisions had not changed the previous approach of the courts, and expressly declined to make any lump sum or earmarking order compensating for pension loss.

Then Mr and Mrs Burrow took their case to court (*Burrow versus Burrow*, 1999). District Judge Bowman (unaware of the decision in *T v T*) interpreted the new laws so as to order that Mrs Burrow should receive a half of her husband's pension lump sum and a half of his pension income – that is, one half of his pension as a whole. But on appeal, Mr Justice Cazalet set aside that part of her order relating to the pension income, rejecting entirely the concept of an entitlement in the sense of some accrued right acquired by one spouse against the other spouse's pension fund.

The effect of these two cases was that it would only be in rare instances that the law could be used to create pension interests for women. In any event, the 'earmarking' provisions did not give divorced wives a pension of their own, and any rights they were given were lost on remarriage without further compensation. These provisions were little used. In four-and-a-half years, fewer than 2,000 orders were made, while divorces were occurring at a rate of 150,000-180,000 per year (Eversheds Pensions Law Team, 2000).

In a qualitative study at about this time of the way in which solicitors approached the 'pension issue' after divorce, Arthur and Lewis (2000) found that even though pensions had to be considered in every case, solicitors focused on the assessment of immediate needs, with future needs being less emphasised unless a couple were close to retirement age. The 'clean break' was generally said to underpin consideration of options in a case. Pension rights were not much considered for couples far off retirement, in short marriages, or where the rights were considered relatively small. State earnings-related pension schemes (SERPS) – often of substantial value to a husband – were seen as of low importance and rarely valued or taken into account.[7] Yet most divorcing couples are far off retirement and are likely to have young children, and a divorced wife is likely to become sole carer for some years.

'Offsetting' pension rights against other assets

So, even after 'earmarking', the practice of the law for most divorcing couples,[8] by combination of lack of legislative principle and conservative judicial interpretation, remained lawfully to terminate economic dependence by wives on their former husbands as soon as practical, and to leave women without pensions, and/or without the means to acquire sufficient pensions. This was principally achieved in the courts by marginalising the new earmarking laws, but also by focusing on the immediately foreseeable needs of the parties – usually for housing – with priority in this respect to the needs of any children.

Since most divorcing parties coming before the courts who have assets have at most a house and a pension, with perhaps some modest savings or insurance policies (Prior and Field, 1996), this has for many years meant that in the financial settlement the carer of the children (almost invariably the mother) retains the house or sufficient share of it to ensure rehousing with the children.[9] Deliberation about the future ability of the carer to earn sufficient money to contribute to pensions that might mean that she could live comfortably in retirement has been sacrificed to these considerations (Davis et al, 2000).

It is in this context that the reluctance to embrace 'earmarking' of pensions took place in the late 1990s. Arthur and Lewis' (2000) study and an associated survey of solicitors (Field, 2000) both found that where pension rights were taken into account, the preference was to 'offset' these rights against other assets – usually a house – rather than give an interest in the pension to a wife. 'Offsetting' as a mechanism was not new, and the process of 'taking the pension into account' is obscure. Field (2000) found that the whole of the value[10] of a pension was 'offset' against other assets in less than a third of cases where a husband had occupational pension rights[11] and these were mostly cases of older men, long marriages, and/or where substantial sums of money were involved.

Even these findings do not suggest, however, that in 'offsetting' pension rights lawyers and judges are departing from long-standing judicial practice, whereby a home would be preserved or provided if at all possible for children and (almost invariably) their mother. Prior and Field (1996) found in June 1995 prior to the implementation of the 'earmarking' legislation that of the cases in their study,[12] the median value of pensions where either party had been in any sort of pension scheme for five or more years was £46,000 for husbands and £5,800 for wives. In these cases, the median equity in the former matrimonial home was £59,200. Although the results are not cross-tabulated, in a third of cases, the house was sold with a division of the proceeds, and in 40 per cent of cases, the house was awarded to the wife, although in an unspecified proportion of these – possibly more than half – she had to buy her husband's share or part of it with a lump sum. In all cases husbands retained their pensions, but in over 90 per cent of cases pension rights were said to be offset against the matrimonial home.

This can be seen as a device: in these cases, it is almost certainly the case that because of the presence of dependent children, the disposal of the matrimonial home would have been identical regardless of the pension rights. Now, simply, by a husband retaining his pension, the transfer of a house to preserve a home for children might be seen as a less unequal division of capital assets where a wife is necessarily awarded the larger share of equity in the family house in order to preserve a home for children.[13] In addition, a husband's abilities to earn on the labour market (with its associated acquisition of pensions for men) and to acquire other assets post-divorce remain intact. His ability to rehouse himself is one of the primary considerations of the divorce court process (Davis et al, 2000). A wife – particularly a younger wife – does not in this trade-off herself acquire pension assets, nor does she somehow, having never had it before, acquire the ability to accumulate pension or other assets in the future, particularly if she has children to care for. Few divorced women in this situation participate in pension accumulation post-divorce (Ginn and Price, 2002).

Pension sharing but principles unchanged

With the 1997 election of the Labour Party, which had supported pension sharing in opposition, the smooth passage of a new pension sharing law was assured and on 1 December 2000 in England and Wales 'pension sharing' became possible on divorce.[14] Now, as part of the financial claims of either party to a divorce case, a claim can be made against a former spouse's pension: both state earnings-related pensions and private pensions. If the claim is successful, the original pension is effectively split into two pensions, one for the former husband, and one for the former wife. The size of the share can be anything from 0 per cent to 100 per cent of the pension fund, and can be agreed, or determined by a judge. In introducing the law, the government declared that pension sharing was "an important step towards security in retirement for women" (DSS, 1998, Foreword by the Secretary of State).

Yet, the matter of pension sharing has been left to the judiciary, to continue to determine on a case-by-case basis. The government has said:

> We do not consider that legislation is needed to require the courts to give higher priority to retirement incomes ... broadly speaking, the courts in [the UK] **may** look at the longer term position of the parties when considering pensions.... We would not wish to give greater priority to retirement incomes *at the expense* of the welfare of dependent children. [bold – author's emphasis; italics – original emphasis]. (Select Committee on Social Security, 1999, paras 16-17)

So framed, if women are to obtain any fair outcome in retirement, it is explicitly at the expense of the welfare of their own children. The courts are permitted to consider this but, so framed, the answer is posed as self-evident, for who would wish to jeopardise the welfare of dependent children? There is no data presented, no critical evaluation of the operation of the law, nor any analysis of whether this dichotomous approach is empirically, theoretically, or politically supported.

The judiciary are already interpreting the new law as they did the old. In the first case to come before the Court of Appeal since the new law was introduced, they have made it clear that pensions are not to be seen as 'equal' to other capital assets in any process of division. They are to be interpreted as worth much less than even their paper valuation[15] (*Maskell versus Maskell*, 2001).

Between 1 December 2000 when this legislation came into force, and 15 April 2002, only 367 pension-sharing orders had been made,[16] when there are likely to have been in excess of 140,000 divorces.[17]

Conclusion

Successive governments have failed to address directly the poverty of older women resulting from their economic dependence on men through the medium of family life, their low wages and their low participation in pension schemes, all of which are connected. At the same time, the higher courts in binding judgments have shown a consistent bias against considering the longer-term financial consequences of divorce for women, in favour of considerations of terminating wives' financial dependency on their former husbands.

Neither result is surprising. Legislation relating to pensions in the UK has been deeply gendered in its effects on those of working age in the accumulation of pensions, with an assumption of virtually complete financial dependency by women on husbands in later life, and this has barely changed within pension policy 'logics' since the 1950s. This inequality is supported by a gender culture, which manifests itself in financial inequalities in the private realm of the household. Domestic arrangements between men and women are exposed on marital or relationship breakdown, and in the same way that lone motherhood is seen as a paradigm to illustrate the gender bias of state welfare regimes, financial provision on divorce is equally revealing.

The power of the law as a social institution has been examined through its treatment of pension rights on divorce. The 'law' is not a neutral, independent thing. It is interpreted and implemented by individual judges, who use their discretionary power to reinforce and embed the strength of the breadwinner/ homemaker model in its deliberations, and thereby assist in the assurance of its reproduction. This is not only by encouraging the same cultural norm in second marriages, but by leaving women without financial support as they age, meaning that the gender-system ensures re-partnering and financial dependence once again on a male partner as the easiest route to escape from poverty.

The selection of the law of divorce as the solution to the 'problem' of poverty for older divorced women is itself revealing. This is a private law, with hearings held in private, and applied on a case-by-case basis to the private circumstances of each couple. It is in keeping with the liberal ideology underlying welfare in Britain whereby state and family are kept distinct. The liberal insistence on separation of state and family is key to many gendered outcomes. Here, this choice of vehicle marginalises the wider institutional processes of the state whereby divorced women as a group are disadvantaged in pension outcomes.

The mobilisation of the middle classes to seek pension sharing did not reflect even subtle changes in the position or role of women, nor has any institutional or macro-level change resulted. In Pfau-Effinger's (1999) terms, the change in the law and the political process by which it was negotiated did not reflect a change in the gender culture, nor in the gender system, and so without more is relatively ineffectual in changing the position of most women.

Embracing the law as a vehicle for social change fails to conceive of the law as part of the institutionalisation of gender inequality. To effect change would require scrutiny of gender differences in the workplace and in the home, and understanding the cultural and institutional reasons for the financial dependency of women on men. It would also involve resolution of the competing ideologies of husband versus state support for divorced women and their children and the role to be played by marriage in long-term financial provision. This in turn requires examination of the complex world of gender and welfare, and the state and private pension systems, and an understanding of the causes of poverty in old age. By implicitly reducing this social complexity to a new 'pension sharing' law the prospects for divorced women in old age must remain poor.

Notes

[1] Scotland has a different legal system.

[2] Esping-Andersen has to some extent accepted the gender critique of his original thesis (1999, pp 47-94).

[3] The corresponding figures for men are 25 per cent of those over 65, and 33 per cent of those over 75.

[4] For a full list of current factors, see section 25 1973 Matrimonial Causes Act (as amended).

[5] With the introduction of the assessment and enforcement of child support by the Child Support Agency in 1991.

[6] Sections 166 and 177 of the 1995 Pensions Act, which amended the 1973 Matrimonial Causes Act.

[7] See also Costley-White (2002) and Field (2000, pp 141-3).

[8] The exceptions are those approaching retirement, and those with substantial assets.

[9] In the 1970s it had been popular for courts to order that the non-carer, usually the husband, retain a share in the house to be realised when the children had grown up,

but these orders, known as *Mesher* orders after the case in which the mechanism was first used, became increasingly unpopular as preventing a 'clean break' and forcing a sale of the house when a wife was in her 50s with nowhere else to go and no ability to raise a mortgage or capital.

[10] The question of valuations used in these cases is itself highly contested – the chosen method almost invariably *undervalues* the pension loss to a wife, and is only departed from in cases involving the very wealthy. This issue is complex – for further details see Joshi and Davies (1998), Brindley (2000a, 2000b) and Salter (2002).

[11] 45 per cent of 71 per cent of cases.

[12] It is clear from the financial profiles of the couples in this study, and in a similar study conducted a few years later (Field, 2000) that these couples (who by selection used solicitors to resolve their financial affairs on divorce) were wealthier than the general population and almost certainly therefore than the average divorcing couple.

[13] Field's 2000 study undertaken in 1998 had broadly similar findings in this respect, but these later results should be treated with caution, as the response rate to the survey was less than 50 per cent.

[14] By the coming into force of Parts III and IV of the 1999 Welfare Reform and Pensions Act. The Act also applies in Scotland, but the legal system for the division of matrimonial property in Scotland is quite different.

[15] See footnote 10: these valuations themselves already undervalue most pensions.

[16] Written Answer to Parliamentary Question, *Hansard* 15 April, 2002, column 703W.

[17] The last available data are for 1999: divorces in the last few years of the 1990s were running at between 140,000 and 150,000 each year: see www.statistics.gov.uk/statbase/

References

Arber, S. and Ginn, J. (1995) *Connecting gender and ageing: A sociological approach*, Buckingham: Open University Press.

Arthur, S. and Lewis, J. (2000) *Pensions and divorce: Exploring financial settlements*, DSS Research Report no 118, Leeds: Corporate Document Services.

Barlow, A., Duncan, S., James, G. and Park, A. (2002) 'Just a piece of paper? Marriage and cohabitation', in A. Park et al (eds) *British social attitudes: Public policy, social ties: the 18th report* (2001/2002 edn), London: Sage Publications, pp 28-53.

Beveridge, Sir W. (1942) *Social insurance and allied services*, Cm 6404, London: HMSO.

Brindley, B. (2000a) 'An actuary's view of pension sharing, part 1', *Family Law*, vol 30, no 11, pp 845-48.

Brindley, B. (2000b) 'An actuary's view of pension sharing, part 2', *Family Law*, vol 30, no 12, pp 918-21.

Burrow v Burrow [1999] 1 Family Law Reports 508.

Costley-White, T. (2002) 'SERPS – the forgotten asset', *Family Law*, vol 32, no 3, pp 222-23.

Cretney, S.M. (1986) 'Money after divorce – the mistakes we have made?', in M.D.A. Freeman (ed) *Essays in family law 1985*, London: Stevens & Sons, pp 34-56.

Daly, M. (1994) 'Comparing welfare states: towards a gender friendly approach', in D. Sainsbury (ed) *Gendering welfare states*, London: Sage Publications, pp 101-17.

Daly, M. (2000) *The gender division of welfare: The impact of the British and German welfare states*, Cambridge: Cambridge University Press.

Daly, M. (2002) 'Care as a good for social policy', *Journal of Social Policy*, vol 31, no 2, pp 251-70.

Daly, M. and Lewis, J. (2000) 'The concept of social care and the analysis of contemporary welfare states', *British Journal of Sociology*, vol 51, no 2, pp 281-98.

Davidson, K. (1999) 'The second time around: romantic relationship choices for older men and women', paper presented to Gerontological Society of America conference New perspectives on ageing in the post-genome era, 19 November, San Francisco, CA.

Davis, G., Pearce, J., Bird, R., Woodward, H. and Wallace, C. (2000) 'Ancillary relief outcomes', *Child and Family Law Quarterly*, vol 12, no 1, pp 43-64.

DSS (Department of Social Security) (1998) *Pension sharing on divorce: reforming pensions for a fairer future. Part 1: consultation*, London: DSS.

Ermisch, J. and Francesconi, M. (2000) 'Patterns of household and family formation', in R. Berthoud and J. Gershuny (eds) *Seven years in the lives of British families: Evidence on the dynamics of social change from the British household panel survey*, Bristol: The Policy Press, pp 21-44.

Esping-Andersen, G. (1990) *The three worlds of welfare capitalism*, Oxford: Polity Press.

Esping-Andersen, G. (1999) *Social foundations of post-industrial economies*, Oxford: Oxford University Press.

Eversheds Pensions Law Team (2000) *Pensions law handbook 2001*, London: Eversheds.

Falkingham, J. and Rake, K. (2001) 'Modelling the gender impact of British pension reforms', in J. Ginn, D. Street and S. Arber (eds) *Women, work and pensions*, Buckingham: Open University Press, pp 67-85.

Falkingham, J. and Victor, C. (1991) 'The myth of the Woopie?: incomes, the elderly, and targeting welfare', *Ageing and Society*, vol 11, no 4, pp 471-93.

Field, J. (2000) *Pensions and divorce: The 1998 survey*, Leeds: Corporate Document Services.

Field, J. and Prior, G. (1996) *Women and pensions: DSS research report 50*, London: The Stationery Office.

Ginn, J. (2001) 'Pensions for women of all ages', in *All our tomorrows*, proceedings of a conference organised by the Southward Pensioners Action Group, London: Eunomia Publications, pp 6-18.

Ginn, J. (2003) *Gender, pensions and the lifecourse*, Bristol: The Policy Press.

Ginn, J. and Arber, S. (1994) 'Heading for hardship: how the British pension system has failed women', in S. Baldwin and J. Falkingham (eds) *Social security and social change*, Hemel Hempstead: Harvester Wheatsheaf, pp 216-34.

Ginn, J. and Arber, S. (1999) 'Changing patterns of pension inequality: the shift from state to private sources', *Ageing and Society*, vol 19, no 3, pp 319-42.

Ginn, J. and Arber, S. (2001) 'A colder pension climate for British women', in J. Ginn, D. Street and S. Arber (eds) *Women, work and pensions: International issues and prospects*, Buckingham and Philadelphia: Open University Press, pp 44-66.

Ginn, J. and Price, D. (2002) 'Do divorced women catch up in pension building?', *Child and Family Law Quarterly*, vol 14, no 2, pp 157-73.

Haney, L.A. (2000) 'Feminist state theory: applications to jurisprudence, criminology, and the welfare state', *Annual Review of Sociology*, vol 26, pp 641-66.

Haskey, J. (1999) 'Divorce and remarriage in England and Wales', *Population Trends*, no 95, pp 18-22.

Hobson, B. (1994) 'Solo mothers, social policy regimes and the logics of gender', in D. Sainsbury (ed) *Gendering welfare states*, London: Sage Publications, pp 170-87.

Joshi, H. and Davies, H. (1991) 'Pension splitting and divorce', *Fiscal Studies*, vol 12, no 4, pp 69-91.

Joshi, H. and Davies, H. (1992) 'Pensions, divorce and wives' double burden', *International Journal of Law and the Family*, vol 6, pp 289-320.

Joshi, H. and Davies, H. (1998) 'Memorandum from Professor Heather Joshi and Dr Hugh Davies: comments on consultation document and draft Bill', in *House of Commons Social Security Committee, Fifth Report, Pensions on Divorce. Together with the proceedings of the committee relating to the report, minutes of evidence and appendices to the minutes of evidence*. HC 869, pp 221-24, London: The Stationery Office.

Law Commission (1966) *Report on the reform of the grounds of divorce: The field of choice*, no 6, London: HMSO.

Leitner, S. (2001) 'Sex and gender discrimination within EU pension systems', *Journal of European Social Policy*, vol 11, no 2, pp 99-115.

Lewis, J. (1992) 'Gender and the development of welfare regimes', *Journal of European Social Policy*, vol 2, no 3, pp 159-73.

Lewis, J. (1997) 'Gender and welfare regimes: further thoughts', *Social politics*, vol 4, no 2, pp 160-77.

Lister, R. (1994) 'The child support act: shifting family financial obligations in the United Kingdom', *Social Politics*, vol 1, no 2, pp 211-22.

Maskell v Maskell [2001] Family Court Reporter 296.

McKay, S., Heaver, C. and Walker, R. (2000) *Building up pension rights*, DSS Research Report, no 114, Leeds: Corporate Document Services.

Milne v Milne [1981] 2 Family Law Reports 286.

O'Connor, J.S. (1993) 'Gender, class and citizenship in the comparative analysis of welfare state regimes: theoretical and methodological issues', *British Journal of Sociology*, vol 44, no 3, pp 501-18.

O'Connor, J.S. (1996) 'From women in the welfare state to gendering welfare state regimes', *Current Sociology*, vol 44, no 2, pp 1-124.

O'Connor, J.S., Orloff, A.S. and Shaver, S. (1999) *States, markets, families: Gender, liberalism and social policy in Australia, Canada, Great Britain and the United States*, Cambridge: Cambridge University Press.

Orloff, A.S. (1993) 'Gender and the social rights of citizenship: the comparative analysis of gender relations and welfare states', *American Sociological Review*, vol 58, no 3, pp 303-28.

Orloff, A.S. (1996) 'Gender in the welfare state', *Annual Review of Sociology*, vol 22, pp 52-78.

Pahl, J. (1989) *Money and marriage*, Basingstoke: Macmillan Education.

Pfau-Effinger, B. (1999) 'The modernization of family and motherhood in Western Europe', in R. Crompton (ed) *Restructuring gender relations and employment: The decline of the male breadwinner*, Oxford: Oxford University Press, pp 60-79.

Pierson, P. (2001) 'Post-industrial pressures on the mature welfare states', in P. Pierson (ed) *The new politics of the welfare state*, Oxford: Oxford University Press, pp 80-104.

Price, D. and Ginn, J. (2003: forthcoming) 'Sharing the crust? Gender, partnership status and inequalities in pension accumulation', in S. Arber, K. Davidson and J. Ginn (eds) *Gender and ageing: Changing roles and relationships*, Buckingham: Open University Press.

Priest v Priest [1978] 1 Family Law Reports 189.

Prior, G. and Field, J. (1996) *Pensions and divorce*, DSS Research Report, no 49, London: The Stationery Office.

Rake, K., Falkingham, J. and Evans, M. (2000) 'British pension policy in the twenty-first century: a partnership in pensions or a marriage to the means test?', *Social Policy and Administration*, vol 34, no 3, pp 296-317.

Sainsbury, D. (1994) 'Women's and men's social rights: gendering dimensions of welfare states', in D. Sainsbury (ed) *Gendering welfare states*, London: Sage Publications, pp 150-69.

Salter, D. (2002) 'The pitfalls of pension sharing', *Family Law*, vol 32, no 8, pp 598-603.

Schiewe, K. (1994) 'German pension insurance, gendered times and stratification', in D. Sainsbury (ed) *Gendering welfare states*, London: Sage Publications, pp 132-149.

Select Committee on Social Security (1998) *Fifth report: pensions on divorce*, HC 869, London: The Stationery Office.

Select Committee on Social Security (1999) *Pensions on divorce. The government response to the committee's fifth report of session 1997–98*, HC 146, London: The Stationery Office.

Shaw, C. (1999) '1996-based population projections by legal marital status for England and Wales', *Population Trends*, vol 95, spring, pp 23-32.

Smart, C. (1984a) 'Marriage, divorce, and women's economic dependency: a discussion of the politics of private maintenance', in M.D.A. Freeman (ed) *State, law and the family: Critical perspectives*, London and New York: Tavistock Publications/Sweet and Maxwell, pp 9-24.

Smart, C. (1984b) *The ties that bind: Law, marriage and the reproduction of patriarchal relations*, London: Routledge.

Smart, C. (1989) *Feminism and the power of law*, London and New York: Routledge.

Smart, C. and Neale, B. (1999) *Family fragments*, Cambridge: Polity Press.

T v T (Financial Relief: Pensions) [1998] 1 Family Law Reports 1072.

Titmuss, R.M. (1963) 'The social division of welfare: some reflections on the search for equity', in R.M. Titmuss (ed) *Essays on 'the welfare state'*, London: Unwin University Books, pp 34-55.

Waine, B. (1995) 'A disaster foretold? The case of the personal pension', *Social Policy and Administration*, vol 29, no 4, pp 317-34.

Walker, A., Maher, J., Coulthard, M., Goddard, E. and Thomas, M. (2001) *Living in Britain: General Household Survey 2000*, London: The Stationery Office.

Weitzman, L.J. and Maclean, M. (1992) *Economic consequences of divorce: The international perspective*, Oxford: Clarendon Press.

Index

W

Z